MARIA WICKERT

Studies in John Gower

MEDIEVAL AND RENAISSANCE TEXTS AND STUDIES

VOLUME 486

MARIA WICKERT

Studies in John Gower

2nd Edition

Translated from the German by

Robert J. Meindl

ARIZONA CENTER FOR MEDIEVAL
ACMRS
AND RENAISSANCE STUDIES
Tempe, Arizona
2016

THE ARIZONA CENTER FOR
MEDIEVAL &
RENAISSANCE
STUDIES

Published by ACMRS (Arizona Center for Medieval and Renaissance Studies)
Tempe, Arizona

Originally published in German as *Studien zu John Gower* by the University of Cologne Press, 1953.

Library of Congress Cataloging-in-Publication Data

Names: Wickert, Maria, author. | Meindl, Robert J. (Robert James), translator.
Title: Studies in John Gower / Maria Wickert ; translated from the German by Robert J. Meindl.
Other titles: Studien zu John Gower. English | Medieval & Renaissance Texts & Studies (Series) ; v. 486.
Description: 2nd edition. | Tempe, Arizona : ACMRS, 2016. | Series: Medieval and Renaissance Texts and Studies ; volume 486 | Includes bibliographical references and index.
Identifiers: LCCN 2016015234 | ISBN 9780866985413 (hardcover : alk. paper)
Subjects: LCSH: Gower, John, 1325?-1408. Vox clamantis. | Gower, John, 1325?-1408--Criticism and interpretation. | Latin poetry, Medieval and modern--England--History and criticism.
Classification: LCC PA8520.G74 S813 2016 | DDC 871/.04--dc23
LC record available at https://lccn.loc.gov/2016015234

∞
This book is made to last. It is set in Adobe Caslon Pro,
smyth-sewn and printed on acid-free paper to library specifications.
Printed in the United States of America

Table of Contents

Introduction — *vii*
R. F. YEAGER

Translator's Note — *xi*

Author's Preface — *xiii*

1. The Text and Development of the *Vox Clamantis* — 1

2. The Vision of the Peasants' Revolt — 21

3. The *Vox Clamantis* and the Medieval Sermon — 53
   A. The Homilist and the Archer — 53
   B. The Topology of the Prologue — 74

4. The Mirror for a Prince — 99

5. Gower's Sense of Order — 131

6. Gower's Narrative Technique — 165

Bibliography — 189

Introduction

R. F. Yeager

Although Maria Wickert's *Studien zu John Gower* was published in 1953, it remains in 2016 the richest treatment of Gower's great Latin poem, the *Vox Clamantis*. It may be as well the least-recognized important book ever written about a major work by a major medieval English poet. The purpose and the hope of the present translation is to bring this exceedingly learned, insightful study—long unavailable either in German or in Robert Meindl's earlier small-run English translation from a coterie press—to the attention of Gower's English-speaking readers, to that wider audience commensurate with its scholarly worth.

In this there is significant irony. Brushing aside seemingly insurmountable research obstacles, Wickert decided in the late 1940s to leave criticism of Gower's English works (for the most part) to others in order to concentrate on his far more difficult Latin poem, a decision that was exactly in the best and the rightest scholarly tradition. She did what was most needed, because it *was* needed—most apparently for no other reason—and because she had the broad knowledge to tackle it. Her training in the exacting traditions of the German university qualified her superbly for the task.

The qualities of her scholarship and critical insight have made the difference. Although first-hand readers of the German text of *Studien zu John Gower* in the years since its publication have been relatively few, the work's influence, spreading slowly and by most gone unnoticed, has nevertheless been profound. Few now would disagree that, after G. C. Macaulay, the great nineteenth-century editor of the *Complete Works*, contemporary Gower studies most owe their shape to the pioneering efforts of John H. Fisher. His biographical monograph, *John Gower, Moral Philosopher and Friend of Chaucer*, set the outline of the field for twenty-five years.[1] Yet as Fisher himself often acknowledged in its pages

[1] New York: New York University Press, 1964. Credit of a lesser kind is also owed to C.S. Lewis's chapter on the *Confessio Amantis* in *The Allegory of Love* (Oxford: Oxford University Press, 1936), which has led scholars such as Derek Pearsall ("Gower's Narrative Art," *PMLA* 81 [1966]: 475–84) and most recently Peter Nicholson (*Love and Ethics in Gower's Confessio Amantis* [Ann Arbor: University of Michigan Press, 2005]) to focus on the tales in the *Confessio*, and to two articles by George R. Coffman, "John Gower in

(and not infrequently, too, when he did not), his own work is inconceivable without Wickert's. Fisher incorporates nearly wholesale Wickert's reconstruction of Gower's process of revision from the different versions of the *Vox* and accepts her chronology for Gower's major poems. Indeed, the guiding premise of his principal argument—which itself has guided so many later studies—that Gower conceived of the *Mirour de l'Omme*, the *Vox Clamantis*, and the *Confessio Amantis* as segments of a vast, single poem, can be traced directly back to Wickert's assertion that a concern for self-knowledge "is the central problem of Gower's three major works and it, more than anything else, unites the *Mirour*, the *VC*, and the *Confessio*."[2] Scholarly studies that, since Fisher, have incorporated "his" conception of Gower's single vision thus echo, however inadvertently, the original insight of Maria Wickert.

Of course, for the five or so decades since Wickert and Fisher first saw print, Gower scholarship has been focused primarily upon the *Confessio Amantis*. Without a doubt this has further served to hold *Studien zu John Gower* in the background, obscuring Wickert's contribution further. Undeservedly even here, one must assert, for surely her illuminating analysis of the tales of "Acteon," "Pygmaleon," and "Florent" in her final chapter, "Gower's Narrative Technique," is among the very best delineations of those narratives from the *Confessio* and ought to be better known. Still, her primary subject being not the more accessible Middle English *Confessio* but the demanding Anglo-Latin *Vox Clamantis*, it should not be surprising that the book languished, little read, except by the especially perceptive such as Fisher. Wickert's learned commentary on Gower's Latin poems apparently seemed of little use in the pursuit of the *Confessio Amantis* and its meanings, and her chapter on the English poem was simply overlooked. A major boost occurred in 1981, to be sure, with the publication of the earlier version of this translation by Robert J. Meindl—though "major," again, needs qualifying. Although Meindl's labor rendered Wickert's scholarship available to readers in English, their number remained small due to the obscure manner of the translation's appearance.

One is reminded, however, of Milton, writing for "fit audience, though few." As scholarship addressing the Latin poetry has accumulated slowly, the influence of Wickert's study has grown along with it. Eric W. Stockton's English

---

His Most Significant Role," in *Elizabethan Studies and Other Essays in Honor of George F. Reynolds*, University of Colorado Studies, Series B, II, 4 (Boulder: University of Colorado Press, 1945), 52–61; and "John Gower, Mentor for Royalty: Richard II," *PMLA* 69 (1954): 953–64, both of which have been seminal for a body of later readers headed by Russell A. Peck, who configures Gower as an outspoken citizen (*Kingship and Common Profit in Gower's Confessio Amantis* [Carbondale and Edwardsville: Southern Illinois University Press, 1978]). R. F. Yeager, *John Gower's Poetic: The Search for a New Arion* (Woodbridge: Boydell & Brewer, 1990), falls somewhere in between Coffman and Peck.

[2] See below, 155–56.

translation of the *Vox Clamantis* and the *Cronica Tripertita*, published in 1962, is generous in its recognition of *Studien zu John Gower*.[3] Wickert's identification of Book I of the *Vox* (which she designated as the *Visio*, subsequently amended by A. G. Rigg and David Carlson to *Visio Anglie*) as a separately composed addition, not the poem's original beginning, also determined Rigg's discussion of Gower in his watershed *History of Anglo-Latin Literature 1066–1422*.[4] After Wickert, Rigg may be our most careful reader of Gower's Latin—though David R. Carlson threatens to unseat him. Carlson has devoted much recent attention to Gower's Latin, especially in several strongly-argued articles, and—teamed with Rigg—in a new edition and translation of the *Visio* (*VC* I) and the *Cronica Tripertita*.[5] To these contributions must be added also a burgeoning number of new essays that indicate a growing recognition among literary scholars of the importance of Gower's Latin poetry, the *Vox* and the *Cronica* especially (although historians have mined them both for years, often rather credulously).[6] Excellent work by Eve Salisbury, Siân Echard, and Andrew Galloway, all of whom, like Miller, Rigg, and Carlson, represent some of the best work in current Gower studies, have had occasion to draw upon Wickert more than casually; Lynn Arner, too, has read her Wickert carefully. These all stand in their ways on the shoulders of *Studien zu John Gower*—as do all of us who seek to know and appreciate the difficult, but profound and often moving poetry of John Gower. The translation by Robert J. Meindl brilliantly captures Wickert's thoughtful, nuanced voice, as well as her capacious learning. Having it available once again in a more attractive version, with improved translations of the many Latin sources Wickert cites, is indeed a great gift to Gower studies. It should ensure wide access to Maria Wickert's wisdom for many years to come.

---

[3] *The Major Latin Works of John Gower: The Voice of One Crying and the Tripartite Chronicle*, trans. Eric W. Stockton (Seattle: University of Washington Press, 1962).

[4] (Cambridge: Cambridge University Press, 1992), 287.

[5] D. R. Carlson, "Gower's Early Latin Poetry: Text-Genetic Hypotheses of an *Epistola ad regem* (c.1377–1380), from the Evidence of John Bale," *Mediaeval Studies* 65 (2003): 293–317; "Gower's Beast Allegories in the 1381 *Visio Anglie*," *Philological Quarterly* 87 (2008): 257–75; "The Parliamentary Source of John Gower's *Cronica Tripertita*," in *John Gower, Trilingual Poet: Language, Translation, and Tradition*, ed. Elisabeth Dutton, with John Hines and R.F. Yeager (Cambridge: D.S. Brewer, 2010), 98–111; *John Gower: Poems on Contemporary Events: The Visio Anglie (1381) and Cronica tripertita (1400)*, ed. Carlson, with a verse trans. by A. G. Rigg (Toronto: Pontifical Institute of Mediaeval Studies, 2011).

[6] E.g., Matthew Irvin, "Genius and Sensual Reading in the *Vox Clamantis*," in *John Gower, Trilingual Poet: Language, Translation, and Tradition*, ed. Dutton et al., 196–205; Malte Urban, "Gower's *Vox Clamantis* and the Authority of History," in idem, *Fragments: Past and Present in Chaucer and Gower* (Bern: Peter Lang, 2010), 57–84.

Translator's Note to the Second Edition

I have undertaken a second English edition of Maria Wickert's important study of John Gower's Latin (and English) poetry because it has been long out of print, because I needed to redo my translations of the many Latin texts she quotes in illustration and support of her positions, and, above all, because her work deserves to be made accessible to medieval scholars in an attractive and durable format that more accurately reflects the significance of her contribution to Gower studies.

I have used the translation of A.G. Rigg for Book I of the *Vox Clamantis* and the *Cronica Tripertita* (*John Gower: Poems on Contemporary Events*, ed. David R. Carlson and trans. A. G. Rigg [Toronto: Pontifical Institute of Medieval Studies, 2011]). I have used my own version of Book VI from the Gower Project Wiki Translation and everywhere else the prose translation done a half-century ago by Eric W. Stockton and still in most cases the sole English text available (Eric W. Stockton, *The Major Latin Works of John Gower* [Seattle: University of Washington Press, 1962]). Where I have relied upon other translators for various texts, I indicate the borrowing at the place where it occurs. Otherwise the translations are in all cases my own, although I am deeply indebted to my friend and colleague Mark Riley for his generous and learned assistance with the bulk of them. The responsibility for their final form is, of course, mine, but they are substantially better for his patient and detailed critiques. Kim Zarins and Georgiana Donavin read the manuscript and made many valuable suggestions for its improvement. I am grateful to them for their assistance, friendship, and support. My valued friend Robert F. Yeager has once again demonstrated the depth of his commitment to Gower studies in both reading the manuscript and providing an introduction that lends his enormous scholarly energy and *gravitas* to my project. I have added, often silently where dates make clear my presence, material that updates Wickert's notes.

The past several months have returned me, if only through awakened memories of a long-ago summer in Cologne, to the warm and genial company of Lothar Wickert, who once welcomed a woefully unprepared young student into his magisterial presence and generously helped him prepare to translate his late wife's book. To both their memories I dedicate this second edition.

California State University, Sacramento
October, 2016

Author's Preface

Gower's claim to a place in the literary history of the fourteenth century is based upon the poems *Mirour de l'Omme* (*Speculum Meditantis*), *Vox Clamantis,* and *Confessio Amantis.* They are written in three different languages: the *Mirour* in a dialect that the author designates, with the necessary proviso, as French,[1] the *Vox Clamantis* in a tolerably correct Middle Latin, and the *Confessio* in the Middle English of the London area that was destined to provide the basis for a standard written language.

The destiny of the three works is closely connected with the fate of the three languages on English soil. When Gower selected French at the beginning of his literary career, and when he returned to French at its end, he clearly did so with the intention of addressing the entire educated world in the cultural language of the time:[2]

> *Al université de tout le monde*
> *Johan Gower ceste Balade envoie.*
>
> [To the community of all the world
> John Gower sends this ballad.] *Traitie* 18.22–23

---

[1] See *Traitie* 18.24–27 in George C. Macaulay, ed., *The Complete Works of John Gower*, 4 vols., EETS E.S. 81–84 (Oxford: Oxford University Press, 1899–1902; repr. Grosse Pointe, MI: Scholarly Press, 1968), 1:391:

> *Et si jeo n'ai de François la faconde,*
> *Pardonetz moi qe jeo de ceo forsvoie:*
> *Jeo sui Englois, si quier par tiele voie*
> *Estre excusé . . .*
>
> [And if I lack a Frenchman's eloquence,
> Forgive me my straying from it:
> I am an Englishman and therefore
> Ask to be excused . . .]

The language of the *Mirour* is a late literary form of Anglo-Norman.

[2] See J. Wogan-Browne, ed., *Medieval Britain: The French of England, c. 1100–1500* (York: York Medieval Press, 2009) for a recent consideration of Anglo-Norman. Trans.

In the *Livres dou Tresor*, Brunetto Latini had similarly preferred French, as the common language of the educated classes, to his mother tongue.[3] However, what might have been suitable for the thirteenth century in Italy as well as England became less and less so in England in the fourteenth. English replaced French as the language of education around the middle of the century and by its end had already appeared in royal decrees and the deliberations of Parliament. Chaucer's humorous characterization of his Prioress' knowledge of French and the wretched grammar of many private letters from so-called educated circles show how French slowly died out as a living language in England. Gower deluded himself when he believed the language of the *Mirour* capable of a broad consequence. The work stands at the end of Anglo-Norman literature. It was scarcely circulated in manuscript and not printed until the end of the nineteenth century. Unrecognized, it survived in a single truncated manuscript until Macaulay discovered it and identified it as Gower's.

The opposite fate was allotted the *Confessio Amantis*. Here Gower's choice of English was an experiment to which he may have been stimulated by Chaucer's example. Nevertheless, the attempt seemed novel and daring, and for that reason Gower experimented on a subject that was less important to him than that of his earlier writings. The extent to which the royal commission, which he himself so charmingly describes in the Prologue, was a determining factor for Gower's new course, and the extent to which doubt in the success of his moral mission occasioned the genesis of the *Confessio* can hardly be ascertained.[4] Certainly the new work was of lesser significance in the author's eyes than everything that he had previously written. Thus it may not have been very important to him to address a national audience instead of the educated world, and to increase the modest stock of literature in the vernacular:

And for that fewe men endite
In oure englissh, I thenke make
A bok for king Richardes sake.[5]

---

[3] *Et se aucuns demandoit por quoi cist livres est escriz en romans selonc le langage des François, puisque nos somes Ytaliens, je diroie que ce est . . . porce que la parleure est plus delitable et plus commune a toutes gens* [And if anyone asks why this book is written in Romanic after the manner of the French language, since we are Italian, I would say that it is . . . because the parlance is more delightful and more common to all people]. Quoted in Charles Victor Langlois, *La Vie en France au Moyen Age*, 3 vols. (Paris: Hachette, 1925–1928), 3:337. [See *Li livres dou tresor*, ed. S. Baldwin and P. Barrette, MRTS 257 (Tempe: ACMRS, 2003), 2. Trans.]

[4] See lines 33–92 of the earlier version of the Prologue (Macaulay, *Works*, 2:2–6) and *Confessio Amantis* 1.1–10.

[5] *Confessio,* Prologue, 22–24. The later version has "A bok for Engelondes sake."

It seems an irony of fate that he thereby, and only thereby, found entry into the history of his land's literature and was able to maintain his place as a father of English poetry, full of honor alongside Chaucer, into the early seventeenth century.

The *Vox Clamantis* lies in time between the *Mirour* and the *Confessio*. The choice of Latin points to the importance of the subject, the passion of the language to the intensity of the inner concern that urged Gower to the composition of this work, and the number of manuscripts is evidence of its circulation up to the second half of the fifteenth century. It is respectfully mentioned in the literary histories, but seldom looked at closely. Two circumstances appear to me to have been involved. The first is the opinion that the Latin works of an English author do not belong to the history of English literature. Then, of course, nothing remains but to parcel a phenomenon like Gower out to the three disciplines of English, Romance Languages, and Middle Latin. The notion seems to me absurd. One should seek to understand a poet from the totality of his work and, indeed, one should begin where he himself was most strongly interested, not at the points that have become important for a later development in literary history. Gower can be understood in his entirety only in the light of the *Vox Clamantis*.

The second difficulty lies in the theme of the *Vox*, which is barely accessible to modern taste. Whatever Chaucer had in mind when he bestowed upon Gower the epithet "moral,"[6] the word implies for modern readers a stigma to which not only Gower, but, moreover, almost all fifteenth-century poetry is subject, for while the school of Chaucer followed his form, its spirit was Gower's.

The present investigations endeavor to understand this spirit. They are concerned with the technical problem of textual criticism because the work's development, as it is revealed in the different rescensions, is very closely interwoven with its aim. Moreover, the connection with the tradition of sermon and devotional literature alluded to in the title *Vox Clamantis* needed clarification. Since Gower considered the state to be first of all a moral institution, his moral mission was at the same time a political mission, and it was therefore necessary, in at least one section, to show his political ideas. I have also attempted to form from scattered statements the coherent conception of man's place and duty within the creation that was in the author's mind. In order not to overlook the formal side of Gower's poetry, I have added a chapter concerning his narrative technique and interpreted a few tales from that work in which it is most powerfully developed, namely from the *Confessio Amantis*.

The work was accepted as an inaugural dissertation by the Faculty of Philosophy of the University of Cologne. To the German Research Society, which made publication possible, I give my deepest thanks. For untiring assistance, I thank the librarians of the Bodleian. Paul G. Buchloh was kind enough to read the proofs with me.

---

6 See *Troilus and Criseyde*, 5.1856. [All Chaucer citations are from F. N. Robinson, ed., *The Works of Geoffrey Chaucer*, 2nd ed. (Boston: Houghton Mifflin, 1957).]

Abbreviations

EETS O.S.	Early English Text Society, Original Series
EETS E.S.	Early English Text Society, Extra Series
MGH	Monumenta Germaniae Historica
MLR	*Modern Language Review*
MP	*Modern Philology*
ODMA	*Oxford Dictionary of the Middle Ages*
PL	*Patrologia Latina*
PMLA	*Publications of the Modern Language Association of America*
TSMAO	Typologie des Sources du moyen âge occidental
Visio	Gower, *Vox Clamantis*, Book 1
VC	Gower, *Vox Clamantis*, Books 2–7

Chapter One

The Text and Development of the *Vox Clamantis*

Gower's *Vox Clamantis* has survived in eleven manuscripts.[1] It was first printed in 1850 and since 1902 has been available in a critical edition that one may consider definitive in the event that no new manuscript material of crucial importance should come to light.[2] The work comprises seven books. The first deals in visionary fashion with the events of the summer of 1381 and surpasses the others in

---

[1] S = Oxford, All Souls College, MS. 98;
G = Glasgow, University Library, Hunterian MS. T.2.17;
C = London, British Library, MS. Cotton Tiberius A.iv;
H = London, British Library, MS. Harley 6291;
E1= San Marino (California), Huntington Library, MS. HM 150 (Ecton Hall);
D = Oxford, Bodleian Library, MS. Digby 138 (SC 1739);
L = Oxford, Bodleian Library, MS. Laud (Misc.) 719 (SC 1061);
L2 = Lincoln, Cathedral Library, MS. A.72 (235);
T = Dublin, Trinity College, MS. D.4.6 (214);
H2= Hertfordshire, Hatfield House MS. (Marquess of Salisbury);
C2 = London, British Library, MS. Cotton Titus A.xiii (incomplete).
[Wickert used the symbols and manuscript descriptions from Macaulay's edition (see note 2), *Works* 4:lix–lxxi. I have adjusted them to conform to present usage as employed in Derek Pearsall, "The Manuscripts and Illustrations of Gower's Works," in *A Companion to Gower*, ed. Siân Echard (Cambridge: D. S. Brewer, 2004), 73–97, at 78. Wickert's account of the *Vox Clamantis'* genesis in the ensuing discussion is foundational to the current understanding of the poem. See John H. Fisher, *John Gower: Moral Philosopher and Friend of Chaucer* (New York: NYU Press, 1964) and A.G. Rigg, *A History of Anglo-Latin Literature 1066–1422* (Cambridge: Cambridge University Press, 1992); also M. Urban, ed., *John Gower: Manuscripts, Readers, Contexts* (Turnhout: Brepols, 2009). Trans.]

[2] In the first instance by H. O. Coxe, *Poema quod Dicitur Vox Clamantis necnon Chronica Tripertita* (London: Nicol for the Roxburghe Club, 1850) and in the second by George C. Macaulay, *The Complete Works of John Gower*, 4 vols., EETS E.S. 81–84 (London: Oxford University Press, 1899–1902; repr. Grosse Pointe, MI: Scholarly Press, 1968), vol. 4.

literary and historical significance. The remainder of the *Vox Clamantis* is an extensive class critique framed by general observations about the nature and destiny of mankind. The theme of class critique had already emerged in an earlier Anglo-Norman poem of the author, and it recurs in a compressed form in the prologue of that English frame-narrative to which he owes his literary significance.[3] However, in neither the earlier nor the later work is it induced by a contemporary political crisis. As a mirror image of the convulsion of 1381 and as an expression of a profound moral and political awareness occasioned by the Peasants' Revolt, the *Vox Clamantis* is thought to be unique.[4]

The historical transmission of the work presents no difficulties. The four oldest manuscripts appear to have originated during the poet's lifetime, perhaps under his supervision.[5] The rest are easy to classify, with the exception of one manuscript (L) that presents the poem in only six books.[6] The first book is missing—except the prologue and first chapter—and the remaining books are consequently numbered from one to six. As a result, Macaulay questioned whether the first book, the vision of the Peasants' Revolt, was a part of the poem's original design or whether the author had actually added it belatedly.[7] Some inner criteria appear to support the testimony of manuscript L: Books II–VII seem totally independent of the vision, and the prologue of the second book—with its whole series of exordial *topoi* and with the first mention of the title—appears to intro-

[3] Gower, *Mirour de l'Omme,* 18421–27480, Macaulay, *Works,* 1:214–305. *Confessio Amantis*, Prol. 93–1088, Macaulay, *Works*, 2:7–34.

[4] See Bernhard ten Brink, *Geschichte der englischen Literatur,* ed. Alois Brandl, 2 vols. (Strassburg: Trübner, 1891–1893), 2:102–3: "Der Bauernaufstand d. J. 1381 machte dem Dichter, dessen engere Heimat von den Schrecknissen jener Tage vorzugsweise heimgesucht wurde, einen gewaltigen Eindruck . . . So beschloß er, in seiner *Vox Clamantis* der Welt zugleich ein Bild jener Schreckenstage, behufs Erregung heilsamer Furcht, und einen Spiegel vorzuhalten, in dem sie ihre eigene Gestalt and ihr innersten Wesen schaudernd erblicken sollte" [The peasants' insurrection of the year 1381 made a powerful impression upon the poet, whose own locality was chiefly afflicted by the horrors of those days . . . Thus he determined in his *Vox Clamantis* to hold up to the world at the same time a picture of those days of terror, for the sake of arousing a wholesome fear, and a mirror in which it was supposed to see with shuddering its own form and innermost being]. There is a similar evaluation of the work in Emile Legouis and Louis Cazamian, *A History of English Literature*, trans. Helen Douglas Irvine, rev. ed. (London: Macmillan, 1940), 125, and Walter Schirmer, *Kurze Geschichte der englischen Literatur* (Halle: M. Niemeyer, 1945), 46.

[5] See Macaulay, *Works*, 4:lix.

[6] L = Oxford, Bodleian Library, MS. Laud (Misc.) 719 (SC 1061).

[7] Macaulay, *Works*, 4:xxxi-ii, and also in *The Cambridge History of English Literature*, ed. A. W. Ward and A. R. Waller, 14 vols. (New York: G. P. Putnam's Sons, 1907–1921), 2:144.

duce an independent *opus* rather than join together two parts of a larger work.[8] In any case, Macaulay did not attach a great deal of importance to the condition of the Laud manuscript because the family relationships of the Latin Gower manuscripts suggest an omission rather than the preservation of an older version. He did not pursue the inner criteria further. Thus he left suspended the question of the original form of the *Vox Clamantis*, chiefly because the final redaction, which includes the vision, unquestionably originated with Gower himself.

The problem of the development of the *Vox Clamantis* appears to me worthy of investigation not only on compositional grounds. For the question of the date of composition for the *VC* (Books II–VII) would have to be raised anew in the event that the *Visio* (Book I) was indeed added belatedly either after or near the completion of the *VC*.[9] Macaulay failed to observe that the most important key to dating the poem disappears when the *Visio* is separated from the original assemblage of the *Vox Clamantis*. In that case the possibility arises that the *VC* was written before the Peasants' Revolt.[10] It is not, however, advisable to suppose a very lengthy span of time between the early version of the *VC* and its enlargement through the *Visio*, since no reliable separate manuscript tradition of the *VC* has survived. It is, however, conceivable that the events of 1381 surprised the author during work on the *VC* or shortly after its completion. In the event that the *VC* was planned before 1381, and perhaps in the main already executed, that would indicate that the motives which might have compelled the author to the composition of this work are not derived from the shock felt by a country squire of Kent whose property has been threatened, that his pessimism did not spring from the passing darkness on the political horizon, that not sudden panic but tranquil reflection determined his scathing critique of man and society. Thus the much more important problem of the origin and object of the *Vox Clamantis* arises from the question of its date.

This chapter will investigate the origin of the work; the one following, its object. We shall handle the problem in reverse chronology, in order to advance from the secure basis of the transmitted redaction, or redactions, to the traces of an earlier recension. The material for such an investigation consists in the text, the prose summaries of the individual chapters, and a brief colophon of Gower's literary productions that has been preserved in four codices of the *Vox Clamantis*

[8] Book II, Prol.83: *Vox clamantis erit nomenque voluminis huius.*

[9] Hereafter Book I will be designated the *Visio* and Books II-VII the *VC*.

[10] Macaulay expresses himself very cautiously: "As to the date of composition, all that we can say is that the work in its present form is later than the Peasants' rising . . . it was evidently composed while the memory of that event was fresh" (Macaulay, *Works*, 4:xxx). He is inclined to establish it after, rather than before, Richard's wedding (the end of 1382), although he chooses to draw no compelling chronological conclusion from the admonition to marital fidelity in 6.913–916. [Richard wed Anne January 20, 1382. Trans.]

and in most manuscripts of the first recension of the *Confessio Amantis.*[11] This colophon occurs in three versions, the earliest of which almost certainly, the latest of which perhaps originated with the poet himself.[12] For our purposes the middle version can be excluded.[13] The other two, however, give divergent information about the content and thesis of the *Vox Clamantis.*

The later version (hereafter designated B) reads:

> *. . . Secundus enim liber sermone Latino metrice compositus tractat de variis infortuniis tempore regis Ricardi secundi in Anglia contingentibus: unde non solum regni proceres et communes tormenta passi sunt set et ipse crudelissimus rex, suis ex demeritis ab alto corruens, in foveam quam fecit finaliter proiectus est. Nomenque voluminis huius* Vox Clamantis *intitulatur.* [The second book, composed in Latin verse, deals with the various misfortunes that occurred in England during the reign of King Richard II, when not only were tribulations suffered by the magnates and commons of the realm, but also the cruel king himself, falling from on high because of his own misdeeds, was finally cast into the ditch that he had dug. And the volume is entitled with the name of *The Voice of One Crying.*][14]

This version mentions neither the Peasants' Revolt nor the class critique, but alludes tersely to the unfortunate vicissitudes of Richard II's reign that led to the monarch's deserved downfall. Were the title *Vox Clamantis* not given, one would associate the summary with the *Cronica Tripertita*, which treats English history from 1387 to the deposition of Richard in 1399. Because the title is named, it

---

[11] It is important for the dating of the *Vox Clamantis* that the three recensions of the *Confessio Amantis*, which are represented by three manuscript groups, be kept distinct. Macaulay's chronological estimate, until now unopposed, reads as follows:

Confessio—1st Recension—concluded 1390;
Confessio—2nd Recension—concluded 1390/91;
Confessio—3rd Recension—concluded 1392/93.
See Macaulay, *Works*, 2:xxi-xxvi and cxxvii-clxvii.

[12] Both appear in manuscripts that, according to Macaulay, were prepared under the eyes of the author. The earlier version, moreover, exhibits Gower's characteristic stylistic properties, for example, a predilection for the unwarranted use of the comparative of adverbs and an excessive use of particles.

[13] The middle version originates in a manuscript group of the *Confessio Amantis* that contains a contaminated text, the so-called 2nd Recension. The colophon also appears to have been contaminated after Gower's death, if one can so understand the phrase, found only here, "while he lived" (*. . . tres precipue libros per ipsum dum vixit . . . compositos*) (Macaulay, *Works*, 3:480).

[14] *Works*, 4:360. The translation is by R. F. Yeager, *John Gower: The Minor Latin Works,* 39, where this last variant of the colophon, the B Version, occurs as the third stanza of *Quia Unusquisque.* The biblical allusions are to Matthew 3:3 / Mark 1:3 / Luke 3:4 / John 1:23 = Isaiah 40:3; also Psalm 7:15 / Ecclesiastes 10:8.

is clear that for the author of colophon B the *Vox Clamantis* was a work that included the *Cronica Tripertita* and that meant to specify the particular symptoms of the king's fatal misrule that ended with his downfall. In this view the Peasants' Revolt is only one among several symptoms, and so subordinate in the presentation of the whole trend that it appears to merit no special emphasis.

On the other hand, one reads in the earlier version (hereafter designated A):

> . . . *Secundus enim liber, sermone latino versibus exametri et pentametri compositus, tractat super illo mirabili eventu qui in Anglia tempore domini Regis Ricardi secundi anno regni sui quarto contigit, quando serviles rustici impetuose contra nobiles et ingenuos regni insurrexerunt. Innocenciam tamen dicti domini Regis tunc minoris etatis causa inde excusabilem pronuncians, culpas aliunde, ex quibus et non a fortuna talia inter homines contingunt enormia evidencius declarat. Titulusque voluminis huius, cuius ordo Septem continet paginas,* Vox Clamantis *nominatur.* [The second book, composed in the Latin language in hexameter and pentameter verses, treats of the astounding event which took place in England during the time of King Richard II in the fourth year of his reign, when the lowly peasants violently revolted against the freemen and nobles of the realm. Nevertheless, pronouncing upon the innocence of the said lord the king as excusable in this matter because of his minor age, the book declares that the blame, because of which—and not through Fortune—such enormities take place among men, clearly lies elsewhere. And the name of this book, which is arranged in seven sections, is called *The Voice of One Crying.*][15]

Colophon A reveals an entirely different conception of the contents of the *Vox Clamantis*. It places total emphasis on the Peasants' Revolt—everything else is subordinated to an investigation of the question of blame and to a disclosure of the causes that led to the monstrous event. The king is absolved of responsibility because of his minority. This, plus the mention of the fact that the book is divided into seven parts (*paginae*), excludes the *Cronica Tripertita* from consideration.[16] Colophon A, therefore, sees in the *Vox Clamantis* a work in seven parts whose theme is the Peasants' Revolt and whose purpose is instruction in the question of who must bear the blame for it. Nothing indicates a causal nexus between this event and the collapse of Richard II's rule.

Colophon B appears in four manuscripts in which the *Cronica Tripertita* follows the *Vox Clamantis*, and in one manuscript of the last recension of the *Con-*

---

[15] Macaulay, *Works*, 3:479–80 in the critical apparatus. [The translation is by Eric Stockton, *The Major Latin Works of John Gower* (Seattle: University of Washington Press, 1962), 14. I have throughout used Stockton's translation of Books II-V and VII. Trans.]

[16] Whether the seven *paginae* are identical with the seven books of the received text cannot be determined with absolute certainty. The mention of Richard's innocence points to Book VI, the allusion to *Fortuna* to Book II. One may infer the class critique from *culpas aliunde . . . declarat* (Books III-IV).

fessio.[17] It can have originated, according to its contents, only after the conclusion of the *Cronica Tripertita*, that is, after 1400. Colophon A does not occur in any Latin Gower manuscript, but in numerous codices of the first recension of the *Confessio Amantis,* where it immediately follows the *Confessio.* It was probably written at the same time that the *Confessio* was completed or shortly thereafter. The two versions of the colophon indicate that Gower altered the political tendency of the *Vox Clamantis* in the course of a decade (ca. 1390–1400), and that the alteration was paralleled by a quantitative modification, namely the inclusion of the *Cronica Tripertita*.

The text of the *Vox Clamantis* itself reveals two redactions, represented by the manuscript groups SCEHGL (hereafter designated B-Text) and TH2 (designated A-Text).[18] The two redactions differ at the point in the class critique that deals with the special duties of the king, that is, at the beginning and end of the brief Mirror for a Prince in Book VI.[19] Here the A-Text agrees with the judgment of Richard in Version A of the colophon, while the B-Text sounds a pessimistic tone and occasionally breaks out into open censure of the youthful ruler.[20] The passage in question at the beginning of the Mirror for a Prince occurs in the seventh chapter of Book VI. The Latin chapter heading reads the same in both recensions; however, since its content asserts Richard's innocence, it corresponds only with the A-Text:

> *Hic loquitur quod sicut homines esse super terram necessario expedit, ita leges ad eorum regimen institui oportet, dummodo tamen legis custodes verum a falso discernentes unicuique quod suum est equo pondere distribuant. De erroribus tamen et iniuriis modo contingentibus innocenciam Regis nostri, minoris etatis causa, quantum ad presens excusat.* [He says that, just as it is expedient by necessity that men be on the earth, thus it is necessary that laws be instituted for their governance, provided however that the guardians of the law, discerning the true from the false, should distribute in equal weight to each man what is his. However, as far as concerns the crimes and injustices occurring at the present time, he alleges the innocence of our king because of his minor age.][21]

---

[17] SCHG and F (= Oxford, Bodleian Library, MS. Fairfax 3). See Macaulay, *Works*, 2:clvii.

[18] Three versions appear in some few places. Only the two chief recensions are important for our purposes. See above, 1, n. 1, for an explanation of the symbols.

[19] 6.545–580 and 1159–1200. In the second passage D, a contaminated manuscript, follows the A-Text, while in the LL2 group the A- and B-Texts follow consecutively.

[20] See 6.555 and 569–572 in the B-Text.

[21] Macaulay, *Works*, 4:243. The legal allusion is to Justinian *Inst.* 1.1.3. The comprehensive synopsis that precedes the work in some manuscripts has the same wording. See Macaulay, *Works*, 4:14.

The redactor of the B-Text clearly performed his work carelessly and forgot to correct the headnote when he changed the chapter's ending. Furthermore, the headnote has influenced the wording of Version A of the colophon of 1390. The literal correspondences are obvious; only the sense is not the same.[22] While the chapter headnote attests to Richard's innocence in the decay of the administration of justice, Version A of the colophon absolves him of responsibility for the Peasants' Revolt. Indeed, it is possible to establish a connection indirectly by maintaining that the Peasants' Revolt was a consequence of the intolerable state of justice in the country; however, that contradicts the whole tenor of the *Visio*. Nowhere, as will be shown in the following chapter, does the *Visio* admit the possibility that the *legis custodes* or the king are to blame; rather, it one-sidedly condemns the insurgents as rebels against divine as well as human law. One cannot escape the impression that the reference in Version A is belated and artificial, and that the seventh chapter of Book VI of the *Vox Clamantis* originally had nothing to do with the Peasants' Revolt or the *Visio*. However, more will be said on the subject later. For the time being, it suffices to establish that the A-Text of the *Vox Clamantis* furnished the basis for Version A of the colophon. Since Version A presupposes the existence of the *Confessio*—it enumerates Gower's three major works—it cannot have originated before 1390. Therefore, in 1390 the A-Text is still the officially recognized form of the *Vox Clamantis*. Thus we obtain the year 1390 as the *terminus ante quem non* for the redaction of the B-Text.

As soon as one attempts to arrive at a more exact dating of the B-Text, however, one encounters considerable difficulties. To place it at the time of the composition of Version B of the colophon, that is, about 1400, will not do because Richard is also still alive at the time of the B-Text. The direct addresses and admonitions to the king would otherwise be pointless. Thus an authorial adjustment to the altered political circumstances after Richard's fall does not appear to have been the cause of the new recension. The textual history of the *Confessio Amantis* indicates a change in Gower's attitude toward Richard II analogous to that in the textual history of the *Vox Clamantis*. Macaulay had to date this change of opinion to 1391/92, but was unable to set forth a sound reason for so doing. The estimate originates solely in the constraint of the tight chronological sequence of the three *Confessio* recensions as Macaulay establishes it and will become untenable as soon as an editor resolves to date the third recension after 1393. But even if the assumption of a crisis in Gower's political convictions for the year 1391/92 were more secure, the analogy of the *Confessio* is still to be used with caution. Richard was between the ages of twenty-five and twenty-seven in 1391–1393, and the designation *puer*, which is applied to him conspicuously often and emphatically in the divergent passages of the B-Text, is not really ap-

[22] Version A: *innocenciam tamen dicti domini Regis (tamen . . . innocenciam Regis nostri,* A-Text); *tunc minoris etatis causa (minoris etatis causa)*; *excusabilem pronuncians (excusat).*

propriate to that age. It would be difficult to justify it at all after 1390, the year of Version A of the colophon and thus of the authoritative A-Text. To be sure, statements of age of this kind are always relative and the use of *puer* alone proves nothing, especially when one considers that Gower himself may have then been in his sixties.[23] However, Richard's youthfulness does appear to have been so strongly emphasized with a definite intention.

If one were to compare 6.555–80 in the A- and B-Texts,[24] one would find the designations *puer*, *puerilis*, *iuvenis*, and *iuvenilis* five times in the earlier version

[23] The date of his birth is unknown. The literary histories commonly place it in 1330.

[24] A-Text:

Stat puer immunis culpe, set qui puerile
Instruerent regimen, non sine labe manent:
Sic non rex set consilium sunt causa doloris,
Quo quasi communi murmure plangit humus.
Tempora matura si rex etatis haberet,
Equaret libram que modo iure caret:
. . . . .
Hoc set eum tangit discretum quem probat etas,
Non puerum, quia tunc fit sibi culpa minor.
Non est nature lex nec racionis, ut illud
Quod mundum ledit sit puerile malum;
Non dolus, immo iocus, non fraus set gloria ludi,
Sunt pueris, nec ibi restat origo mali.
Dixit enim Daniel, quod de senioribus orta
Exiit impietas, quam furor orbis habet:
Omne quod est mundi vicium plantant veterani,
Et quasi de peste spersa venena serunt.
Horum namque scelus fertur maculare figuras
Tocius mundi, quo furit ira dei. 6.555–578

[The boy stands absolved of fault, but those who audit
The boyish reign are not without blemish.
The council, not the king, thus cause our grief, for which
The land as if with common murmur mourns.
If the king were in the mature times of age, he
Would balance the scales that now lack justice.
. . . . . .
But this pertains to him whom age has proved discreet,
Not to a boy, because his fault is less,
It is not nature's law nor reason's that boyish
Bad behavior is what injures the world.
Not guile but rather jest, not fraud but glorious play
Such are to boys; not there is evil's source.
For Daniel says the sin the madness of the world

Embraces goes forth born from old men.
Old men plant all the wickedness that's in the world,
And they sow poisons as if strewn by plague.
Their wickedness is said to stain the characters
Of all the world, for which God's wrath rages.]

B-Text:

Rex, puer indoctus, morales negligit actus,
In quibus a puero crescere possit homo:
Sic etenim puerum iuvenilis concio ducit,
Quod nichil expediens, sit nisi velle, sapit.
Que vult ille, volunt iuvenes sibi consociati,
Ille subintrat iter, hiique sequntur eum:
Vanus honor vanos iuvenes facit esse sodales,
Unde magis vane regia tecta colunt.
Hii puerum regem puerile more subornant,
Pondera virtutum quo minus ipse gerit.
Sunt eciam veteres cupidi, qui lucre sequentes
Ad pueri placitum plura nephanda sinunt:
Cedunt morigeri, veniunt qui sunt viciosi,
Quicquid et est vicii Curia Regis habet.
Error ad omne latus pueri consurgit, et ille,
Qui satis est docilis, concipit omne malum:
Non dolus immo iocus, non fraus set gloria ludi
Sunt pueris, set ei sors stat aborta doli.
Sunt tamen occulte cause, quas nullus in orbe
Scire potest, set eas scit magis ipse deus:
Nescit enim mater nato que fata parantur,
Fine set occultum clarius omne patet.
. . . . .
Sic ego condoleo super hiis que tedia cerno,
Quo Regi puero scripta sequenda fero. 6.555–580

[The king, an untaught boy, neglects the moral deeds
By which a man can grow up from a boy.
Indeed a youthful council guides the boy so that
He knows nothing useful, only his will.
What he wants, his youthful companions also want,
He goes upon a road, they follow him.
Vainglory makes these young comrades idle, whereby
They idle dwell beneath the royal roofs,
Suborn the boy king in his childish way, in which
He seldom dons the burdens of the virtues.
There are, too, the greedy old men, who for their gain
Allow much wickedness at the boy's plea.

but no fewer than twelve in the later. The reason for the increase is readily apparent. The A-Text absolves the boy of all responsibility and directs its major attack against the mature men who should educate and counsel him. They are heaped with reproaches and represented in a very unflattering biblical parallel.[25] The B-Text, however, mentions them in only a few words. They are in their avarice certainly an additional evil (see lines 565–568), but not *fons et origo mali*. The cancerous sore is, rather, the *concio iuvenilis*, the king's corrupt and corrupting young associates. The B-Text enlarges upon this theme, whereas the A-Text makes no mention of youthful comrades. Thus the emphatic repetition of the word *puer* and its synonyms. This attitude of the B-Text points to a political position characteristic of the period between 1385 and 1387. Thus one arrives at a starting date of somewhere around 1386–1387 for the second redaction of the *Vox Clamantis*. Such an estimate, however, is impossible unless one assumes a continual fluctuation in Gower's attitude toward Richard: initially positive (A-Text), pessimistic in 1386–1387 (B-Text), hopeful if not enthusiastic in 1390 (*Confessio Amantis* and Version A of the colophon), and finally negative in 1391–1392 (the third recension of the *Confessio*).

A substantial simplification of the complicated chronological problem results if one assumes that Gower made *post eventum* corrections within the second recension of the *Vox Clamantis* when he joined the work with the *Cronica Tripertita* after Richard's fall and attempted an organic transition. The *Cronica* begins with a statement of the year (1387),[26] followed by a passage of nine lines that in

---

Indulgently they yield, those who are sinful arrive,
And the king's court has every vice there is.
Sin rears up on all sides of the boy, and he, who
Is attentive, conceives every mischief.
To boys this is not guile but jest, not fraud but splendid
Sport, yet his fate miscarries by deceit.
There are, moreover, hidden causes, which no one
On earth can know, but God Himself knows well.
A mother knows not what the fates ordain her child,
But in the end each secret is made clear.

. . . . .

Thus I grieve the loathsome things I see upon them,
Whereby I bear these words to the boy king.]

[25] See 567: *Hoc set eum tangit discretum quem probat etas;* 555–556: *. . . set qui puerile / Instruerent regimen, non sine labe manent;* 575: *Omne quod est mundi vicium plantant veterani;* 577: *Horum namque scelus.* See 573–576: they are the lascivious elders from the story of Susanna in the Book of Daniel.

[26] *Cronica Tripertita, Pars* I:1–2. Macaulay, *Works* 4:314.

Tolle caput mundi, C ter et sex lustra fer illi,
Et decies quinque cum septem post super adde.

[Take mundus's head, three C's, six fives, and add to these
Five tens, and then another seven if you please. (Trans. Rigg.)]

all the manuscripts is written over an erasure.[27] What may have been there originally cannot be determined. What is there now represents a rather inept attempt to join the *Cronica Tripertita* to the chronicle of the Peasants' Revolt,[28] that is, to the *Vox Clamantis*. The *Cronica Tripertita* itself begins after the erasure with attacks upon the king's *consilium iuvenile*:

Rex induratum cor semper habet, neque fatum
Tale remordebat ipsum, qui iure carebat:
Stultorum vile sibi consilium iuvenile
Legerat, et sectam senium dedit esse reiectam:
Consilio iuvenum spiraverat ille venenum,
Quo bona predaret procerum, quos mortificaret:
Sic malus ipse malis adhesit, eisque sodalis
Efficitur, tota regis pietate remota. 1.13–20

[King Richard's heart was ever hard, and this event
Did not restrain him from his constant foul intent.
Unsound advice from foolish youth he took as guide;
The wiser thoughts of older men he cast aside.
By young men's counsel he breathed out a deadly breath
To seize the nobles' goods and bring them to their death.
Thus he became their friend, as bad with bad combined;
All royal sense of mercy was put out of mind. (Trans. Rigg.)]

---

[27] Lines 4–12:

Dum stat commotus Ricardus amore remotus,
Principio Regis oritur transgressio legis,
Quo fortuna cadit et humus retrograda vadit.
Quomodo surrexit populus, quem non bene rexit,
Tempus adhuc plangit super hoc, quod cronica tangit.
Libro testante, stat cronica scripta per ante;
Est alibi dicta, transit nec ab aure relicta:
Audistis mira, vulgaris que tulit ira:
Omnibus in villis timuit vir iustus ab illis.

[As Richard's reign began, the law was set far back,
When fortune fell and earth went backward in its track.
The people then rebelled, for he had ruled them ill;
The chronicles report these deeds, we mourn them still.
The book attests, this chronicle was told before;
It's said elsewhere, but ears retain it evermore.
You've heard what peasant rage achieved, their fearful deeds;
In all the towns the just man flinched from such as these. (Trans. Rigg.)]

Lines 9–10 are a direct reference to the composition of the manuscript.

[28] The *Vox Clamantis* is called *cronica* in the *incipit* of two manuscripts of the B-Text.

That is, in a somewhat sharper tone of voice, the same complaint that the B-Text of the *Vox Clamantis* substitutes for the accusation against the corrupt elders. At the same time, the king is reproached for not having taken to heart the lesson of the Peasants' Revolt—or should one say of the *Vox Clamantis*? Gower appears to have proceeded in the following manner: when he realized that the history of Richard was a continuous development in the direction of catastrophe, the Peasants' Revolt became for him the first symptom of irreversible decline. The *Vox Clamantis* and the *Cronica Tripertita* formed in this new view of things a unity that was outwardly established by effacing a number of lines in the beginning of the *Cronica* and substituting a reference to the *Vox Clamantis*. At the same time, Gower deleted his favorable statements about Richard in the *Vox* and inserted a passage that pointed to the beginning of the *Cronica*. The result is that the reader of the B-Text receives the impression that the *Vox Clamantis* is a last futile warning to the young king, the ignoring of which led to the situation of 1381. Perhaps several dark and oracular lines in the introduction to the Mirror for a Prince already allude to the ending of the *Cronica Tripertita*:

> *Nescit enim mater nato que fata parantur,*
> *Fine set occultum clarius omne patet:* B-Text, 6.575–576
>
> [A mother knows not what the fates ordain her child,
> But in the end each secret is made clear.]
>
> . . . *set ei sors stat aborta doli;* 6.572
>
> [. . . yet his fate miscarries by deceit].

The keenness with which Gower criticizes the king personally also indicates that a reinterpretation of the motivation for the Mirror for a Prince, derived from the conditions of the 1380s, first appeared after the king's deposition. With the second and third recensions of the *Confessio Amantis*, Gower unobtrusively replaced the lines concerning Richard II with a new version. This was all the less conspicuous since it was done—at least in the case of the third recension—in a private dedicatory copy, while the mass of codices continued to circulate the first recension. On the other hand, the second recension of the *Vox Clamantis* appears, to judge from the number of codices, officially to have replaced the earlier version. It criticizes in a tone that would have during Richard's lifetime brought the author to the Tower instead of yielding him, shortly after its appearance, a royal commission for the composition of the *Confessio Amantis*.

We arrive at the following conclusion: the latest recension of the *Vox Clamantis*, that is, the B-Text, does indeed simulate the situation of *ca*. 1387, but is, as colophon A testifies, to be dated after 1390 and in all likelihood originated, as its political attitude shows, in the period after Richard's fall, when the *Vox Clamantis* was joined to the *Cronica Tripertita*. It forms the basis for Version B of the colophon. The older recension, that is, the A-Text, underlies Version A and was consequently concluded before 1390. The year 1381 provides the *terminus post quem* for the *Visio*; however, it would be valid for the remaining books only if they were not composed before the *Visio*.

If we return to our original concern, namely to the question of whether textual history is able to provide information concerning the relationship of the *Visio* to the *VC*, then we must consider the third book of the *Vox Clamantis*. The alterations in Book VI have attracted such a strong interest because of their historical significance that a divergence in the textual tradition of the third book has remained practically unnoticed. It involves the first twenty-nine lines of Book III. They exist in three redactions, of which two are represented by the manuscript group of the B-Text, while the third occurs only in the small manuscript group of the A-Text.[29] The two versions of the B-Text differ from each other only stylistically. They will hereafter be designated B1 (CHGEDL) and B2 (S). In contrast, the A-Text version differs distinctly in its content from the B-Text group. The important lines in this context are 1–8:

A-Text:

Sunt clerus, miles, cultor, tres trina gerentes;
Hic docet, hic pugnat, alter et arua colit.
Quid sibi sit clerus primo videamus, et ecce
De reliquis fugiens mundus adheret eis.
Primo prelatos constat preferre sequendos,
Nam via doctorum tucior illa foret.
Morigeris verbis modo sunt quam plura docentes,
Facta tamen dictis dissona cerno suis.

[There are the cleric, the knight, and the peasant, the three carrying on three {different} things. The one teaches, the other fights, and the third tills the fields. First let us see what the clergy are. Behold, the whole world cleaves to them and shuns the rest of us. Evidently, prelates prefer to be waited upon first, for the pathway of learned men ought to be quite secure. I observe how much they teach with their moral words, but their deeds are not in harmony with what they say. (Trans. Stockton.)]

B-Text:

Sunt Clerus, Miles, Cultor, tres trina gerentes;
Hic docet, hic pugnat, alter et arua colit.
Quid sibi sit Clerus primo videamus, et ecce
Eius in exemplis iam stupet omnis humus.

[29] SCHGEDL and TH2.

Scisma patens hodie monstrat quod sunt duo pape,
Unus scismaticus, alter et ille bonus:
Francia scismaticum colit et statuit venerandum,
Anglia sed rectam servat ubique fidem.
Ergo meis scriptis super hoc ubicumque legendis
Sint bona dicta bonis, et mala linquo malis.

[There are the cleric, the knight, and the peasant, the three carrying on three {different} things. The one teaches, the other fights, and the third tills the fields. First let us see what the cleric is. Behold, the whole world is now stunned by his example. The schism of today shows plainly that there are two popes, one a schismatic and the other the proper one. France favors the schismatic and declares that he ought to be revered, but England everywhere preserves the right faith. I accordingly bequeath the good things said by my writings about this matter to good readers wherever they may be, and I bequeath the bad things to the bad. (Trans. Stockton.)]

B-Text (B2):

Sunt Clerus, Miles, Cultor, tres trina gerentes,
Set de prelatis scribere tendo prius.
Scisma patens hodie monstrat quod sunt duo pape.
(from here identical with B1)

[There are the cleric, the knight, and the peasant, the three carrying on three {different} things. But I intend to write about the prelates first. The schism evident today shows that there are two popes. (Trans. Stockton.)]

The B-Text mentions the Schism; the A-Text, like the prose summary of the chapter headnote, which reads the same in all redactions,[30] says nothing about it. Thus there is the same correspondence of summary and A-Text as in the analogous passage of Book VI. Should the A-Text of Book III therefore be dated before the autumn of 1378? An *argumentum ex silentio* is, naturally, hazardous; nevertheless, one must clarify the situation at the beginning of Book III in order to determine what the Schism signifies for this part of the *Vox Clamantis.*

[30] *Hic tractat qualiter status et ordo mundi in tribus consistit gradibus, sunt enim ut dicit, Clerus, Milicies, et Agricultores, de quorum errore mundi infortunia nobis contingunt. Unde primo videndum est de errore cleri precipue in ordine prelatorum, etc.* [Here he treats of how the state or order of the world consists of three estates. They are, as he says, the clergy, knighthood, and peasantry. Through their going astray, the misfortunes of the world befall us. Hence we must first examine the waywardness of the clergy, especially among the rank of prelates, etc. (Trans. Stockton.)] See Macaulay, *Works*, 4:105.

In the second book Gower rejects the cheap excuse of the masses that *Fortuna* is responsible for the decline of the times. Supported by the authority of the Bible, he advocates the view that man's moral behavior defines his fate. Like the destiny of the individual, the destiny of human society in its organization in church and state is dependent upon the moral integrity of its institutions. After this general observation, the third book begins with a moral inventory of the three estates of society. The church has precedence. First the secular, then the regular clergy are treated in hierarchical gradation from the top downwards. The Schism would have constituted not only the natural point of departure for a criticism of the church in root and branch, but at the same time an extraordinarily effective beginning for a mercilessly negative judgment such as Gower heavy-heartedly delivers. Moreover, it would have provided, according to the organic conception of the nature of the state as well as of the church that the author shared with his public, the natural explanation for all the symptoms of disease in the body of the church, for the branches, too, will suffer the disease of the root. Gower himself speaks of this causal nexus in the class critique of the *Mirour de l'Omme*, where it is said of pope and cardinals:

> *Ce dist qui sapience enfile,*
> *Du bonne mere bonne file,*
> *Et par contraire il est auci*
> *Mais c'est tout voir, qant chief s'avile,*
> *La part des membres serra vile.*
> *Au Court de Rome il est ensi.* 18841–18846

> [The wise man says that
> Good daughters come of good mothers,
> The reverse of which is also true.
> Certainly it is true that when the head
> Becomes vile, so do the limbs.
> Thus things are at the court of Rome.]

It is scarcely credible, or rather improbable to a high degree, that in the *Vox Clamantis* Gower should have voluntarily renounced the strongest and most palpable argument for the necessity of a moral regeneration of the church. The belated insertion of the Schism into the B-Text shows that he was well aware of the significance of this event for his class critique, even though from lack of space—he was limited to the number of lines of the erasure—he could not make full use of it but had to be satisfied with a brief reference. The redaction of the A-Text, therefore, appears at this point to refer back to the time before the Schism. If this supposition is correct, the *VC*, or more precisely the third book of the *Vox Clamantis*, originated during the span of time between Richard's accession and the outbreak of the Schism, that is, during the period from 1377 to the autumn of 1378.[31]

With that the series of textual-historical reference points for the development of the *Vox Clamantis* is exhausted. The internal criteria remain to be investigated. There are in the *VC* neither direct references to the *Visio* nor allusions to the events of 1381. A reference to the Peasants' Revolt in the seventh chapter of Book VI, as shown above,[32] was interpolated belatedly into the text from Version B of the colophon and cannot be considered authentic. The compositional connection of the *VC* with the *Visio* is very loose and indistinct. The last chapter of the last book retrospectively mentions a dream inspiration, but gives no details nor makes any clearly recognizable reference to the *Visio*.[33] At the point of transition between the *Visio* and the *VC*, that is, in the prologue of the second book, in which—if anywhere—the juncture ought to have become visible, a clear allusion is absent from the text. Only the prose summary makes a connection to the *Visio*, whereas one cannot be read into the text without doing violence to the wording.[34]

---

[31] In the *Mirour de l'Omme*, which nobody doubts was composed before the accession of Richard II, Gower has also inserted the Schism belatedly. Because only one manuscript exists, no more can be known about the original version.

[32] See above, 5–7.

[33] See 7.1461 and, above all, 1443–1444:

Hos ego compegi versus, quos fuderat in me
Spiritus in sompnis: nox erat illa gravis.

[I have compiled these verses, which a spirit uttered within me during my sleep. That was a hard night. (Trans. Stockton.)]

These lines are hardly compatible with those that immediately follow (1445–1448), in which the author represents himself as the spokesman of public opinion.

[34] The summary states: *Hic dicit quod ipse iam vigilans, secundum vocem quam in sompnis acceperat, intendit scribere ea que de mundo vidit et audivit.* [Here he says that now that he is awake he intends to write, in accordance with the voice which he understood in his dreams, of the things which he saw and heard concerning the world. (Trans. Stockton.)] Then the text begins:

Multa quidem vidi diversaque multa notavi,
Que tibi vult meminens scribere penna sequens. 2.Prol.1–2

[I have seen and noted many different things, which my reminiscing pen is eager to write down for you now. (Trans. Stockton.)]

However, it mentions no dreams. Rather, it seems to attempt to express the same material that is more fully explained, with reference to a quotation from Seneca (*Ep.* 84.3), at the end of the Prologue, namely the origin of the material in countless oral and written sources:

The *VC*'s only actual point of contact with the *Visio* is its critique of the peasantry in the ninth and tenth chapters of Book V. Macaulay even remarks in the notes his surprise that there is not one word of mention in these chapters of the events of 1381. He does not attempt an explanation. However, it is a matter not only of the absence of any reference to the Revolt, but of Gower's attitude toward the peasants. One is here in the fortunate position of being able to compare, by means of the *Mirour* and the *Visio*, Gower's attitude before and after 1381. Of course, one does not expect sympathies for the agricultural worker, be he bound or free, in a country squire of the time—even before the Peasants' Revolt. The relationships between the two classes had been strained to the utmost since the Statute of Labourers; complaints in Parliament were the order of the day, warnings from the pulpit numerous, and acts of violence frequent. The state of affairs was equally intolerable for both parties.[35] However, even for a biased onlooker—as Gower probably was because of his station in life—there is a difference between the critique of a class that does not fulfill its duties and the condemnation of a class that in organized rebellion endangers the existence of the state. The *Visio*'s judgment of damnation will be treated extensively in the next chapter. It is of a severity unmitigated by any missionary endeavor, by any intercession on behalf of the peasants. In the *Visio* the rebellious peasant is Satan incarnate. In the *Mirour*, on the other hand, and also in the *VC*, the peasantry ranks as one among the various classes that in their totality comprise the state and that the poet calls upon to come to their senses and return to their divinely ordained duties. The blame for the decline of the times rests with all the classes; the peasantry is only partially responsible. Indeed, one could conclude from the scant space that is granted the failings of this class in the *Mirour* and the *VC*, and from the meager emphasis that is allotted to clergy or jurists, that Gower assigns the main guilt to the other classes. That may be in part because the root of all evil is the disappearance of justice, for which the upper classes are more responsible than the lower, and it may be grounded in part in the practice of the homily, which

Non tamen ex propriis dicam que verba sequntur,
Set velut instructus nuncius illa fero.
Lectus ut est variis florum de germine favus,
Lectaque diverso litore concha venit,
Sic michi diversa tribuerunt hoc opus ora,
Et visus varii sunt michi causa libri. 2.Prol.75–80

[I shall not, however, speak of my personal affairs in the words which follow, but I shall report them just like a well-informed messenger. As the honeycomb is gathered from the bud of various flowers and the seashell is found and gathered from many a shore, so many different mouths have furnished me with the matter of this work; and my several visions are the reason for the book. (Trans. Stockton.)]

[35] See George Macaulay Trevelyan, *England in the Age of Wycliffe*, 4th ed. (London: Longmans, Green, and Co., 1946), 183.

in principle directed itself equally to all classes and spared none,[36] but which in practice somewhat overlooked the lower classes because they were already expiating a part of their punishment through difficulty and hardship—*tribulationes* is the *terminus technicus*—in their mortal existence. One may read in the Book of Wisdom: *Horrende et cito apparebit vobis, quoniam iudicium durissimum his, qui praesunt, fiet. Exiguo enim conceditur misericordia; potentes autem potenter tormenta patientur* [Horribly and swiftly will he appear to you, for a most severe judgment shall be for them that bear rule. For to him that is little, mercy is granted, but the mighty shall be mightily tormented] (Wisdom 6:6–7). Gower, whose class critique has to a considerable extent the character of a homily, could have made this his guiding principle.[37]

In the details of the *VC*'s argument, Gower follows his own model from the *Mirour*. The class vices of the rural populace are sloth (*Mirour* 26434; *Vox Clamantis* 5.573, 577, 581, 587–588), excessive wage demands (*Mirour* 26435–26448; *Vox Clamantis* 5.579–582), gluttony (*Mirour* 26449–26458; *Vox Clamantis* 5.637–648), and presumptuous dress (only in the *Mirour* 26458–26464). The stylistic characters of the two works are, however, different. In the *Mirour*, Gower sketches a melancholy description of the old, simple, rustic, Horatian way of life, which he contrasts to the evil present, finally clothing the moral of his observations in the garb of an epigram.[38] In the *VC* he provides a theological foundation for peasant labor. Common to both works are allusions that appear to refer to *jacquerie*;[39] common also is the tendency to symbolize the peasant malady through botanical comparisons.[40] In the *Mirour*, the metaphor of the nettle provides the occasion for a prediction of impending catastrophe that is evidence of Gower's political sensitivity and that guarantees a pre-1381 date.[41]

---

[36] According to the words of the Bible: *Loquere ad populum, et cunctis audientibus praedica* [Judges 7:3: Speak to the people, and proclaim in the hearing of all]. On this passage, see Bromyard, *Summa Praedicantium* (Venice: D. Nicolinus, 1586), *s.v. praedicatio: Et sicut praeco nulli parcit, nec diviti, nec potenti, vel pauperi, sed omnes tangit, qui contra illud quod clamat fecerunt, vel faciant, ita vos praedicate evangelium omni creaturae* [And just as the herald spares none—neither the wealthy, nor the powerful, nor the poor—but touches all who have acted or who do act against that which he proclaims, thus must you preach the Gospel to every creature (Mark 16:15)].

[37] See below, 53–55, 109–11.

[38] *Mirour* 16497–16508.

[39] *Mirour* 27229–27234; *Vox Clamantis* 5.599–628.

[40] *Mirour* 16489 *urtie; Vox Clamantis* 5.601 *cardo.*

[41] *Mirour* 26485–26496:

Me semble que la litargie
Ad endormi la seignourie,
Si qu'ils de la commune gent
Ne pernont garde a la folie,
Ainz souffront croistre celle urtie

However, it has not been observed until now that a similar premonition of the catastrophe occurs in the *VC*. The critique of the peasants in Book V ends with an urgent warning in the twelfth hour:

> *Hiis, nisi iusticia fuerit terrore parata,*
> *Succumbent domini tempore credo brevi.* 5.653–654

> [I believe that in a short time the lords will submit to them, unless justice shall have been obtained by means of fear. (Trans. Stockton.)]

The time reference, *tempore brevi*, points clearly to the future, and indeed to the near future. The situation is still exactly the same as at the time of the *Mirour*, strained to the utmost, the eruption immediately at hand. This part of the *VC* was obviously written before 1381. Gower's attitude toward the peasant question agrees in all respects with that of the *Mirour*, as does his gaze into the political future. The tone has become somewhat sharper, but the catastrophe of 1381 is still to come.

For the time being we come to the following conclusion: beyond the fact that there are two redactions, the B- and A-Texts, certain inner criteria indicate a stage in the development of the *Vox Clamantis* that is to be located before 1381. At that time the greater part of the class critique, that is Books II-V, already existed. Whether the Mirror for a Prince of Book VI[42] and the frame of Books II and VII were already a part of the nascent work cannot be ascertained by the means employed to this point.[43] Book I, the *Visio*, was obviously missing because it presupposes the Peasants' Revolt. It is probable that at least Book III was begun before the Great Schism. From this one can posit an earliest redaction (Alpha), which comprises Books III-V, perhaps even Books II-VII, and which was written in the years 1377–1381.

> *Quelle est du soy trop violent.*
> *Cil qui pourvoit le temps present*
> *Se puet doubter procheinement,*
> *Si dieus n'en face son aie,*
> *Qe celle urtie inpacient*
> *Nous poindra trop soudainement,*
> *Avant ce q'om la justefie.*

> [It seems to me that lethargy has rocked the nobility to sleep, so that the commoners are not on their guard against folly, and will rather allow this nettle to grow whose nature is too violent. Any man who observes the present time can only expect to see, in the near future, unless God helps him, this impatient nettle sting us all too suddenly, and before anyone has a chance to examine it with moderation.]

42 Book VI, Chapters 8–18.

43 The question will be taken up once more after the interpretation of the Mirror for a Prince and after the discussion of Books II and VII; see below, 132–34.

It is, therefore, no longer possible for us to view the convulsion of 1381 as the motive force that aroused the author to political and moral awareness and that found its expression in the *Vox Clamantis*. This convulsion can at most be held responsible for the final form of the work. The main part of the *Vox Clamantis*, the *VC*, does not describe Gower's contribution to the solution of a current political problem. In order to recognize the purpose of the *VC*, one must exclude the *Visio*. Therefore, in the following chapters *Visio* and *VC* will be examined separately.

Chapter Two

The Vision of the Peasants' Revolt

The first book of the *Vox Clamantis* reports the events of the summer of 1381 in a series of dream visions. The author avails himself of the conventional frame for allegorical tales. He describes a spring morning in an awakening nature, a walk to a *locus amoenus*, the onset of evening, and finally the transition from day's weariness to a restless sleep and dream. The prologue that introduces the scene explains the four *causae* of the work: the *causa materialis*, that is, the subject of the book (lines 13–18 and 29–30); the *causa efficiens*, that is, the writer (19–24); the *causa finalis*, that is, the instruction or entertainment that is the book's object (25–28 and 47–52); and the *causa formalis*, that is, its meter and arrangement (53–54). The prologue also includes a few of the *regulae* according to which the work should be received and understood by the reader. It does not include, however, a title for the book, any reference to a direct divine commission,[1] or a mention of *gloria dei* among the *causae finales*. A formal analysis of the prologue will not be given here in order to avoid duplication with a later section.[2] However, it is important to investigate the prologue and the allegorical narrative frame as they establish the mood for the vision.

The prologue begins with a businesslike discussion of the question of whether or not dreams are invested with a mantic character. The author declines to unravel the problem in its total medieval complexity; instead, he contrasts the testimony of Sacred Scripture with the *communis opinio* and agrees after a presentation of positions with the opinion of those who believe in the veracity of dream visions. The mood of the passage is neutral, as is the mention of the author's name and the disclaimer of literary ambition.[3] A mood-establishing element emerges for the first time in 1.Prol.31–42. It is of great, if not to say compelling, power and reveals gloomy perspectives:

---

[1] The guardian angel in 9–14 is meant to guarantee the credibility of the vision; however, it is clearly not the *causa efficiens* of the work.

[2] See below, 60–64, 74–79.

[3] See lines 19–24 and 25–28, respectively.

Quod michi flere licet scribam lacrimabile tempus,
Sic quod in exemplum posteritatis eat.
Flebilis ut noster status est, ita flebile carmen,
Materie scripto conveniente sue.
Omne quod est huius operis lacrimabile, lector
Scriptum de lacrimis censeat esse meis:
Penna madet lacrimis hec me scribente profusis,
Dumque feror studiis, cor tremit atque manus.
Scribere cumque volo, michi pondere pressa laboris
Est manus, et vires subtrahit inde timor.
Qui magis inspiciet opus istud, tempus et instans,
Inveniet toto carmine dulce nichil. 1.Prol.31–42

[I'll write of tearful times, which I can mourn,
So those to come may thence a lesson learn.
A mournful song befits our mournful state:
The style is suited to the tale it tells.
What's tearful in this work, the reader must
Accept, was written wholly from my tears.
Often its lines are wet with tears I spill
While writing, oft pen too is wet with tears;
And when I want to write, my hand succumbs,
By labour's weight oppressed; fear saps my strength.
If you inspect this work and present times,
In all my song you'll find there's nothing sweet. (Trans. Rigg).][4]

The passage is absolutely tear-soaked, and with tears that are in no small part borrowed.[5] Its forcefulness depends on the following stylistic means: 1) an unexpected appearance in a neutral context; 2) the repetition of emotionally suggestive words in strategic positions;[6] 3) a renunciation of analysis of the emotions expressed; 4) an intensification through the addition of further symptoms (*cor tremit atque manus*) until finally the word *timor* in conspicuous end position

[4] This and all subsequent translations of the *Visio Anglie* and *Cronica tripertita* are from *John Gower, Poems on Contemporary Events: The Visio Anglie (1381) and Cronica tripertita (1400)*, ed. David R. Carlson with a verse translation by A. G. Rigg (Toronto: Pontifical Institute of Mediaeval Studies, 2011).

[5] The loan derives from Ovid's *Tristia*. Macaulay points out the following parallels in his notes: *Vox Clamantis* 1.Prol.33–34 (*Tristia* 5.1.5–6); 36 (*Tristia* 1.1.14); 37–38 in the tradition of GDLTH2 (*Tristia* 4.1.95–98). He overlooked 42 (*Tristia* 5.1.4). One wonders involuntarily whether the choice of elegiac meter instead of epic hexameters could perhaps have anything to do with the lachrymose material and the Ovidian model. However, the influence of the *Speculum Stultorum* and the *Aurora* may have been the determining factor.

[6] Twice *lacrimis* before a caesura (36 and 37); once *flebilis* at the beginning of a line (33); *lacrimabile tempus* (31) and *flebile carmen* (33) at the ends of lines; also *flere* (31) and another *lacrimabile* (38).

names the emotion explicitly.[7] Thus Gower establishes an important coupling of sorrow and fear for the entire vision.

Ovid's significance for the tears passage is limited to providing convenient forms of expression. The tears themselves are not of Ovidian extraction, although there is a superficial similarity between the situation of the exiled poet in Pontus and that of the anxious author in mutinous London. Both have a lively sense of threatened safety and of the decline of law and order.[8] Ovid's barbarian hordes, which fall like wolves upon the defenseless Roman citizens,[9] resemble Gower's mob of peasants, who are transformed into raging beasts. For the reader versed in Ovid this potpourri from the *Tristia* doubtless calls up associations which prepare for the content of the *Visio*. However, Ovid's tears flow from fear and pity for his own situation and depend upon the reader's sympathetic identification. Gower's tears and those of his audience are intended, as rueful tears of the sacrament of penance, to lead to reconciliation with God and regeneration of the individual as well as of the people.[10]

The fear and sorrow motif is intensified in its gloomy effect through contrast with the detailed description of the June morning that intervenes between the prologue and the start of the first vision. It is, despite certain lovely touches, scarcely more than a skillful treatment of *topoi*. It is also conventional insofar as the spring day is among the customary requisites of medieval allegorical poetry. It is interesting because of Gower's clever utilization of contrast and because of an awkwardness that seems to me important for the poem's interpretation. When the courtly love allegory describes a May morning and leads the poet into

---

[7] If one wishes, one can view lines 39–40 as an exordial *topos* of trepidation before the matter which lies ahead; see E. R. Curtius, *European Literature and the Latin Middle Ages*, trans. Willard R. Trask (New York: Pantheon, 1953), 83–84. However, the trepidation *topos* appears again shortly afterwards in a more extensive form (43–52).

[8] See *Tristia* 4.1 and 5.10.15–28.

[9] *Tristia* 5.7.45–48. Translations of the *Tristia* are throughout those of Arthur Leslie Wheeler (Cambridge, MA: Harvard University Press, 1924):

> *Sive homines, vix sunt homines hoc nomine digni.*
> *Quamque lupi saevae plus feritatis habent.*
> *Non metuunt leges, sed cedit viribus aequum,*
> *Victaque pugnaci iura sub ense iacent.*
>
> [If I look upon the men, they are scarce
> men worthy the name; they have more of cruel
> savagery than wolves. They fear not laws;
> right gives way to force, and justice lies
> conquered beneath the aggressive sword.]

[10] This development is not yet fully clear in the prologue. However, the end of the first book, as well as that of the entire work, permits no uncertainty; see 1.1885–1892, 7.1121–1124, and above all 7.1417–1442.

a meadow in bloom, it usually does so with the intention of having him fall asleep there, whereupon the dream apparatus is set in motion. So it is in the *Roman de la Rose*, in Chaucer's *Legend of Good Women*, and in Gower's *Confessio Amantis*, to name but a few examples. In the *Visio*, on the other hand, the spring morning serves no real purpose, since the dream first ensues at night and in bed. The author obviously had difficulty padding out the day until evening in order to be able, finally, to begin with the visions. Why he made the effort is not readily apparent. Couldn't he have fallen asleep to the song of the birds if the cliché was so important to him, or gone straight to bed—as Chaucer did in the *Book of the Duchess*—if he absolutely had to dream at night? I wish tentatively to propose the hypothesis that the awkwardness arises because on the one hand Gower did not wish to give up the traditional spring morning scheme, but on the other was obliged to place the dream at night in order to satisfy another tradition.

This tradition is not properly literary, stemming rather from the practice of medieval biblical exegesis. The four levels of interpretation—the *sensus historicus, tropologicus* or *moralis, allegoricus,* and *anagogicus*[11]—were entrusted not only to professional theologians, but to every sermon listener and every reader of edifying works. Moreover, the method had taken possession, beyond the limited sphere of the Scriptures, of secular literature, for it offered a welcome means of reinterpreting heathen authors in a Christian sense. Bernardus Silvestris's interpretation of the *Aeneid,* the *Integumenta Ovidii*, and the *Ovide Moralisé* are testimony to the influence of this form of biblical exegesis in the Middle Ages. Gregory the Great's *Moralia in Job* provided, however, the classic model for biblical exposition in the Middle Ages.[12]

There is one chapter in the *Moralia* that treats of the significance of the time of day in biblical *exordia.*[13] The prologue in heaven from the Book of Job provides the occasion. Gregory begins with 1:6: *Quadam die cum venissent filii Dei, ut assisterent coram Domino, adfuit inter eos etiam Satan* [On a certain day when the sons of God came to stand before the Lord, Satan also was present among them]. He then shows how precisely the Scriptures indicate through statements of time and place, especially in the beginning of a narrative, a story's positive or negative

[11] They are most concisely explained in the first prologue of Nicolas de Lyra's *Expositio in Biblia:*

> *Littera gesta docet, quid credas allegoria,*
> *Moralis quid agas, quo tendas anagogia.*
>
> [The letter teaches the deeds, the allegory what you may believe,
> The moral what you should do, the anagogue where you are going.]

Cited from the five-volume edition, *Postilla litteralis super Biblia* (Rome, 1471–1472).

[12] *PL* 75; ed. M. Adriaen, 2 vols., CCSL 143–143A (Turnhout: Brepols, 1979).

[13] *Moralia in Job,* 2.2.

conclusion.[14] Thus it is night when Judas goes out from the Last Supper to betray the Lord (John 13:30). At noon the Lord comes to Abraham when He promises him offspring (Genesis 18:1); in the evening He sends His messengers to proclaim the destruction of Sodom (Genesis 19:1). Since the trials of Job will end in the victory of the good, the prologue in heaven begins during the day.[15] Gregory also applies to visions the rule that the beginning of a story by day predetermines a good ending, but by night a bad. Solomon figures among the above-mentioned examples in this respect. He received the gift of wisdom from the Lord, but at night while asleep, and that is a sign that it would not last.[16] Now Gower's visions do not end with a feeling of relief. We have escaped again, but with the oppressive certainty that the Lord has once more but delayed his wrath; therefore, we must repent and do penance before it is too late.[17] Gower was accordingly obliged to dream by night in order to avoid a contradiction.[18]

The vision proper begins with the third chapter of the first book. It is grouped around three successive central conceptions: 1) the rebellious peasant hordes, which change into raging beasts before the dreamer's eyes; 2) murder and arson in London, striking the dreamer as a second fall of Troy; 3) great distress and salvation at the last moment, experienced by the dreamer as an impending shipwreck and the sudden calming of a storm at sea.[19] For the sake of brevity they shall be designated in the following discussion as the Beast Vision, the Troy Vision, and the Ship Vision. They do not represent independent stages of an historical occurrence, although one could date the Beast Vision in the first week

---

[14] *Historicus sensus. Quam accurate S. Scriptura facta describat.—Intueri libet quomodo sacra eloquia in exordiis narrationum qualitates exprimant, terminosque causarum. Aliquando namque a positione loci . . . aliquando a qualitate temporis signant, quid de ventura actione subjiciant.* [Historical sense. How carefully Sacred Scripture describes details. It is pleasing to consider how the sacred utterances express the properties and the conclusions of cases in the beginnings of narratives. For sometimes by the location of a place . . . sometimes by the nature of the time they signify what they might make subject about the forthcoming action.] *PL* 75:555; ed. Adriaen, 1:59.

[15] So Gregory in any case understands *quadam die.*

[16] *Hinc est quod Salomon, qui sapientiam non perseveraturus accepit, in somnis hanc et nocte accepisse describitur* (3 Kings 3:11) [Hence it is that Solomon, who received wisdom but was not destined to persevere in it, is said to have received it in sleep and at night]. *Moralia in Job*, *PL* 75:556; ed. Adriaen, 1:60.

[17] See lines 1885–1892.

[18] One is tempted to connect the night dream in Chaucer's *Book of the Duchess* with the elegiac character of the work, which treats of the death of Blanche. Unfortunately, the parallel does not work out completely in Chaucer. *The House of Fame* begins at night for no apparent reason.

[19] After the rescue, of course, there follows a second gloomy sea voyage, the motivation of which is insufficient and the interpretation of which is difficult, since clearly it has little to do with the historical event. See below, 45–49.

of June, the Troy Vision on 13–14 June, and the chief events of the Ship Vision on 13–15 June, 1381. The first vision flows almost unnoticeably into the second, so that for a time beast symbolism and Troy myth are intermingled. A genuine pause does occur before the third vision, which is also clearly distinguished in narrative technique from the preceding vision. There are no imagistic overlappings between the second and third visions; instead there appear chronological overlappings, or at least obscurities, which are yet to be investigated. We shall begin with the Beast Vision.

The Beast Vision reveals simultaneously the individuality and the limitation of Gower's talent.[20] Artistically, the idea of describing the Peasants' Revolt of 1381 as an animal uprising could have been extremely fruitful. Models to which a work of this sort can be oriented with little difficulty are found in French treatments of Reynard the Fox. Of course, the beast epic as an artistic vehicle for class

[20] *Vox Clamantis* Book I, Chapters 3–12. There is a summary in Macaulay's introduction to vol. 4 and in Henry Morley, *English Writers,* 10 vols. (London: Cassell, 1864–1894), 4: 177–92. [The first book of the *Vox Clamantis* has received a great deal of attention since Wickert wrote, culminating in Carlson and Rigg's edition/translation in 2011. Important work has been done by David Aers, "*Vox Populi* and the Literature of 1381," in *The Cambridge History of Medieval English Literature,* ed. David Wallace (Cambridge: Cambridge University Press, 1999), 432–53 and "Representations of the Third Estate: Social Conflict and its Milieu around 1381," *Southern Review* (Australia) 16 (1983): 335–49; David R. Carlson, "Gower's Beast Allegories in the 1381 *Visio Anglie,*" *Philological Quarterly* 87 (2008): 257–75; Siân Echard, "Gower's Books of Latin: Language, Politics and Poetry," *Studies in the Age of Chaucer* 25 (2003): 123–56; Andrew Galloway, "Gower in his Most Learned Role and the Peasants' Revolt of 1381," *Mediaevalia* 16 (1993 for 1990): 329–47 and idem, "Reassessing Gower's Dream-Visions," in *John Gower, Trilingual Poet: Language, Translation, and Tradition,* ed. Elizabeth Dutton, John Hines, and R. F. Yeager (Cambridge: D. S. Brewer, 2010), 288–303; Stephen Justice, *Writing and Rebellion: England in 1381* (Berkeley: University of California Press, 1994); Yoshiko Kobayashi, "The Voice of an Exile: From Ovidian Lament to Prophecy in Book I of John Gower's *Vox Clamantis,*" in *Through a Classical Eye: Transcultural and Transhistorical Visions in Middle English, Italian and Latin Literature in Honour of Winthrop Wetherbee,* ed. Andrew Galloway and R. F. Yeager (Toronto: University of Toronto Press, 2009), 363–80; Maura Nolan, "The Poetics of Catastrophe: Ovidian Allusion in Gower's *Vox Clamantis,*" in *Medieval Latin and Middle English Literature: Essays in Honour of Jill Mann,* ed. Christopher Cannon and Maura Nolan (Cambridge: D. S. Brewer, 2011), 113–33; A. G. Rigg, *A History of Anglo-Latin Literature 1066–1422* (Cambridge: Cambridge University Press, 1992), 286–93; Eve Salisbury, "Violence and the Sacrificial Poet: Gower, the *Vox*, and the Critics," in *On John Gower: Essays at the Millennium,* ed. R. F. Yeager (Kalamazoo: Medieval Institute Publications, 2007), 124–43. See also S. Echard and J. Lauz, "A Chronology of Gower Criticism," in *A Companion to Gower,* ed. Echard, 251–73 and the online bibliography of the John Gower Society. (Trans.)]

satire was scarcely developed in England at the time.[21] It is unimportant for our purposes whether the causes actually lie in the English national character or in the fact that the reading public to whom the mentality of the Reynard epics was accessible still understood enough French to delight in the original. The introduction of a new genre would hardly have presented an insurmountable obstacle in a century of receptiveness for nearly all branches of continental literature. The transformation of the beast allegory might have proved more difficult, for by its nature it concretizes abstractions in an artistic statement that reproduces specific events in a code language that utilizes animals. But even if such requirements did not exceed Gower's talent, they contradicted his intellectual posture. He was inclined to be not ironic but apocalyptic. For him the intrusion of chaos into the divinely ordained order of the world was an experience that could not be expressed by means of an ironic, aloof estates satire. The force of moral outrage, the priority of morals over aesthetics, inhibited his artistic development throughout his life.

Therefore, Gower's first vision is not a beast allegory. That is apparent even superficially from the fact that, while the rebellious peasants do indeed assume animal forms, the harried free men (*ingenui*) do not. In this way Gower's Beast Vision distinguishes itself at the same time from the genre of political prophecy, which, however, is not to be disregarded as background for the first book of the *Vox Clamantis*. Political prophecy comes, at least quantitatively, into an astonishing heyday in England in the fourteenth century. For example, *Six Kings to Follow King John* (probably composed before the death of Edward II in 1327), *The Prophecy of Thomas à Becket* (Hatton version, shortly after 1356), *The Prophecy of John of Bridlington* (*circa* 1364), *When Rome is Removed into England* (oldest surviving version 1382), and *Thomas of Erceldoune* (*circa* 1400), to name only the most important.[22] Richard II is said to have been especially receptive to this kind of literature.[23] Towards the end of the century, prophecy played such a role in the political battles of ethnic groups as well as factions that Henry IV felt forced to take legal steps against it. Nevertheless, these prophecies were often not much more than literary exercises that translated historical events into a cryptic style of

[21] Caxton first translated and printed a Reynard tale in 1481. Previously there had existed in England only the story of "The Fox and the Wolf" and Chaucer's *Nun's Priest's Tale*. Nevertheless, Chaucer's tale presupposes his public's familiarity with the Reynard story. See Henry Morley, ed., *The History of Reynard the Fox* (London: George Routledge and Sons, 1889). Also J. M. Ziolkowski, *Talking Animals: Medieval Latin Beast Poetry, 750–1150* (Philadelphia: University of Pennsylvania Press, 1993), and J. Mann, "Beast Fable and Epic," *ODMA* 1:237–39.

[22] The dates are from Rupert Taylor, *The Political Prophecy in England* (New York: Columbia University Press, 1911), 48. For *When Rome, etc.* see Reinhard Haferkorn, *When Rome is Removed into England: eine politische Prophezeiung des 14. Jahrhunderts*, Beiträge zur englischen Philologie 19 (Leipzig: Tauchnitz, 1932), 92–98.

[23] See Taylor, *Political Prophecy*, 83.

expression that had become traditional, and cloaked the author's glance into the political future in a similar prophetic *obscuritas.*[24]

Now animal symbolism is typical of the English form of political prophecy, which at first arbitrarily, later according to fixed conventions, introduced its chief figures in beast form:[25] thus the King of Scotland usually appears as a crab, the Black Prince as a cock. Gower's *Cronica Tripertita* is rife with this characteristic style of the English political prophecy: no names are mentioned at all in the first part and all persons are concealed behind animal designations which, according to the tendency of the fourteenth century, are often taken from heraldry. Moreover, one finds traces of the so-called sibylline, that is, the original continental form of prophecy, when Gower employs initials as ciphers. Insofar as the *Visio* was influenced by the political prophecy, it reveals the English type, as for example when the author transforms the ringleader of the rebels, Wat Tyler, into a jay (*graculus*). The total conception of the uprising of the beasts, however, is difficult to explain in terms of the political prophecy. That becomes evident when one compares the *Visio* with the prophecies that were circulated under the name of John of Bridlington.[26]

At first glance, Gower and John of Bridlington show a certain similarity. Both wrote *post facto* prophetic visions of historical events. The *John of Bridlington* author uses every means to maintain the illusion of true prophecy. He professes to have found and annotated a poem from the first years of the reign of Edward III, a poem that predicts the future in bleak words and images. That the prophet and commentator are identical, there can be no doubt; the aim of the artificial schizophrenia is altogether too obvious. Both works make use of animal symbolism. In *The Prophecy of John of Bridlington* it is a code language, a form of prophetic *obscuritas* without artistic ambitions, conditioned by its purpose and consistently maintained from start to finish.[27] Gower uses it not for camouflage, but for elucidation. The apocalyptic mood that is produced by this means is only a secondary effect. Gower is not interested in the cheap nimbus of alleged political prophecy. His Beast Vision has the sole purpose of expressing with almost mathematical precision an easily intelligible, scathing value judgment.

This value judgment is theologically and philosophically founded and thus perhaps not as evident to the modern reader as to the contemporary public. The crucial passage upon which an understanding of the first vision depends occurs

[24] Taylor, *Political Prophecy,* 89–90.

[25] Taylor names this type "Galfridian" because it first appears in Geoffrey of Monmouth.

[26] Edited by Thomas Wright, *Political Poems and Songs*, 2 vols., Rolls Series (London: Longman, Green, Longman, and Roberts, 1859–1861), 1: 123–215.

[27] The commentator knows ten forms of *obscuritas*, which he conscientiously introduces and explains in the second prologue of the work.

just at the beginning, when the peasant hordes are transformed into beasts before the astonished eyes of the dreamer:

> *Ecce dei subito malediccio fulsit in illos,*
> *Et mutans formas fecerat esse feras.*
> *Qui fuerant homines prius innate racionis,*
> *Brutorum species irracionis habent.* 1.175–178

> [Then suddenly the curse of God blazed down
> On them and changed their form and made them beasts.
> Thus men endowed with reason at their birth
> Take on the form of beasts irrational. (Trans. Rigg.)]

The usual view of the divinely ordained hierarchy (*ordo*) of the creation underlies the passage. The plant stands one step above the stone by virtue of its *anima*, the beast one step higher than the plant by virtue of its *animus*, the man one step higher than the beast by virtue of his *ratio*. Reduced to a simple equation, man equals animal plus *ratio*. By a reversal of the equation, man, if his *ratio* loses control, becomes an animal. That is neither allegory nor poetic display, but a kind of theological mathematics. God bestowed reason upon man in order that it guide his life. If his animal instincts gain the upper hand, then man is degraded to beast and sins against the law of God and of Nature. Thus the Bible warns: *Nolite fieri sicut equus et mulus, quibus non est intellectus* (Psalms 31:9) [Do not become like the horse and the mule, who have no understanding]. Gower develops the same train of thought more fully in Book VII of the *Vox Clamantis*:

> *Et sic bruta quasi perit humane racionis*
> *Virtus, dum vicium corporis acta regit.*
> *Est homo nunc animal dicam, set non racionis,*
> *Dum vivit bruti condicione pari.*
> *Nescia scripture brutum natura gubernat,*
> *Iudicis arbitrium nec racionis habet:*
> *Est igitur brutis homo peior, quando voluntas*
> *Preter naturam sola gubernat eum.* 7.1171–1178

> [And so the power of human reason perishes as if it were that of a beast, so long as vice governs the actions of the body. Now, I should say that man is an animal, but not a rational animal, as long as he lives in a condition like a brute beast's. A nature ignorant of learning governs a beast, and it has no power of judgment or reason. Man is therefore worse than a beast when his will alone governs him contrary to nature. (Trans. Stockton.)]

The passage goes one step beyond what Gower says at the beginning of the *Visio*. There man's sin and punishment consisted in his becoming like an animal; here, on the other hand, he is animal-like in status but beneath the beasts in morality.

The thought is wholly in accord with the orthodox exegesis of another passage from Psalms, often commented upon by the church fathers. I quote, from the chapter *De Homine* of the pseudo-Bonaventura's *Pharetra,* the following citation from John Chrysostom:

> *Comparatus est, ait propheta, homo iumentis insipientibus, et similis factus est eis. Peius est comparari quam nasci. Naturaliter non habere rationem tolerabile est, verum ratione decoratum irrationabili creature comparari voluntatis est crimen non nature.*
>
> [Man is compared, says the prophet, to the foolish beasts of burden, and he has become like them. It is worse to be likened to one than to be born one. To lack reason by nature is bearable, but to liken a creature endowed with reason to a brute beast is to level an accusation against his will and not his nature.][28]

If the *Visio* does not execute this second step dogmatically, it nevertheless expresses it artistically through a second metamorphosis, which I will now discuss.

The dream transforms speculative lines of thought into lively, visible figures. The peasant horde also become animals externally. The divine judgment is that the voluntary inner degradation be followed by an involuntary outer.[29] It is natural enough that the peasants and rural laborers are changed into domestic farm animals. However, the author goes further, and the terror that he seeks to suggest to the reader—and here and there is actually able to arouse—does not originate in this simple metamorphosis but in a further transformation. To the degeneration of man into beast is joined a further degeneration in which the domestic animals become untrue to their nature and acquire the *proprietates* of wild animals:

> *Devia natura sic errat ab ordine, mores*
> *Porcus quod porci non habet, immo lupi.* 1.319–320

[28] *Liber Salutaris Beati Bonaventure Cardinalis Ordinis Minorum Pharetra Vocatus* (Paris: Berthold Rembolt, 1518), 1.7. The passage from Psalms referred to [48:13] reads in the Vulgate: *Et homo, cum in honore esset, non intellexit; comparatus est jumentis insipientibus, et similis factus est illis* [And man when he was in honor did not understand; he is compared to senseless beasts, and is become like to them].

[29] The standard biblical example is Nebuchadnezzar, who, as punishment for his arrogance, was turned into a grass-eating ox (Daniel 4:25–34). Gregory comments in the *Moralia*: . . . *quia elatione cogitationis se super homines extulit, ipsum, quem commune cum hominibus habuit, sensum hominis amisit* [. . . because in the exaltation of thought he raised himself above men, he lost that very thing—the human faculty—which he had in common with men]. *Moralia in Job,* 5.11.20, *PL* 75:688; ed. Adriaen, 1.230. Gower describes the episode vividly and a bit touchingly in the *Confessio Amantis* 1.2785–3042.

[Disordered nature runs awry: the pig
Behaves not like a pig but like a wolf. (Trans. Rigg.)]

The ox is not only an ox, but at the same time lion, panther, and bear (293–294); the rooster wears unlawfully the claws and beak of the falcon (521). This transformation is more than a play of fancy or a cheap artificial device employed in order to produce an impression of the monstrous; it is the artistic equivalent of the second part of the line of thought from Book VII cited above. Gower designates the event now as *retrogradus ordo*, now as *natura denaturans*. When man surrenders his *ratio* and becomes an animal, he sins against the divine and natural *ordo* of the cosmos.[30] When the beast, moreover, conducts himself *contra naturam*, therein lies a superlative instance of *parekbasis*. The phenomenon may be explained stylistically as metamorphosis plus *adynaton*, from the point of view of literary history as an influence of Revelation. However, such an explanation is unfair to the author, who is principally interested in moral instruction.

Now the hierarchical order of the class-organized state is also anchored in a tightly-linked hierarchy of the entire creation. The church fathers saw in the institution of the state—and for medieval man that denotes the state organized in classes—either God's punishment or his instrument of education. In either case a social revolution is also a rebellion against a divine institution. Accordingly, Gower nowhere poses the question of social justice. The *ordo*, the divine principle for the preservation of the world, has been violated, as Gower most emphatically remarks:

Perfida stulticia tunc temporis omne negavit,
Quod natura sibi vel deus ipse petit:
Non timet ipsa deum neque mundi iura veretur,
Set statuit licitum criminis omne malum:
Ordine retrogrado sic quilibet ordo recessit,
Nec status ipse sapit quid sit habere statum. 1.1307–1312[31]

---

[30] In this connection Gower often mentions God and Nature in the same breath; see 1.1092 and 1308. The relationship of God and Nature, of the *lex dei* and the *lex naturae*, will be discussed later.

[31] See also 979–982:

O denaturans urbis natura prioris,
Que vulgi furias arma movere sinis!
O quam retrograda res est, quod miles inermis
Expavit, que ferus vulgus ad arma vacat!

[The old world's nature is denatured now,
By letting furies of the mob take arms.
The world is upside down: the knight, unarmed,
Is filled with fear; the savage mob takes arms. (Trans. Rigg.)]

[Their foolish treachery refused then to
Obey what God and Nature granted them.
They don't fear God or have respect for laws
Of man: they judged all evil was allowed.
All orders thus reversed with backward step:
No rank now knew what having rank entailed. (Trans. Rigg.)]

It is only a natural consequence that such a violation of the *ordo* summons the forces of chaos to battle. He who will not obey God must serve the devil (John 8:34):

Demonibus homines subici culpis meruerunt,
Tunc quia non hominem nec timuere deum. 1.1319–1320

[Through sin mankind became the devil's slaves,
And rightly, for they feared not man or God. (Trans. Rigg.)]

Thus Gower achieves a final gloomy intensification by causing the degenerate beasts to be possessed or inspired by furies and demons, and the swine, after the example of the New Testament (Matthew 8:28–33; Mark 5:1–20; Luke 8:26–37), by Satan in person.[32] To these are joined the plagues of Egypt (frogs and flies) and Philistia (mice). Thus the bestial rebel becomes the demonic, and the temporal as well as the eternal judgment of damnation is sealed:

Scit deus hos homines silvestres igne perhenni
Dignos et reprobos a racione vagos. 1.1017–1018

[God knows, these savages deserve to burn
For ever, lacking reason, reprobates. (Trans. Rigg.)]

The conclusion of the awakened poet's dream experience is the dogmatic counterpart to the value judgment implicitly contained in the Beast Vision. The peasantry lie once more in bondage. Satan's power has been broken with God's help; however, the devil slumbers always in the peasants and can erupt anew. He must be repressed with relentless severity.[33] The antithesis of bondsmen and free men

[32] See 377–378:

Hii fuerant porci, maledictus spiritus in quos
Intravit, sicut leccio sancta refert.

[These were those pigs in which the cursed ghost
Once entered, as the holy scriptures tell. (Trans. Rigg.)]

[33] 2093–2106:

Sic cum rusticitas fuerat religata cathenis,

is shown throughout the entire *Visio* with a crassness that aligns Satan in person on the one side and the Christian martyrs on the other. Gower is not writing a class critique, which according to its nature is always a criticism of the abuses within a social group without thereby questioning its right to be, but a harsh condemnation, unmitigated throughout, which divinely sanctions every action against the peasantry. This is understandable in light of the unique situation of 1381; it in no way, however, accords with the attitude that Gower adopts in the following books of the *Vox Clamantis* and in the *Mirour de l'Omme*.

The Troy Vision (Chapters 13–15) spotlights the seizure of London with a peculiar, solemnly macabre light. The scene changes from country to city, and the city is London, the new Troy:

> *A dextrisque novam me tunc vidisse putabam*
> *Troiam, que vidue languida more fuit.* 1.879–880
>
> [Then to my right I thought I saw New Troy:
> It languished like a widow, filled with grief. (Trans. Rigg.)][34]

Over the events of June 13 is diffused the atmosphere of the fall of ancient Troy, which forms the background to the looting, murder, arson, and drunkenness of the mob and rabble soldiery. Well-known individuals, no longer recognizable to

---

> *Et paciens nostro subiacet illa pede,*
> *Ad iuga bos rediit, . . .*
> *Sic ope divina Sathane iacet obruta virtus,*
> *Que tamen indomita rusticitate latet;*
> *Semper ad interitum nam rusticus insidiatur,*
> *Si genus ingenuum subdere forte queat.*
> . . . .
> *Forcius ergo timor stimulans acuatur in ipsos,*
> *Et premat hos gravitas quos furit illa quies.*
>
> [When peasantry had now been bound in chains
> And lay in sufferance beneath our feet,
> The ox returned to yoke, . . .
> Thus, by God's help, Satanic might is crushed
> But still it lurks, for peasants are untamed.
> The peasants always plot towards our death,
> If they can subjugate the noble class.
> . . . .
> Let stabbing fear be sharpened at those serfs;
> Severity must crush those peace drives mad. (Trans. Rigg.)]

[34] Note also the allusion to Lamentations 1:1 in line 880.

a modern reader, are hidden behind a catalogue of Trojan heroes (961–970).[35] The Queen Mother appears in the role of Hecuba (997–998) and the youthful Richard II must then bear comparison with the hoary Priam (995–996 and 1115). The description attains its climax with the execution of Archbishop Simon Sudbury, who is identified with the high priest Helenus (Chapter 14). Thus the historical events receive an impressive epic heightening.[36] It remains to be considered whether this was the sole or just the most compelling concern that led the author to the Troy theme. Once again it appears as if rational rather than artistic considerations influenced him. For the Trojan model brings into the production, besides the epic flavor, an important new element that indicates Gower's position on the philosophy of history. The history of Britain began in a hazy prehistory with the fall of Troy, which led via the wandering of Aeneas and the exile and divine rescue of his grandson Brutus to the founding of a New Troy on the island of Brutus. Obviously, Gower's public knew the legend of London's founding. Geoffrey of Monmouth, Wace, Layamon were considered historical authorities. Although critical spirits such as William of Newburgh had expressed doubts, the prevailing opinion was still far from willing to separate history from legend.

Perhaps the designation of London as New Troy was especially the fashion in court circles. It appears three times in a 1393 court poem by Richard de Maidstone.[37] In any case, the association of old with New Troy lay ready to hand. Going beyond their common name, Gower implies to the reader that they may share a common fate. Might not the New Troy be about to fall as did the old? Names have a fateful significance for medieval man; history can repeat itself. The Trojan destiny hovers menacingly over the city on the Thames. When one considers what significance historical or pseudo-historical analogies have had for English history, one cannot take Gower's Troy Vision too lightly. It is to a modest extent an equivalent of the Arthurian renaissance of Tudor times. In the prosperous days of Elizabeth the legendary analogy promised a golden future. In the times of class unrest and national insecurity under Richard II the historical parallel

---

[35] They comprise a curious catalogue, for it names only Greek victors, whereas one would expect representatives of the conquered Trojans. Clearly Gower is not overly concerned with the precision of the historical analogy. A second catalogue of mixed derivation, which is probably to be taken as an outdoing *topos*, appears in 985–994.

[36] The Beast Vision, in order that it might be brought to the same stylistic plane, was studded throughout with frequent classical tropes, often in the form of outdoing *topoi*: see 263–276; 349–358; 441–460; 579–580.

[37] "The Reconciliation of Richard II with the City of London," in Wright, *Political Poems and Songs*, 1:282, *Trenovantes;* 283, *Troia* and *Nova Troia*; 286, *Troia novella.* [A modern edition of the poem is available. See Richard Maidstone, *Concordia (The Reconciliation of Richard II with London)*, ed. David R. Carlson, with a verse translation by A. G. Rigg (Kalamazoo: Medieval Institute Publications, 2003). Available online from TEAMS. (Trans.)]

proclaimed imminent downfall. For Gower the case of Troy is a kind of dumb show that masks the English tragedy and makes clear what conclusion is to be expected; the play itself stands in the midst of the last act, and the anxiety that has gripped the author imparts itself to the reader:

Sic amor ecce vetus Troie mutatur in iram,
Cantus et ex planctu victus ubique silet:
In lacrimas risus, in dedecus est honor omnis
Versus, et in nichilum quod fuit ante satis. 1.1333–1336

[Thus Troy's old love is now turned into wrath,
And song, by lamentation quelled, grew still.
Then laughter turned to tears; all honour was
Disgrace: what once sufficed was nothing now. (Trans. Rigg.)][38]

Here the Troy Vision ends. There follows Chapter 16, which suddenly projects the figure of the dreamer into the foreground and forms a bridge to a new series of visions. In Chapter 17 a ship appears, and it is so unexpected and unmotivated that the unity of the poem is seriously endangered. According to the prose summary, it symbolizes the Tower of London, the refuge of the royal party.[39] The remainder of the vision revolves about the ship and the fate of its passengers, above all the author. Of Troy, old or new, nothing more is said.

There are several questions to be clarified here. The first concerns the imagistic sphere in which Gower's visions move. First there was the picture of the uprising of the beasts, frighteningly distorted by *adynaton*; then the vividly epic portrayal of a burning Troy; now a ship in greatest danger on a storm-tossed sea. The factor of fear is common to all three; otherwise they have little in common. Why is a single historical episode such as the Peasants' Revolt divided into three different images, the inner coherence of which remains vague?

The second question concerns the ship itself. The historical occurrences are centered on the Tower. It would have been natural to remain within the Trojan sphere and to identify the citadel with Priam's stronghold. Instead, Gower forces upon the reader the image of a ship, which is much further from the matter. True, the Tower stands on the Thames; one could imagine it as a ship. But this

[38] Note the allusion to James 4:9 in line 1335.

[39] *Hic eciam secundum visionem sompnii describit quasi in propria persona angustias varias que contingebant hiis qui tunc pro securitate optinenda in Turrim Londoniarum se miserunt, et de ruptura eiusdem turris: figurat enim dictam turrim similem esse navi prope voraginem Cille periclitanti.* [Here, as though in his own person, he describes, according to the vision of his dream, the various torments that afflicted those who betook themselves to the Tower of London, in order to find safety, and he describes the incursion into the Tower. He portrays the Tower as like a ship endangered near the whirlpool of Scylla. (Trans. Rigg.)] In the text the comparison first appears in the next chapter, lines 1743–1770.

ship puts at once to sea and has to battle with an infernal storm. Thus Gower places considerable demands upon the reader's capacity for illusion and her willingness to submit to it. Why was the ship so important to the author at this moment? What process of the imagination transformed the Tower into a ship?

The third question concerns the chronology of the events in their relationship to the chronology of the visions. Until the end of the Troy Vision both run parallel. Then they suddenly overlap. The Troy Vision deals with the 13th and 14th of June, 1381, that is, with the seizure of London, the concessions of the king in Mile End (?), the storming of the Tower (?), and the murder of Sudbury.[40] Even if the allusions to Mile End and the Tower are uncertain, the surrender of the Tower in any case should precede the murder of the archbishop, who had sought refuge there. At the beginning of the Ship Vision, which follows from the Troy Vision according to the dream chronology, the storming of the Tower has yet to occur. It is symbolically accomplished before the eyes of the reader in the shipwreck. What reasons compelled the author to alter the sequence of events in the dream?

The reasons for the abandonment of the Trojan setting are easy to see. An accurate retelling of the history of Troy would end with its complete collapse and so would not match the facts of English history. The analogy is maintained as closely as possible until the moment of the catastrophe in order to make clear the gravity of the situation and the importance of the warning. Then it is abandoned.

The reasons for the choice of the ship metaphor—the word "metaphor" is used here as the collective name for all the possibilities of figurative usage—is to be sought in the area of the associations that the author could evoke in his public with it. The ship plays a not insignificant role in literature and preaching. It appears peripherally in the sphere of exordial *topoi* when the composition of a work is compared to the perils of a sea journey.[41] The ship gains varying degrees of importance, however, when viewed as a symbol of the human soul, mankind, the church, or the state.[42] It would be tempting to trace the ship of state in a straight

[40] Lines 995–996 appear to be a reference to the king's concessions: *Nec solito Priamus fulsit tunc liber honore, / Set patitur dominus quid sibi servus agat* [Bereft of glory, Priam did not shine / As once: the lord endures the slave's commands. (Trans. Rigg.)] The storming of the Tower is probably implicit in 997–998; Froissart also mentions the molestation of the Queen Mother. Sudbury's murder occurs in Chapter 14.

[41] Curtius, *European Literature and the Latin Middle Ages*, 128–30, gives an abundance of examples that indicate a continuity of the *topos* from classical antiquity to the Renaissance. I would add from my limited knowledge of the material the very detailed ship metaphor in the prologue of the eighth book of the *Policraticus*. John of Salisbury renews the *topos* by using it to justify his writing. Gower is less original; See *Vox Clamantis* 3.Prol.105–106 and perhaps 81–82.

[42] The soul, for instance, in Hugh of St. Victor's *De Arca Noe Morali*. The relationship has already been reduced to a short formula in the second book, *De Vanitate Mundi:* . . . *Mundus diluvium est, cor autem hominis, si per amorem mundanorum se deorsum inclinat,*

line back to Horace[43] and regard the remaining ship metaphors as a development from biblical origins. However, it will not do to let the religious and secular ships steer neatly separated courses. The isolation of individual areas and their traditions is impossible for a mentality that sees all classifications as expressions of the same divine principle of creation. Thus the concept of the world as an organic whole clarifies the nature of the church as the *corpus Christi* as well as the nature of the class-organized state; it would be absurd to wish to break it down into its classical and New Testament origins. Likewise there are no separable religious and secular traditions of the ship metaphor.

Take, for example, Gower's contemporary, the anonymous author of the poem *Heu Quanta Desolatio.* Does he have Horace in mind when, in the first stanza, he compares England to a menaced ship,[44] and is he conscious of the ecclesiastical traditions when, in a later verse, he extols Wyclif and his disciples as the divinely-sent saviors of St. Peter's ship, that is, the church?[45] In this poem the ship metaphors have only a peripheral significance. There is, however, from the same time or shortly before, in any case from the years of Richard's minority,

---

naufragatur inter fluctus saeculi [The world is a deluge, and the heart of man, if for love of worldly things it inclines itself downward, is shipwrecked among the waves of the world]: *PL* 176:715. Mankind, for example, in Sebastian Brant's *Narrenschiff* and the church in Hugh of St. Victor's *De Arca Noe Mystica* (*PL* 176:669C).

[43] *Carmina*, 1.14.

[44] Wright, *Political Poems and Songs*, 1:253:

> *Heu! quanta desolatio Angliae praestatur,*
> *Cujus regnum quodlibet hinc inde minatur,*
> *Et cujus navigium pene conquassatur.*
>
> [Alas! how much desolation is at hand in England,
> Whose kingdom is threatened on all sides,
> And whose ship is nearly crushed.]

[45] Wright, *Political Poems and Songs*, 1:258:

> *Tantos motus intuens Dominus in mari,*
> *Quosdam viros nobiles fecit magistrari.*
> *Ut fides ecclesiae possit restaurari,*
> *Wyclif et discipulos voluit vocari.*
> With an O and I, *hi sunt viri nautae,*
> *Ducentes a Domino navem Petri caute.*
>
> [Seeing such great motions upon the sea, God
> Caused certain noble men to be the pilots.
> So that faith can be restored to the church,
> He wanted Wyclif and his disciples to be called.
> With an O and I, they are the mariners,
> Safely leading Peter's ship through God.

a political song in English that has the ship of state as its chief theme. It is usually named after its refrain, "Seldom Seen is Soon Forgot," and is found in the Vernon Manuscript, a commonplace book of the fifteenth century.[46] It behooves one to consider it if one wishes to recreate those possibilities of association for his ship vision that Gower could assume in his public.

The anonymous author carefully examines the inner decay of England and the foreign political menace during the Regency. He awakens the memory of the glorious past in order to urge concord and conjures up the figures of Edward III, the Black Prince, and Henry of Lancaster in order to strengthen loyal devotion to the young Richard. The poem goes as follows: once England was a noble and seaworthy ship that defied every storm. In the whole world there was not her equal. She was steered by a strong and steady rudder (Edward III). Nowadays, however, ship and rudder have become separated. The ship is the knighthood of the realm, citizens and peasants are the mast, prayer the wind that fills the sails. Alas, however, piety is no longer in fashion, and so forth.

It is a typical medieval ship of state, whose individual parts are interpreted with reference to class,[47] akin to the comparison between the political cosmos and the human body in all its individual limbs. The vague outlines of Gower's ship have little in common with the systematic-rational enumeration of detail in the English poem. Moreover, the anonymous poet celebrates, with a touch of historical romanticism, the ship in the times of its glory, while Gower describes its decline as near. On this point Gower is in accord with the sermon of an unknown monk from the beginning of the fifteenth century.[48] The text is Ecclesiasticus 43:26: *Qui navigant mare, enarrent pericula ejus; et audientes auribus nostris admirabimur* [Let them that sail on the sea tell the dangers thereof, and when we hear with our ears, we shall wonder]. The preacher, too, proceeds from a pessimistic view of the present, that basic mood that had prevailed in England ever since the last third of the fourteenth century. He, too, casts his eyes backward to happier times, to when England was a proud ship on the sea of prosperity and

---

[46] Frederick F. Furnivall and Carl Horstmann, eds., *The Minor Poems of the Vernon Manuscript,* 2 vols., EETS O.S. 117 (London: Kegan Paul, Trench, Trübner, 1892–1901), 1:715.

[47] The ecclesiastical estate is probably omitted because the vessel is a man-of-war. The accommodation of the Black Prince and his uncle in the class organization obviously proved difficult. Thus Henry of Lancaster is a bark that escorts the ship, while the Black Prince is aboard the ship but not identified with any part. See S. Wenzel, *Macaronic Sermons: Bilingualism and Preaching in Late-Medieval England* (Ann Arbor: University of Michigan Press, 1994).

[48] Bodleian Library MS. 649, fols. 129v–130r. G. R. Owst, *Literature and Pulpit in Medieval England* (Cambridge: Cambridge University Press, 1933), 72–73, gives a lengthy excerpt; however, he does not preserve the macaronic character of the original but translates the Latin parts.

fortune.[49] The clergy formed the bow; the nobility, the stern; the third estate, the hull of the ship. As long as virtue was at the helm and the three estates lived harmoniously in fulfillment of their particular tasks, it sailed on a sea of wealth and happiness. However, once Vice took command, the ship became frail and *Fortuna* averted her face.

Here, then, is the opportune moment for the moralizer to begin. What interests us in his performance is that he cites the Peasants' Revolt as an historical example of an imminently threatening shipwreck. And what links him with Gower beyond that is the conviction that such catastrophic situations are the wages of sin:

> Thus, thoroo pride and synne, *a prosperite navigavimus* in to wo. Mech wo and tribulacion *fuit in hoc regno* for synne: many mishappys mownt up *inter nos*: stormes of debate and dissencioun piryyd up fast. *Nostra navis* was so hurlid and burlid *inter ventos et freta quod erat in grandi periculo et sepe in puncto pereundi. Fuit in grandi periculo quando communes surrexerunt contra dominos. Fuit iterum in grandi periculo quando domini litigabant inter se . . .* (further examples follow). Qwo-so hath sailed the see and abidde thes bittur stormys, he may sauele telle our schip hath be in perlis: *fuit in periculis* withinne, *in periculis* without, in perles of oure selue, in perlis *hostium, in periculis alti maris, in periculis portus.*
>
> [Thus through pride and sin we have sailed from prosperity into woe. There was much woe and tribulation in this kingdom because of sin: many mishaps mounted up among us: storms of debate and dissension piled swiftly up. Our ship was so hurled and burled among the winds and seas that it was in great danger and often on the point of perishing. It was in great danger when the commons rose up against the lords. It was in great danger when the lords quarreled among themselves . . . Whosoever has sailed the sea and endured these bitter storms, he may safely tell that our ship has been in perils: it was in dangers within, in dangers without, in perils from ourselves, in perils from the enemy, in dangers on the high seas, in dangers in port.][50]

If this sermon derives from the time of Henry V, it must, to conclude from the overall tenor, be dated before Agincourt; its pessimism would otherwise have been somewhat moderated. The preacher could naturally have been influenced by Gower; that would indicate that Gower's ship was understood in the beginning

---

[49] *Magna navis que navigauit multos dies in mari prosperitatis est illud copiosum regnum, regnum anglie. Deus per suam passionem salvet illud et conservet* [The great ship that has sailed many days on the sea of prosperity is that fruitful kingdom, the kingdom of England. May God preserve and keep it safe through his passion]. Bodleian Library MS. 649, fol. 129v.

[50] Bodleian Library MS. 649, fol. 130. The biblical quotations are from 1 Corinthians 11:26.

of the fifteenth century as a ship of state. More probable, however, is a common dependence upon an older tradition. The anonymous poet may have followed a sermon convention that also helped shape Gower's imagination, no longer or not yet again evident to us, by which the secular (in any case not noticeably ecclesiastical) author of "Seldom Seen is Soon Forgot" was also stimulated. One detail that appears in the poet as well as in the preacher perhaps helps to explain Gower's transformation of the Tower into a ship. Both provide the ship of state with a tower, and the tower appears to be the particular mark of its strength. The English poem states:

> Sum tyme an Englisch Schip we had,
> Nobel hit was and heih of tour;
> Thorw al cristendam hit was drad.[51]

The sermon implies the same thing with *ffuit etiam adeo fortis quod fortissima nauis* of toure *super mare non audebat nostram expectare* [it {the ship} was also so mighty that the mightiest ship of tower upon the sea did not dare to await ours],[52] and farther on it names a type of ship "brave turyeres." If "turyere" is not in this case a corruption of the word *triere*, which might have been unknown to the scribe, one might assume it to be an otherwise unrecorded synonym for "ship of tour" modeled after the pattern of French. A ship designation of this kind could have facilitated for Gower the transformation of the Tower into a ship.

Is Gower's visionary ship therefore the Tower on the one hand and the English state on the other? I suspect that both notions were current and that Gower intended to evoke them both. However, I also suspect that there dominates another conception, which is easily brought into harmony with the idea of the ship of state and which also ties the last vision organically to the one preceding. If the author saw the events up to 14 June as an *Ilias Anglicana*, wouldn't it then be logical to seek in the Ship Vision a counterpart to the *Odyssey*? The ship, Scylla and Charybdis, the wandering, all point in this direction.[53] And yet the literary tradition and the historical consciousness of those times speak against such an assumption.[54] The matter of the *Odyssey* never acquired the same significance in the literature of the Middle Ages as the Troy myth. The *Aeneid*, not the *Odyssey*, was regarded as the natural continuation of the *Iliad*. In part that was due to patriotic reasons. Britain meant "the island of Brutus," and Brutus was a fictitious descen-

51 Furnivall and Horstmann, eds., *The Minor Poems of the Vernon Manuscript*, 1:716, lines 17–19.

52 Bodleian Library MS. 649, fol. 129v.

53 Scylla and Charybdis are both named in 1723 and 1741. Scylla alone appears in 1768, 1842, 1951–1952, 2085. References to wandering begin on line 1945.

54 See A. B. Taylor, *An Introduction to Medieval Romance* (London: Heath Cranton, 1930; repr. New York: Barnes & Noble, 1969), 120–24.

dent of Aeneas. The fall of Troy and the wandering of Aeneas together formed a piece of the English national past, or past perfect. When Gower portrays the escape from a burning *Troya nova* aboard a rescuing ship, his literary as well as his historical model is the *Aeneid* and not the *Odyssey*. He derives even Scylla and Charybdis, Iris, and the unruly winds not from Homer but from Virgil's third book.[55] With the Ship Vision as a reflection of the *Aeneid*, Gower found an appropriate continuation for his Troy Vision. It guarantees the continuity of action as well as the epic elegance. At the same time it shows the only possible way out of the menacing analogy of the Trojan catastrophe that still corresponds to the actual events.

In his visions Gower manipulates historical account and allegorical interpretations in such a manner that they never fully coincide. Everything fluctuates. The author leaps continuously from one manner of presentation to the other. Within the same series of visions the peasant hordes are now animals, now men, without a transition having been clearly marked. Likewise, the Trojan analogy is a magical illumination in which events are from time to time bathed, rather than a consistently carried out, pseudo-historical equation. Gower thereby attains—perhaps without having intended it—a realism in his nightmare such as otherwise seldom occurs in medieval dream allegories. In the third series of visions, however, the author abandons this technique of presentation and simultaneously undertakes a change in the role that he plays as dreamer and as subject of the *angst* dreams. Thus before we continue with the investigation of the vision as an interpretation of reality, we shall stop for a moment and turn to the figure of the dreamer.

The genre of the dream-narrative requires that the action focus upon the person of the dreamer at the beginning and end. He is the medium through which the dream is transmitted to the reader. Whether he appears again at intervals in this medial function depends on how concerned the author is with maintaining the unity of the dream illusion. Continuity is the rule, interruption the exception. In the visionary prophecy that was in circulation under the name of John of Bridlington in the second half of the fourteenth century, the dream occurs in three waves that are interrupted by the awakening of the dreamer exhausted from the tremors of fever. Gower is careful not to endanger the unity of the illusion through occasional interruptions of the dreams. He has found another means of introducing realistic characteristics into his dream: he distinguishes

[55] Gower's sea storm is, of course, not purely Virgilian, but a mixture of Ovid (*Metamorphoses* 11.410–748, "Ceyx and Halcyone") and Virgil. Whether Gower came to Ovid independently, drawn by his personal preference, or whether he followed the Troy romances of Benôit de Sainte Maure and Guido delle Colonne—who had used Ovid liberally—cannot be determined for sure.

between *somnus* and *somnium*.[56] While the author's sleep, or half-sleep, maintains unity, the individual dream stories rush along in terrifying crescendo until the whirlpool of events in London draws everything together into one single nightmare.[57] The figure of the dreamer becomes visible at the boundaries of the individual dreams. He assumes the role of chorus in the tragedy and functions as audience and commentator. He can be terrified (181–182), paralyzed with fear (240 and 505–506), express dread and alarm in lengthy lamentations;[58] above all, he can evaluate and explicate.[59] At first he is not drawn, either actively or passively, into the events of the dream itself.

This role changes abruptly in Chapter 16, which links the Troy Vision to the Ship Vision. This chapter belatedly establishes the figure of the author as having been active in the first two visions and uses him as a transition to the last vision, in which he becomes the central figure. One may see the influence of the *Aeneid* in the dreamer's differing participation in the events of the second and third visions. According to the account of the *Iliou Persis*, Aeneas is little more than an onlooker and reporter, whereas the flight and wandering appear in a concentrated first-person narrative. Yet this is only a problem of external form. More important is the question of the poetic ego's functional significance for the vision. Because Gower actually experienced June 1381, it is logical to look for autobiographical reminiscences in visionary garb in his appearance in Chapter 16.[60] Since next to nothing is known of Gower's life, however, there are no controls for such an effort. Moreover, the chapter heading warns against hasty autobiographical inferences. It reads:

> *Hic plangit secundum visionem sompnii quasi in propria persona dolores illorum, qui in silvis et speluncis pre timore temporis illius latitando se munierunt.*
>
> [Here, according to the vision of his dream, he laments, as though in his own person, the griefs of those who, out of fear of that time, protected themselves by hiding in woods and caves. (Trans. Rigg.)]

---

[56] Cf. C. S. Lewis, *The Discarded Image* (Cambridge: Cambridge University Press, 1964), 63–65.

[57] See 299, 461–462, 565–566, 1595–1596; each is at the beginning of a new chapter.

[58] See the variation on the theme of the sequence *Dies irae, dies illa* in 635–678. The impetus for this passage may derive from the *Speculum Stultorum*; see Macaulay's note on 635. However, Macaulay did not consider the sequence, to which Gower is much nearer in mood than to an ironic paraphrase of Wireker. That is especially clear toward the end, where verbal and contentual reminiscences of Thomas of Celano prevail. Another lamentation passage is the six elegiac distiches with the anaphora *O res mira nimis* [O what a most astonishing thing], 623–634.

[59] The numerous outdoing *topoi* (263–276, 349–358, 441–460, etc.) are primarily scathing value judgments, not only solemn hyperboles.

[60] For example, in 1381–1398 or 1585–1590.

Whoever may have been the author of the prose summary, the formula *quasi in propria persona* makes one thing clear: the will of the author or the understanding of the contemporary editor speaks against a concrete autobiographical interpretation.

The sixteenth chapter is in form a *cento* of Ovidian citations in a density such as seldom occurs in Gower. I count no fewer than fifty literal borrowings of different lengths in 233 verses;[61] presumably there are still more. Most derive from the *Tristia*, which is indeed similar to Chapter 16 in mood and content. The prose statement *hic plangit* causes the chapter to appear as a *planctus* that is resolved through action and reflection. Both concentrate on the figure of the dreamer, who is suddenly drawn from the periphery into the vortex of events, thus compelling the attention of the reader. Of course, what happens to the author is, as the summary suggests, of a universal nature. The effect that the events produce is more important than the events themselves. Gower thus requires a psychological mirror to reflect them and so he projects his own ego as exponent of a universal experience.

What then is the relationship of the poet's reportorial and entirely passive self to his active dream self? In his essay on the "poetic and empirical I" in medieval authors, Leo Spitzer establishes a hypothesis concerning the different significance of the two *ego*s that with a few modifications is applicable to the *Visio*.[62] According to it, both forms are necessary, the one (the "poetic I") in order to push beyond the limits of individuality to an experience of universal, paradigmatic significance; the other (the "empirical I") in order to record and portray the subject of this experience. Gower's "poetic I" serves not to communicate his personal sufferings and fears in the summer of 1381 but to convey metaphysical insights that arise from these sufferings. The hitherto scattered fragmentary references to the transcendental significance of the events are summarized in Chapter 16 (1369–1379); there is attained through painful individual experience the universally valid knowledge that life can be death and death, life (1583–1584); there is made possible the meeting with the allegorical figure of Sophia, who teaches the author about God's anger (1545–1556).[63]

---

[61] They are: 1359, 1363–1366., 1369, 1379–1380, 1385–1386, 1387, 1395, 1397–1398, 1401–1402, 1403, 1413–1414, 1420, 1424, 1425–1426, 1429–1430, 1433, 1442, 1445–48, 1453, 1459, 1465, 1467–1468, 1469, 1473, 1475, 1485, 1496, 1501–1502, 1503–1504, 1506, 1512, 1514, 1517–1518, 1519, 1521, 1534, 1535–1538., 1539, 1549, 1564, 1565–1566, 1569, 1571, 1573, 1575, 1585, 1589; see Macaulay's comments on these verses in the notes. Macaulay did not register the dependence of 1534 (*Tristia* 5.4.4), 1537 (*Tristia* 1.5.11), and 1538 (freely after *Tristia* 3.3.44).

[62] L. Spitzer, "Note on the Poetic and the Empirical 'I' in Medieval Authors," *Traditio* 4 (1946): 414–22.

[63] The theme was already raised in 1455–1456. This figure seems similar to Boethius's Lady Philosophy.

Its accented stoic tendency distinguishes Chapter 16 from the experiences of the following vision, in which Sophia in person is called upon to console the anguished author with the banality that everything has an end and that patience is the final consequence of wisdom. The question of guilt nowhere attains great importance:

> *Sic tibi fata volunt non crimina . . .* (1.1547)
>
> [The cause is not your crimes but fate; . . . (Trans. Rigg.)]

and

> *Non merito penam pateris set numinis iram:*
> *Ne timeas, finem nam dolor omnis habet* (1.1549–1550)
>
> [Your pain is not deserved: you feel God's wrath.
> Don't be afraid, for every pain has end (Trans. Rigg)],

assures Sophia in Ovid's words.[64]

The *malediccio dei*, which transformed the peasant horde into animals at the beginning of the *Visio*, and the *numinis ira*, which the poet borrowed from Ovid in order to characterize his undeserved suffering, have a certain epic magnitude that allows the idea of human sacrifice in Chapter 19 to appear appropriate. They are, however, far distant from the Christian interpretation of history in the sense of sin, penitence, and forgiveness. In order to give the events a significance in the full sense of the Christian concept of salvation, Gower requires a human being whose inner process of purification in constant correspondence to events leads to the *kairos*, in which the literal rescue, that is, the death of the ringleader, occurs not as simple accident but as inner necessity. The active dream *ego* has the task of developing from the pupil of Sophia into a likeness of the prodigal son. Thus, the last vision is not so much a new stage of the historical events as a new illumination of those events from another level of experience. If one wished to employ the medieval *termini* of biblical exegesis, one could call the Ship Vision the anagogical interpretation of the events of 1381. In an age permeated by the exemplary significance of all substances and all events, such a method was the natural way to true understanding. How an historical event could be anagogically interpreted in secular letters is shown by, for example, Bernardus Silvestris's interpretation of the flight, wandering, and Italian landing of Aeneas as the way of the soul to the heavenly fatherland.[65] Now Gower clearly intended to deal with history in

---

[64] See *Fasti*, 1.483.

[65] *Commentum Bernardi Silvestris Super Sex Libros Eneidos Virgilii*, ed. R. Riedel (Greifswald: J. Abel, 1924); trans. C.G. Schreiber and T.E. Maresca (Lincoln: University of Nebraska Press, 1979).

the *Visio*. The word *cronica* in the *incipit* of three manuscripts[66] and lines 29–30 of the prologue[67] permit no doubt about that. The first two visions sketch events known to the contemporary reader, in the course of which the Beast Vision renders a moral value judgment, the Troy Vision a wide historical perspective of these events. The presentation is relatively objective; thus the role of the author is reduced to a minimum, thus also any direct, personal relationship with God is absent.[68] The last vision, on the other hand, departs from the historical events and is in all essential respects anagogical, that is, it places external events in relationship to inner spiritual events.

The ship's journey begins with a prayer to Christ, the master of wind and wave.[69] It is not much more than a Christian substitute for classical efforts to win Neptune's favor before the beginning of a journey. The objective is physical assistance in a physical emergency. At first the journey promises well, but the dreamer's optimism proves misleading. A violent sea storm breaks out and dashes all hopes, and a fantastic sea monster menaces ship and passengers, whose behavior suits the markedly epic-classical presentation:

Brachia cum palmis, oculos cum menteque tristi
In celum tendens, postulat omnis opem:
Non tenet hic lacrimas, stupet hic, vocat ille beatos.
Proque salute sua numina quisque vocat. 1.1733–1736

[Each stretched his hands and arms and, sad in mind,
His eyes to heaven and he prayed for help.
None checked their tears; one gapes, one calls on saints,
And each one begs salvation from the gods. (Trans. Rigg.)]

Apart from the mention of the *beati*, the passage distinguishes itself more through the quality of its Latin than through a specifically Christian coloring of classical parallels.

---

66 SCE according to Macaulay's designations.

67 *Quos mea terra dedit casus novitatis adibo,*
Nam pius est patrie facta referre labor.

[I'll treat the new events my land's endured:
To write one's country's deeds is pious work. (Trans. Rigg.)]

68 It is striking that the *Visio* contains no prayer in a Christian sense until Chapter 16. All starts in this direction are epically traditional and religiously neutral; see 1471–1472, 1555–1556.

69 It is unimportant for our purposes whether the prayer has Christ in mind with the designation *stella maris* and appeals to him alone, or whether it is a double prayer to Christ and Mary. See Macaulay, Notes ad loc.

At first the author implicitly includes himself (*omnis*). However, that changes with the impression of the storming of the Tower, which he describes as follows:

> *Visa michi Cilla fuit et tunc visa Caribdis,*
> *Devoret ut navem spirat utrumque latus.* 1.1741–1742
>
> [First Scylla, then Charybdis, came in view:
> Each side aspires to swallow up the ship. (Trans. Rigg.)]

His soul achieves an insight into the relationship of the outer and inner events; that is, it recognizes its own sin and guilt. Instead of the formula of Chapter 16—*conscia mensque michi fuerat, culpe licet expers* (1553) [and my mind had been aware, although devoid of guilt]—there now follow reflection and contemplation:

> *Talia fingebam misero michi fata parari,*
> *Demeritoque meo rebar adesse malum.*
> *Sic mecum meditans, tacito sub murmure dixi,*
> *"Hec modo que pacior propria culpa tulit."*
> *Non latuit quicquam culparum cordis in antro,*
> *Quin magis ad mentem singula facta refert:*
> *Cur michi commemorat scelerum commissa meorum*
> *Ut magis exacuat cordis ymago preces.* 1.1781–1788
>
> [Such things, as I imagined, were my fate:
> I thought that evil came from my own guilt.
> Reflecting thus, I murmured silently
> 'All that I suffer comes from my own fault'.
> No blame lurked in the cavern of my heart
> That did not bring each single sin to mind.
> My intellect recalls the crimes it's done,
> To make imagination sharpen prayer. (Trans. Rigg.)]

It is the parable of the prodigal son that the author experiences, just as Augustine had seen it, in two principal stages of self-contemplation and return to God.[70] Gower accomplishes the first stage in phrases such as *mecum meditans, cordis ymago*; the second in the prayer, *Peccavi, redeo, miserere precor miserendi!* (1.1823) [I've sinned, I'm back: forgive me, I need help!]. Thus is discovered the meaning of

[70] *In nobis ipsis dei imaginem contuentes tanquam iunior ille evangelicus filius ad nosmet reversi surgamus et ad illum redeamus a quo peccando recesseramus* [Beholding the image of God within us, having come back to ourselves just as that younger biblical son, let us arise and return to him from whom in sinning we departed]. In Pseudo-Bonaventura, *Pharetra*, 4.50, cited as a quote from *De Civitate Dei* 11.28 (*PL* 41:342).

earthly suffering, which is to divorce the soul from the world and guide it back to God:

> *Iam prope depositus sum mundo, frigidus, eger,*
> *Servatus per te, si modo server, ego.* 1.1829–1830
>
> [Abandoned almost by the world, cold, sick,
> If now I'm to be saved, I'm saved by you. (Trans. Rigg.)]

The historical events have taken on a metaphysical significance—become anagogical in the true sense of the word. The moment has arrived when the contention that catastrophe can be averted through a process of spiritual purification appears prepared and substantiated. God has mercy on the contrite sinners, removes his judgment of damnation, and the uprising collapses.

At this point the epic cast of the story leads to a striking mixture of pagan and Christian motifs that makes interpretation difficult. Chapter 18, in which the author had become introspective, ended with the word *preces*. Chapter 19 accordingly begins with the effectiveness of the prayer:

> *Clamor in excelsis, lacrime gemitusque frequentes,*
> *Non veniam cassi preteriere dei.* 1.1851–1852
>
> [Our calls on high, our tears and frequent groans
> Were not in vain: God's mercy heeded them. (Trans. Rigg.)]

However, divine forgiveness is attached to a condition. The Ovidian-Virgilian description of the uproar of the elements had brought into the fray Aeolus and the four winds, and especially Neptune. The calming of the sea falls in his province and he demands a sacrifice (1853–1856). The concept of a sacrifice of expiation, and indeed of a human sacrifice, places a heavy demand on the reader and stands in sharpest contrast to the preceding chapter's perception of sin. The epic solemnity may perhaps require it. However, hadn't the offering of human sacrifice been forbidden by Jehovah on Mount Moriah and by the Greek goddess Artemis at Aulis? Of course, Gower tones the matter down by speaking of requital (1867), and by suggesting the possibility that the guilty can make atonement for themselves through death (1872). However, that is not to deny that in the beginning, without any consideration of moral justification, God is offered a sacrifice, a bribe, as it were:

> *Dona valent precibus commixta, per hec deus audit*
> *Micius, et votis annuit ipse precum.* 1.1855–1856
>
> [Gifts mixed with prayers prevailed: God was more kind
> And heard and yielded to our pleas and prayers. (Trans. Rigg.)]

The sacrifice to Neptune as an epic reminiscence is an alien element in Gower's story, as is evident at the point where the account returns to the Christian God. As far as Neptune is concerned, the sacrifice has the desired consequence, for it is a *holocaustum sufficiens* (1883). The storm abates and the elements return to their accustomed courses. The dreamer breathes easily, for the hour of rescue has come. A smooth and clear denouement appears to have been achieved.

However, at this moment a voice sounds *ab excelso*, and God speaks of a postponement, not an appeasement, of his anger. The *sufficiens holocaustum* appears to have been forgotten; the settled account is reopened in all its Christian dubiousness. After God's promise the already solaced author (1881) awakens to a new life (1899), and only then does the already calmed storm first cease. Such repetitions and overlappings persist.[71] And as though he intended to make the confusion complete, Gower fails to distinguish clearly between Neptune and God. At the beginning of the chapter he gives the impression that there are two gods, whose relationship to each other remains unclear.[72] When, however, the sacrifice is over and Neptune has played his role, there sounds the unspecified heavenly voice. There is no perceptible transition. In the event that two gods are still intended, the general concept *deus* covers both. Probably it is one and the same deity, now seen under classical, now under Old Testament aspects.

Between the muddled development of Chapter 19 and its accompanying prose summary occurs an instructive contradiction. The summary reverses the sequence of events. It begins with the heavenly voice, and then God, appeased by prayer, restrains the elements. Only then occurs the death of the ringleader, *quasi in holocaustum*.[73] The human sacrifice is not avoided, but any possibility of considering it as an attempt to influence God is excluded, since it occurs sub-

[71] Compare 1884–1886 with 1927–1928; 1899–1900 with 1933–1934; the conduct of the sailors in 1901–1906 with 1935–1940.

[72] The forgiving God is simply designated *deus* (in 1851–1852), while Neptune is introduced in the following lines as *deus maris*. Because the two distiches are contrasted through an adversative particle, there appear to be two gods:

> *Clamor in excelsis, lacrime gemitusque frequentes*
> *Non veniam cassi preteriere dei;*
> *Attamen ipse maris Neptunus qui deus extat,*
> *At* [sc. *ut*] *mare pacificet, tunc holocausta petit.* 1.1851–1854
>
> [Our calls on high, our tears and frequent groans
> Were not in vain: God's mercy heeded them.
> Yet Neptune, who was ocean's god, required
> A sacrifice to pacify the sea. (Trans. Rigg.)]

[73] *Hic fingit secundum visionem sompnii de quadam voce divina in excelsis clamante, et quomodo deus placatus tandem precibus tempestates sedavit, et quomodo quasi in holocaustum pro delicto occisus fuit ille Graculus, id est Walterus, furiarum Capitaneus* [Here, according to the vision of his dream, he writes about a divine voice proclaiming on high, and describes

sequently and seems designated, through the addition of the words *pro delicto*, as punishment. The sense of such a sacrifice after appeasement must be sought in Genesis. When the Lord pacified the waters of the deluge and bade him go from the ark, Noah constructed an altar and offered a sacrifice: *et tollens de cunctis pecoribus et volucribus mundis, obtulit holocausta super altare* (Genesis 8:20) [and taking of all cattle and fowls that were clean, he offered holocausts upon the altar]. And the Lord took pleasure in the sacrifice and made his covenant of peace with mankind. The analogy does not hold true in all respects, but the basic features of the Noah story are evident in Gower. The situation of the few *ingenui* who succeed in fleeing aboard the rescuing ship corresponds to the fate of the ark's occupants. The sea storm, which Gower industriously intensifies into a colossus, shows a similarity to the deluge. The sacrifice of thanksgiving, the choice of the word *holocaustum* (instead of *sacrificium*), which is inappropriate because there is no fiery sacrifice, point to the Genesis account. Perhaps there is also a connection between the birds of Noah's sacrifice and the statement of line 1863 (*Una peribat avis*—a single bird perished), referring to Wat Tyler the jay. The most important indication of the Noah story, however, probably lies in the accentuation of *pax* restored.[74]

Seen in this way, Chapter 19 dovetails organically with the line of thought of the preceding chapter. The inner story suffers no interruption, the outer adjusts itself without too much difficulty. Both attain their climax and provisional conclusion at the same moment. One is tempted to view the summary as Gower's outline, from which he unintentionally departed (to the disadvantage of the narrative) in working out the details.[75]

The summary of Chapter 20 identifies the ship, vainly seeking a calm harbor, with the *mens turbata* of the dreamer.[76] Finally it lands in Great Britain, an island where, as a worthy old man informs the author upon interrogation, peace never reigns.[77] The shock is so severe that the dreamer loses consciousness. When he awakens, the heavenly voice instructs him for the last time.

---

how God was placated and finally calmed the storms, and how, as though as a sacrifice for sin, the Jay was killed, that is to say Wat, chieftain of the furies. (Trans. Rigg)].

[74] 1920: *Pax redit, atque probis fit renovata salus* [New peace returns, and safety for the good. (Trans. Rigg.)]

[75] It would be possible to hold a careless redactor responsible for the discrepancy. Yet, differences between the summary and the text occur repeatedly and the explanation does not account for several instances where the summary is more knowledgeable than the text, while the supposition that the summary accords with a rough draft accounts for all instances.

[76] *Hic loquitur adhuc de navi visa in sompnis, id est de mente sua adhuc turbata . . .* [He continues to speak of the ship that he saw in his sleep and of his still disturbed mind (Trans. Rigg)].

[77] The idea of peace as the unrealized and unrealizable longing of the poet suffuses the entire *Visio*. It is expressed by *pax, concordia, amor*. This yearning for peace cannot be

From a compositional point of view, it is the task of this last chapter to justify the writing of the work and to sanction its content. That is accomplished in 2047–2050 with a divine commission, as is customary in allegorical dream narratives. Notwithstanding, Gower takes advantage of the opportunity to have the heavenly voice proclaim a considerable amount of banal practical wisdom (2021–2046), which reads like a selection from the *Disticha Catonis* and which is entirely out of place. Even taking into consideration that maxims had to form the ornament of any refined literary work, it is difficult to come to terms with the fact that the trite stoicism recommended here gives the lie to the experiences of the last chapter. It sounds like Chapter 16 with *Sophia* all over again. Even the *Fortuna* concept, which the author elsewhere opposed on ethical grounds,[78] surfaces again. Gower was not enough of a mystic himself to portray convincingly a difficult anagogical theme within the framework of a concrete historical event. He used a meditation and sermon motif without having fully assimilated it. That such an assimilation of outer and inner experience was possible within the metaphor of a dangerous sea journey, and remained possible, is demonstrated by the example of Donne two and one-half centuries later.[79] The decorative value of the ship metaphor appears to have been more important to Gower than its content.

The voyage through the stormy sea of life ends not in the quiet harbor of God's peace, but in a temporary landing place full of unrest and strife that one has to endure with stoic equanimity. Everything remains *in suspenso*. Law and order, or, as the author would say, *pax et concordia*, are still endangered after the collapse of the Peasants' Revolt. Gower's attitude is ambivalent throughout. On the one hand he cannot very well say that God's intervention was inadequate, so he joyfully shouts his thanks[80] and designates himself a new man.[81] On the other hand, his worries on his own and his nation's behalf remain:

> *Non tamen ad plenum fateor mea corda redisse,*
> *Qui mala tam subito tanta per ante tuli.*
> *Qui semel est lesus fallaci piscis ab hamo,*
> *Sepe putat reliquis arma subesse cibis.* 1.2069–2072

---

satisfied because for the Christian author the soul can never find peace in this world. Nor does he find solace in the sense of John 14:27 and 16:33. What Gower has the heavenly voice say in 2025–2046 is strikingly inadequate and can in no way stand as a solution to the problem.

[78] *Vox Clamantis*, Book II *passim*.

[79] See Expostulation 19, in *Devotions upon Emergent Occasions*, ed. John Sparrow (Cambridge: Cambridge University Press, 1923), 114.

[80] See 2064: *exultans*; 2082: *Cum laudis iubilo cantica solvo deo* [I sing a song of praise to God with joy (Trans. Rigg)].

[81] 2067: *Tunc prius ad dominum cordis novitate revivens* [Reviving, first my heart grew new for God]; 2112: *Et velut a sompno sum renovatus homo* [As though from sleep I woke and was renewed (Trans. Rigg)].

[My heart, I grant, had not returned in full,
Since I had borne such sudden ills before.
The fish that's once been hurt by cunning hook
Is wary for the spears beneath the bait. (Trans. Rigg.)]

The conflict of moods is reflected in the wish for England with which the *Visio* concludes:

O mea si tellus, quam non absorbuit equor,
Debita sciret eo reddere vota deo!
Castigavit eam dominus, nec in vicera mortis
Tunc tradidit, set adhuc distulit ira manum. 1.2125–2128

[I wish my land, which sea did not consume,
Knew how to render proper prayers to God.
God chided earth, but did not deal death's wound
For them; his anger still withheld its hand. (Trans. Rigg.)]

The feeling of liberation is coupled with a feeling of continuing menace: *adhuc distulit ira manum.* The author's pessimism is unequivocal. Gower was all too cognizant of the significance of the events of 1381. Sermons and devotional literature leave no doubts about the significance of such *tribulationes*, and it is no accident that the passage on tribulation is one of the longest in Bromyard's *Summa*. Let me cite but one passage:

. . . prosperitas multos a se seu a cognitione sua et a statu proprie salutis alienat; ideo deus tribulationes eis inmittit, ut ad se redeant.

[. . . prosperity estranges many people from themselves or from self- knowledge and especially from a state of salvation; therefore God sends tribulations upon them, that they might return to themselves.][82]

Did Gower achieve his goal? Did the shock of the Peasants' Revolt point the English nation to the way of the prodigal son? *O mea si tellus, quam non absorbuit equor, / Debita sciret eo reddere vota deo!* is a real wish, even though Gower expresses it in an imaginary situation. He had called for soul-searching in the *Mirour de l'Omme*, and in the class critique of the *VC* had attempted to explain the signs of the times. Now in 1381 he believed the catastrophe had begun, and God had granted a reprieve from his wrath only at the twelfth hour. No conversion, however, ensued. The country slid back into the same old rut. The *angst* dream, which had landed the poet *in medio pravae et perversae nationis*, proved in

[82] The last clause alludes to the parable of the prodigal son; see Luke 15:17. Cf. above, 46.

the end to have been correct and, after the removal of the immediate danger, the homilist exhorted deaf ears.

Chapter Three

The *Vox Clamantis* and the Medieval Sermon

A. The Homilist and the Archer

The contents of the *VC*, that is, the *Vox Clamantis* with the exclusion of the *Visio*, are most often described as class critique or estates satire. The concept of estates satire is unfortunate and misleading,[1] and, furthermore, classification of the poem in the category of class critique is justified only to a limited extent. While it is satisfactory for most of the material, it ignores or overlooks the countless philosophical and theological discussions which suffuse and surround the *VC*. They are not simply erudite ballast, strewn about at random, but show the firm outlines of a system, the essence of which is popular theology, that gives the class critique sense and significance. The title, and the accompanying lines about an archer with which Gower sends his poem into the world, together point in the direction of theology—or, more properly, in the direction of the medieval sermon.

The title *Vox Clamantis* first appears in the prologue of the second book and thus refers with certainty to the *VC*. What did the author wish to express with this title? With what expectations did the contemporary reader approach such a work? Did Gower perhaps attempt a sensational "headline" with his *Voice of One Crying in the Wilderness*? Definitely not. For Gower, as for his reader, the figure of John the Baptist signified a concrete programme. John was celebrated in three different aspects in the course of the church year: in February as the greatest among the prophets (according to Matthew 11:11), in June as the first Christian martyr, and in Advent and Lent as the preacher who made ready the

[1] Samuel M. Tucker, *Verse Satire in England before the Renaissance* (New York: Columbia University Press, 1908), denies the existence of satire as a literary genre in England before 1540. His reasons seem valid to me. [Tucker's contention has been convincingly dispelled by Paul Miller, "John Gower, Satiric Poet," in *Gower's* Confessio Amantis*: Responses and Reassessments,* ed. A. J. Minnis (Cambridge: D. S. Brewer, 1983), 79–105. Trans.]

way of the Lord. In this, his chief characteristic, he becomes the epitome of the *vox clamantis*.

In desiring his work to be understood according to the formula *vox clamantis in deserto*, Gower made a statement about his own function, about the form and content of the book, and about the contemporary situation. *Vox Clamantis* is a coinage which the gospels apply to John alone (Matthew 3:3, Mark 1:3, Luke 3:4, John 1:23); however, they take it from Isaiah 40:3 [The voice of one crying in the desert: Prepare ye the way of the Lord, make straight in the wilderness the paths of our God]. It has, therefore, an impersonal, functional significance in addition to its personal and thus unique connection with John the Baptist. Now alongside the current medieval comparisons of the preacher with the *medicus*, the *piscator*, and the *miles*—each of whom displays one of his functions—there appears a comparison with the *praeco*, the herald, who forcefully expresses the weight of divine authority and the medial nature of the preacher's position.[2] In this characteristic the preacher is the instrument, the voice of the Lord, the *vox clamantis*. So says John Waldeby in one of his baptismal sermons:

> *... sicut sol in medio planetarum illuminat omnia celestia luminaria et sicut dux in medio exercitus dirigit omnes tirones in pugna, sic Christus infra id est in anima cuiuslibet predicatoris stans in eo loquitur tamquam in instrumento. Luc. 12° Ego dabo vobis os et sapientiam etc. Et ideo joh. respondit de seipso: Ego vox clamantis in deserto. Non solum joh. sed quilibet predicator ydoneus vox Christi per ipsum clamantis dicitur; alias non dixisset, qui vos audit me audit.*
>
> [... just as the sun in the midst of the planets illuminates all the heavenly lights, and just as a general in the midst of an army directs all the recruits in battle, thus Christ here below, that is, in the soul of every preacher, standing in him speaks as if with an instrument. Luke 12, I shall give you mouth and wisdom, *etc.* And thus John answered concerning himself: I am the voice of one crying in the wilderness. Not only John, but any capable

2 Bromyard, *Summa Praedicantium, s.v. praedicator*, art. 1: *Officium praedicationis assimilari debet officio praeconis ... qui iussa, et ordinationes clamat regia ... Primo quantum ad materiam quam clamat: quia sicut praeco illorum materiam et verba, quae ponuntur in ore suo: quantocumque sint aliquibus terribilia, et gravia, atque displicentia: illa nihilominus aperte clamat, nihil dimittens de hoc, quod ponitur in ore suo? Ita praedicator verba ... et iussa Dei, quae ei ... praecipit.* [Should not the office of preaching be compared to the office of the herald ... who proclaims the royal decrees and laws? ... First, as far as concerns the matter that he proclaims, because just like the herald, {he proclaims} the matter and words which are placed in his mouth; howsoever much they are frightful and oppressive and displeasing to some, he nevertheless proclaims them clearly, omitting nothing from that which is placed in his mouth. Thus the preacher {proclaims} the words ... and decrees of God which to him ... He teaches.]

preacher is said to be the voice of Christ proclaiming through him; otherwise he would not have said, who hears you hears me.][3]

The right with which Gower, a layman, took upon himself the role of preacher and thus the designation *vox clamantis* will be discussed later.[4] We must now come to our second point, the form and content of the Johannine homily.

Among the synoptic Gospels, Luke (3:1–14) provides the most detailed account of the Baptist's sermon. I wish to show how it was understood by reference to one of Bonaventura's commentaries,[5] more suitable as an illustration than a contemporary sermon would be because it interprets the chapter as a whole. The late medieval sermon, rarely treating a biblical text as a unity, instead realizes its own divisions and subdivisions, with appropriate citations, upon a short verse or verse part. The result is that it seldom goes further than *vox—clamantis—in deserto.*[6] Bonaventura, on the other hand, discusses the tone, content, and form of the Baptist's sermon in detail. The tone he characterizes as zealous severity: *Praedicatio Joannis commendatur a zeli severitate.*[7] The content he divides into three parts:

a) Invective (*increpatio*)—Luke 3:7: "He [John the Baptist] said therefore to the crowds that went out to be baptized by him, 'Brood of vipers! Who has shown you how to flee from the wrath to come?'"

b) Exhortation (*exhortatio*)—Luke 3:8: "Bring forth therefore fruits befitting repentance, and do not begin to say, 'We have Abraham for our father'; for I say to you that God is able out of these stones to raise up children to Abraham."

---

3 John Waldeby, *Sermones*, MS. Bodley 687, fol. 84 on the text: *Ego vox clamantis in deserto* (John 1:23); note the quotation of Luke 10:16. See also Alanus de Insulis, *De Sancto Joanne Baptista*: . . . *Et sicut verbum Dei dicitur interior mentis conceptus, sic vox verbi dicitur exterior sonus. Unde, sicut Christus dicitur Verbum, sic vox verbi aliquis praedicans verbum. Sicut quilibet etiam propheta posset dici vox verbi, quasi verbum praedicans, tamen antonomastice Joannes Baptista dicitur vox verbi.* [And just as the word of God is considered an internal concept of the mind, so the articulation of the word is considered an external sound. Whence, just as Christ is called the Word, so the voice of the word {is said to be} anyone preaching the word. Likewise just so can any prophet be called the voice of the word, as if preaching the word, although John the Baptist is called antonomastically the voice of the word.] *Liber Sententiarum ac Dictorum Memorabilium*, *PL* 210:243.

4 See below, 64–69.

5 Bonaventura, *Commentarius in Evangelium Lucae,* in *Opera Omnia*, vol. 7.

6 On the technique of the late medieval sermon, see Etienne Gilson, *Les Idees et les Lettres* (Paris: Vrin, 1932), 93–154; G. R. Owst, *Preaching in Medieval England* (Cambridge: Cambridge University Press, 1926), *passim*; B. M. Kienzle, *The Sermon*, TSMAO 81–83 (Turnhout: Brepols, 2000).

7 Bonaventura, *Commentarius in Evangelium Lucae,* 73.

> c) Threat of Punishment (*comminatio*)—Luke 3:9: "For even now the axe is laid at the root of the trees; every tree, therefore, that is not bringing forth fruit is to be cut down and thrown into the fire."[8]

As for its form, Bonaventura labels the Baptist's a class sermon.[9] The audience is not just a random assortment, but is organized by estates. Whereas in ecclesiastical practice, however, the class sermon usually focused on one class—for example, on merchants or soldiers, the wedded or the widowed—the Baptist's sermon touched all parts of a class-organized community. Bonaventura praises the care with which John satisfied the particular needs of the individual classes, which he reinterpreted as *subditi, ministri,* and *rectores*:

> *Praedicatio Joannis commendatur primo quoad exigentiam populi tripliciter. Quantum ad primum notandum, quod secundum triplicem differentiam personarum audientium diversas instructiones administrat: primo, ad turbas, quae gerunt personam subditorum; secundo, ad publicanos, qui gerunt personam ministrorum; tertio, ad milites, qui gerunt personam rectorum sive praepositorum.*
>
> [The preaching of John is commended in three ways, first in relation to the needs of the people. With respect to the first thing that ought to be observed, that the audience is triply diverse, he directs different instructions: first, to the multitude, who act the role of the governed; second, to the publicans, who act the role of administrators; third, to the knights, who act the role of rulers or commanders.][10]

---

[8] Bonaventura, *Commentarius in Evangelium Lucae,* 73: *Et quia severitati debet adiungi pietas, ideo praemittitur increpatio; secundo vero adiungitur exhortatio, ibi: Facite ergo dignos fructus poenitentiae; tertio vero subinfertur comminatio, ibi: Jam enim securis ad radicem etc. Increpatio est culpae, admonitio poenitentiae, sed comminatio poenalis vindicatae.* [And because piety should be joined to severity, invective is put first; exhortation is added in the second place, to wit "Bring forth therefore the worthy fruits of penitence"; threatening is attached in the third place, to wit "For already the axe is to the root," etc. Invective is for sin, admonition for penitence, but threatening for the punishment of the sinful man.]

[9] The term *status* is not defined very clearly in the medieval sermon manuals. It designates the three estates which comprise the body politic, the different walks of life, and also other categories such as the married, widows, virgins, and the like. Thus Alanus de Insulis, in his *Summa de Arte Praedicatoria* (*PL* 210), places side by side the following examples for the sermon *ad status*: *Ad Milites* (Chap. 40), *Ad Advocatos* (Chap. 41), *Ad Principes et Judices* (Chap. 42), *Ad Claustrales* (Chap. 43), *Ad Sacerdotes* (Chap. 44), *Ad Conjugatos* (Chap. 45), *De Viduis* (Chap. 46), *Ad Virgines* (Chap. 47), and, especially charming, *Ad Somnolentos* (Chap. 48).

[10] Bonaventura, *Commentarius in Evangelium Lucae,* 75.

Inclusive and at the same time detailed class criticism is, therefore, characteristic of the Johannine homily.

Bonaventura is, of course, only one instance of the interpretation of Luke 3. But he brings together, without really adding a new point of view, the components that occur only individually in other ecclesiastical authors and in sermons. One may thus assume that he renders approximately the conceptions and associations that Gower could presuppose in his reading audience when he named his work *Vox Clamantis.* In fact, all the above-mentioned characteristics of the Baptist's sermon recur in Gower's poem. He claims for his person the function of divine spokesman. He pitches the tone of his performance to zealous severity, although on occasion he shifts suddenly to sarcasm or sentimentality. In its essence (Books III-VI) the poem is a critique of a class-organized society *sub specie aeternitatis* with the goal of its moral regeneration; therefore, it is not satire or class criticism, but *increpatio* after the manner of John.[11] Its prelude is Book II, which speaks chiefly of the earlier fortune of the chosen people, of the English.[12] This is clearly a variation on the Father Abraham theme (Luke 3:8) in the Baptist's sermon, hence *exhortatio.* That they are the elect is no guarantee for either the children of Abraham or "God's own people" that the Lord will waive judgment for the sins of the present. There then follows a description of the bitterness and danger in the present situation (2.26–36). It matches the Johannine threat

---

[11] Miller, "John Gower, Satiric Poet," 91n., modifies Wickert's conclusion significantly when he points out that *increpatio* "was already associated with satire in the Vulgate Scholia." He concludes that "Gower's *Vox Clamantis* is an example *par excellence* of medieval satire" (99). [Trans.]

[12] See especially 2.17–36:

Si tamen esse potest quod felix esset in orbe,
Dudum felices nos dedit esse deus:
Quicquid summa manus potuit conferre creatis,
Contulit hoc nobis prosperitatis opus.
Huius erat vite, si que sit, gloria summe,
Nobis pre reliquis amplificata magis.
Tuncque fuisse deum nobis specialius omni
Conversum plebe clamor ubique fuit:
Famaque sic mundi, nobisque beacius omni
Tempus erat populo nuper. . .

[Long ago, God granted that we be happy, if it is possible that one may be happy on earth. Whatever the hand of the Most High could bestow upon His creatures, it bestowed this piece of good fortune upon us: the glory, if such it is, of the highest kind of life was extended to us above all others. And then there was shouting everywhere that God had turned against us in particular, rather than against all people. So ran the common talk of the world, yet times were once happier for us than any people. (Trans. Stockton.)]

that the axe has already been put to the root of the tree and is, according to Bonaventura, *comminatio*—actually *comminatio de praesenti*. To it Gower attaches a discussion of the question of blame that forms a natural transition to the class critique of Book III.[13] At the end of the work, in Chapter 24 of Book VII, the national theme returns, first in the poet's affirmation of his involvement in the national misfortune—one of the most beautiful sections of the work—[14] then in the threat of divine judgment upon the English people (7.1328–1338). Thus one encounters here the Johannine *comminatio de futuro*, corresponding to the second half of Luke 3:9. Gower concludes with an exhortation to remorse and repentance that ends with a prayer for the forgiveness of sin.

Such are, in very concise fashion, the contents of the *Vox Clamantis* with the exclusion of Book I. Such a content, tied to such a title, clearly refers the poem to the area of devotional literature. That in a total of approximately 8,000 verses there are other subjects woven in is obvious. There is, for instance, an exposition of the doctrine of the Trinity and an account of the creation of the world; the Last Judgment, Paradise, and Hell emerge in their turn, accompanied by an

[13] 2.37–50. So much for the first chapter of Book II; for the following chapters, see below, 133–44.

[14] 7.1289–1302:

> *Singula que dominus statuit sibi regna per orbem,*
> *Que magis in Christi nomine signa gerunt,*
> *Diligo, set propriam super omnia diligo terram,*
> *In qua principium duxit origo meum.*
> *Quicquid agant alie terre, non subruor inde,*
> *Dum tamen ipse foris sisto remotus eis;*
> *Patria set iuvenem que me suscepit alumpnum,*
> *Partibus in cuius semper adhero manens,*
> *Hec si quid patitur, mea viscera compaciuntur,*
> *Nec sine me dampna ferre valebit ea:*
> *Eius in adversis de pondere sum quasi versus;*
> *Si perstet, persto, si cadat illa, cado.*
> *Que magis ergo gravant presenti tempore, saltem*
> *Ut dicunt alii, scismata plango michi.*

> [I love all the kingdoms which the Lord has established for Himself throughout the world and which bear standards in Christ's name. But above all I love my own land, in which my family took its origin. Whatever other lands may do, I am not shaken by it, as long as I stand apart at a distance from them. But if the native land which bore me as a young child, and within whose realms I always remain fixed—if she suffers anything, my innermost feelings suffer with her, and she shall not be able to suffer her misfortunes apart from me. I am almost overwhelmed by the weight of her adversities. If she stands firm, I stand firm, if she falls, I fall. Thereupon, I bewail the schisms which, at least so others say, are so oppressive at this present time. (Trans. Stockton.)]

inspection of the deadly sins viewed *sub specie mortis*. It is a property of all these themes that they fit organically into the main theme when one views the poem as a Johannine homily. They are in no way digressions in which the author displays theological knowledge in unbridled liberality, without regard for his subject. They loosen the tightness of the structure, but they do not blur the clarity of the outline.

C. S. Lewis has pointed in another context to Gower's striking compositional talent.[15] His judgment is substantiated by the *Vox Clamantis*. For a medieval work of its scope, the structure is astonishingly tight. Of course, this is not to Gower's credit alone. One must bear in mind that a centuries-old ecclesiastical tradition had made the material available to the author in a well-thought-out and orderly form. While the usually brief Sunday sermon allowed only modest possibilities, Lent, with its duty of a daily sermon, provided the great opportunity for clerics and monks to develop their oratorical gifts. Since the object of their efforts was to arouse remorse and penitence as preparation for the receiving of the Easter sacraments, they thoroughly and exhaustively developed the penitential theme, more intensively than almost any other part of Christian religious dogma with the possible exception of the *Credo* and *Paternoster*.

There were two basic forms of penitential sermon, which recur over and over in countless variations. Either the preacher chose the Seven Deadly Sins as a point of departure and treated them, be it concisely together with their complementary virtues, be it separately in their forms of appearance along with their earthly and heavenly consequences, or he used mankind as a point of departure and showed the classes with their special vices: the merchant in his avarice, the lawyer in his corruptibility, the soldier in his unbridled sensuality. Thus, for instance, all the examples which Alanus de Insulis attaches to his manual on the art of preaching break down into two groups: *Sermones de Vitiis et Virtutibus* and *Sermones ad Status*. The literature *de vitiis et virtutibus* receives a strong impetus in the thirteenth and fourteenth centuries,[16] perhaps because it became especially important when auricular confession was officially introduced as an obligation for both confessor and penitent.

Gower employed both sermon types literarily. His *Mirour de l'Omme* first deals *de vitiis et virtutibus* (1–18420) and then addresses itself to the individual classes (18421–26604). The *VC*, as we saw, is in the form of a Johannine class sermon. Certainly that is not to say that the *VC* is nothing but a versified sermon or sermon collection, although it seems conceivable that the appearance of versified

---

[15] C. S. Lewis, *The Allegory of Love* (Oxford: Oxford University Press, 1936), 198–99.

[16] This is important not only for Latin, but also, above all, for vernacular literature. The history of the adaptations and alterations of the *Somme le Roi* of the thirteenth-century Dominican Lorens d'Orleans provides an instructive example; see W. N. Francis, ed., *The Book of Vices and Virtues,* EETS O.S. 217 (London: Oxford University Press, 1942), Introduction.

sermons in the fourteenth century—they first became the fashion in England in the fifteenth—may have encouraged literary attempts in this direction. For our purposes it is sufficient to note that the *VC* conforms in content as well as in structure to the programme that the title *Vox Clamantis* promised to the contemporary reader.

Before we pass from the title of the work to the accompanying verses, we must again stop for a moment. An unexpected difficulty emerges when one follows the complex of the *vox clamantis* and its associations further, pursuing its appearance in the *Vox Clamantis* and, beyond that, in Gower's total work. Its religious coloring seems to fade occasionally and instead there appears a distinct political shading. Often one cannot ascertain with certainty whether the author perceives himself, in his function as *vox clamantis*, as the spokesman of God or of the public opinion. He leaves it up to the reader to discern periodically, out of the ambivalence of the set phrase, the deciding component. This uncertainty has a very disturbing effect. It is not unreasonable to require of an author that he proclaim clearly whether he wishes to be understood as a homilist (the *vox clamantis* in a biblical sense) or as a political spokesman (the *vox clamantis* as representative of the public opinion). However, one forgets in making such a demand that there was no such alternative for Gower and his contemporaries.

For the modern reader the dilemma begins with the first mention of the book's title, that is, in the prologue of the second book. The author bases the choice of his title on the fact that his poem is a lamentation for the present time:

> *Vox clamantis erit nomenque voluminis huius,*
> *Quod sibi scripta novi verba doloris habet.* 2.Prol.83–84
>
> [And the name of this volume shall be *The Voice of One Crying*, because the work contains a message of sorrow of today. (Trans. Stockton.)]

The Latin prose summary of the prologue expands the explanation, stating that the two significant components of the formula *vox clamantis* derive from the concepts *vox omnium* and *clamor omnium*:

> . . . *et vocat libellum istum Vox Clamantis, quia de voce et clamore quasi omnium conceptus est* [. . . and he calls this book *The Voice of One Crying*, since it was conceived, as it were, by a voice crying over all things (Trans. Stockton.)]

While the distich thus links the title to the elegiac character of the work, the prose summary presents the author as spokesman of the public opinion. Both significations unite in the prologue of the third book, that is, at the start of the class critique proper, where the author stresses in ever-varying expressions that he writes down his lament over the moral decay of the present not in his own person, but in a faithful reproduction of the voice of the people:

A me non ipso loquor hec, set que michi plebis
Vox dedit, et sortem plangit ubique malam:
Ut loquitur vulgus loquor, et scribendo loquelam
Plango, quod est sanctus nullus ut ante status.
. . . . .
Nescio quis purum se dicet, plebs quia tota
Clamat iam lesum quemlibet esse statum. 3.Prol.11–14, 17–18

[I am not speaking of these things on my own part; rather, the voice of the people has reported them to me, and it complains of their adverse fate at every hand. I speak as the masses speak, and even as I write I lament over what I say, namely, that no estate is pious as in days gone by . . . No matter who he is, a man will say he is innocent, for the whole population now cries out that every estate is the injured party. (Trans. Stockton.)]

Here the voice of the people is used in the sense of *consensus omnium* or *communis opinio.* Its value for Gower is that it serves him as an unimpeachable witness for the justification of a radical class critique. Through an accord with the public opinion he gains simultaneously support for his person and weight for his cause. He was already aware of its value as a witness in the *Mirour*, where the frequent recourse to public opinion nearly resembles a stylistic cliché or convenient verse filler. However, it is more than that and in certain passages shows itself to be related to the idea of *vox clamantis.* When, for example, Gower introduces the class critique of the *Mirour* (18421–26604) with an appeal to the *consensus omnium*, employing the dual concept *vois et cry*, the manner of the expression recalls the statement in the prologue of the *Vox Clamantis*' second book (*de voce et clamore quasi omnium conceptus*) and the content recalls the above-cited prologue of the third book:

Ce que je pense escrire yci
N'est pas par moy, ainz est ensi
Du toute cristiene gent
Murmur, compleinte, vois et cry;
Que tous diont je ne desdi. Mirour, 18445–18449

[What I intend to write here
Is not by me, but is rather
Of all Christian people
The murmur, complaint, voice and cry;
I don't contradict what all say.]

Later, in the prologue of the *Confessio Amantis*, the allusion to the voice of the people will confirm the author's objectivity and credibility:

The world is changed overall,
And thereof most in special
That love is falle into discord.
And that I take to record
Of every lond for his partie
The comun vois, which may noght lie. *Confessio,* Prol.119–124

Most instances in which Gower identifies himself with the public opinion or the voice of the people occur, naturally enough, in the *Vox Clamantis.* Without claiming to have located all, I would like to cite the following examples:

Non ego sidereas affecto tangere sedes,
Scribere nec summi mistica quero poli;
Set magis, humana que vox communis ad extra
Plangit in hac terra, scribo moderna mala. 3.Prol.53–56

[I do not aspire to reach the thrones of heaven, or seek to describe the mysteries of the lofty skies. Rather, I write of present-day evils which the common voice of mankind outwardly complains of in this country.]

Non erit in dubio mea vox clamans, erit omnis
Namque fides huius maxima vocis homo. 3.Prol.79–80

[My crying voice will not hesitate, for every man will be a great warrant for its utterance.]

Hec ego que dicam dictum commune docebat,
Nec mea verba sibi quid novitatis habent. 3.1269–1270

[Common talk has taught me what I shall say, and my words contain nothing new.]

Est nichil ex sensu proprio quod scribo, set ora
Que michi vox populi contulit, illa loquar. 4.19–20

[Nothing that I write is my own opinion; rather, I shall speak what the voice of the people has reported to me.]

Talibus iste liber profert sua verba modernis,
Ut sibi vox populi contulit illa loqui. 4.709–710

[To such men of the present this book offers its message, since the voice of the people furnished the things for it to say. (Trans. Stockton.)]

Hoc ego quod plebis vox clamat clamo, nec ullos,
Sint nisi quos crimen denotat, ipse noto. 6.15–16

[I cry out what the people's voice cries out, none do
I charge but those whom the offense denotes.]

The first passage mentions the *vox communis* in the context of exposition, the second refers to the public opinion (*omnis homo*=everyman) as witness to the veracity of the class critique; the remaining distiches are designed to defend the author against the charge of selfish intention or personal animosity.

The voice of the people has a more political sound and a more direct relevance to the present in the frame of the Mirror for a Prince in Book VI, in which instance the A- and B-Texts differ. The introduction in the B-Text has both *vox populi* and *vox plebis*:

Nunc magis in specie vox plebis clamat ubique
Pectore sub timido que metuenda fero. 6.545–546, B-Text

[Everywhere you look the people's voice cries out,
And I have dreadful cares in fearful breast.]

Talia vox populi conclamat ubique moderni
In dubio positi pre gravitate mali:
Sic ego condoleo super hiis que tedia cerno,
Quo Regi puero scripta sequenda fero. 6.577–580, B-Text

[The people's voice everywhere bewails such things,
Shaken by the gravity of evil.
I grieve the loathsome things I see concerning them,
Whereby I bear these words to the boy king.]

The B-Text also appeals to the *vox plebis* at the end of the open letter to the king:

Nunc tamen in plebe vox est, quod deficiente
Lege dolus iura vendicat esse sua. 6.1179–1180, B-Text

[Yet now the plebs' voice says that guile with failing law
Asserts that justice now belongs to it.]

The earlier redaction, the A-Text, has only one passage to set against these three and it speaks not of the *vox plebis* or *populi*, but of the *vox clamantis:*

Nunc magis ecce refert verbi clamantis ad aures
Vox, et in hoc dicit tempore plura gravant. 6.545–546, A-Text

[Behold, the voice crying out brings more to our ears,
Says many things oppress us at this time.]

The interpretation of the original version is unsure because the grammatical referent of the two genitives *verbi* and *clamantis* cannot be clearly determined. Nevertheless, one thing is certain: however the author may originally have intended the lines, the possible biblical association vanishes before the emphatic repetition of the voice of the people in the later B-Text revision. Does that indicate a change in Gower's attitude toward his theme? And if such should be the case, how is it to be explained?

It is not our task here to show how the fourteenth-century English commoner gradually developed and constantly increased in importance as a political and social factor. Also, we must expediently relinquish to the historian the question of the influence which the public opinion—or, to remain in the usage of the time, the voice of the people—exerted on contemporary politics. That Gower continually worked with concepts such as *vox populi, clamor populi* (in the *Vox Clamantis*), *commun vois, commun clamour* (in the *Confessio Amantis*), and *commune voys, commune tesmoygnance du poeple* (in the *Mirour de l'Omme*) demonstrates to us that a political slogan of this kind was readily available. In every passage where Gower employs the *vox populi*, it acts as a lament or grievance, that is, as a negative critique of existing conditions. The necessity and urgency of reform are confirmed through the witness of the people's voice; however, a positive programme of reform is never drafted in its name. Nor is the possibility of self-help for the oppressed, if the voice of the people should remain unheard, a part of Gower's conception of the divine *ordo*. Thus, as political factors, the *vox communis* and *clamor populi* are considerably limited in their direct efficacy. Nevertheless, we must not underestimate the significance of the triple appeal to the people's voice in the later version of the Mirror for a Prince. The latent threat expressed in the *clamor populi* is not, to be sure, directly political in nature but metaphysically anchored and thereby doubly important. This threat arises from the correspondence of the voice of the people with the voice of God. The lament of the common people is heard by God, and God, not the people, threatens the ruler if he refuses to listen:

> *Vox populi cum voce dei concordat, ut ipsa*
> *In rebus dubiis sit metuenda magis.* 3.1267–1268

> [The voice of the people agrees with the voice of God, so that in critical times it ought to be held in greater awe. (Trans. Stockton.)]

Thus Gower moves completely along biblical lines of thought. The Psalter above all is rich in allusions to God as the protector of the poor against the arrogance of the mighty. The Ninth Psalm [9:10, 13b] says of the *clamor pauperum:*

> *Et factus est Dominus refugium pauperum, adjutor in opportunitatibus et in tribulatione . . . non est oblitus clamorem pauperum.*

> [And the Lord is become a refuge for the poor: a helper in due time in tribulation . . . he hath not forgotten the cry of the poor.]

In 9:17–19 the connection between the *clamor pauperum* and God's justice is disclosed:

> *Cognoscetur Dominus judicia faciens: in operibus manuum suarum comprehensus est peccator. Convertantur peccatores in infernum, omnes gentes, quae obliviscuntur Deum. Quoniam non in finem oblivio erit pauperis: patientia pauperis non peribit in finem.*
>
> [The Lord shall be known when he executeth judgments: the sinner hath been caught in the works of his own hands. The wicked shall be turned into hell, all the nations that forget God. For the poor man shall not be forgotten to the end: the patience of the poor shall not perish for ever.]

Yet, not only biblical lines of thought are present, but also concrete historical allusions, appropriate because they give emphasis to the *vox populi* in the crisis years of Richard II's reign.

The formula *vox populi, vox dei* already had a political past at the time. It had played a role in the history of England for the first time in the events of 1327, at which time a legitimate English king was deposed in a kind of civil proceeding and his son chosen as his successor. We know little of the constitutional basis of the event. However, Walsingham, who is a reliable source, reports that the Archbishop of Canterbury, after consenting to the choice with the rest of the prelates, sought to win the concurrence of the people to the accession of Edward III through a public sermon on the theme *vox populi, vox dei.*[17] As a sermon theme it is unusual, for according to ecclesiastical practice the theme of a sermon was always to be taken from the Bible.[18] The unusual situation obviously caused the unusual choice of text. From that it is possible to reason *a posteriori* about the

[17] *Archiepiscopus vero Cantuariensis praesenti consentit electioni, ut omnes praelati; et Archiepiscopus quidem, assumpto themate, "Vox populi, vox Dei," sermonem fecit populo, exhortans omnes ut apud Regem Regum intercederent pro electo.* [Indeed the Archbishop of Canterbury, as did all the prelates, consented to the present choice; and the Archbishop as well, having taken up the subject, "The voice of the people is the voice of God," delivered a sermon to the people, exhorting all that they intercede with the King of Kings for the chosen one.] *Historia Anglicana,* ed. H. T. Riley, Rolls Series, 2 vols. (London: Longman, Green, 1863–1884), 1:186. [Wickert's discussion of the people's voice in Gower anticipates Anne Middleton's important study, "The Idea of Public Poetry in the Reign of Richard II," *Speculum* 53 (1978): 94–114. (Trans.)]

[18] The rule first emerges, to my knowledge, in a letter of Alcuin to Charlemagne; there, however, it appears to be already proverbial. Moreover, Alcuin warns against it: *Epistola CXXXII seu Capitulare Admonitionis ad eundem Carolum* 9, in *Epistolae Karolini Aevi,* ed. E. L. Dümmler, 4 vols., MGH (Berlin: Weidmann, 1895), 2:199.

political significance which the archbishop attributed to the theme. The parallels between Edward II and Richard II, as far as character and fate are concerned, lie ready to hand and may already have been noted in Richard's lifetime. In this connection it is perhaps no accident that Gower placed the greatest stress on the importance of the people's voice in his poem *O Deus Immense*,[19] which according to the witness of three manuscripts is his last poem under the rule of Richard II. It gives, in one hundred and four awkward leonines, the skeleton of a *speculum regis* that agrees essentially in all important respects with that of the *Vox Clamantis*, although in tone far more impersonal and importunately schoolmarmish. The poem distinguishes itself from the analogous section of the *Vox Clamantis* in distribution of emphasis by more conspicuously extolling the significance of the people's voice:

Consilio tali regnum magis in speciali
Undique turbatur, quo regis honor variatur:
Nunc ita sicut heri poterit res ista videri,
Unde magis plangit populus, quem lesio tangit. 43–46

[By such counsel is the kingdom especially
Roiled on all sides, and by it the king's honor changed.
This can be seen at present just like yesterday:
Whence the people, whom the sore afflicts, complain greatly.]

Set qui prescire vult causas, expedit ire,
Plebis et audire voces per easque redire:
Si sit in errore regis vel in eius honore,
Hoc de clamore populi prefertur ab ore. 53–56

[But he who wants to understand causes hastens to go,
And go again to the people to hear through their voices:
If [something] is to the king's blame or his honor,
Is shown by this cry from the people's mouth.]

Nomen regale populi vox dat tibi, quale
Sit, bene sive male, deus illud habet speciale.
Rex qui tutus eris, si temet noscere queris,
Ad vocem plebis aures sapienter habebis. 61–64

[The voice of the people gives you the royal title; of what kind
It may be, good or evil, God takes note.

[19] Macaulay, *Works*, 4:362.

O king who will be secure, if you seek to know yourself,
You will wisely have ears for the voice of the people.][20]

This glorification of the people's voice sounds, in the last years of Richard II, especially relevant and critical. That is not only because Gower confers a somewhat prophetic nature upon it (line 53: *Set que prescire vult causas . . .*), or because he recommends it to the king as the surest source of self-knowledge, but because he links it in a politically taut situation with the voice of God (61–62) so that at least in retrospect it operates as a warning against a repetition of the events of 1327. Gower himself may hardly have been aware of the immediate relevance of his precept of the *vox populi*. He often appeals to the public opinion only in an attempt to protect himself from the charge of personal malice. When, however, in the late version of the *Vox Clamantis* and in the last poem to Richard II he reaches the point at which he sees the manifestation of a divine judgment in the witness of the people's voice, he thus unites the two apparently so different meanings of *vox clamantis*. Whether the poet steps forward as spokesman of God or as representative of the public opinion, his words are upheld in either case by the weight of a divine warning to reverse course.

We have seen which function the title *Vox Clamantis* assigned the author, both with reference to the medieval sermon and to Gower's own conception. The accompanying verses that precede the text in three manuscripts of the *Vox Clamantis* show him in another role. These verses were probably located between the summary of contents and the headnote of Book I[21] in all the B-Text manuscripts, whereas neither summary nor accompanying verses survived in the two A-Text manuscripts (T and H2). The contaminated manuscript L has them, surprisingly, in another place, namely at the beginning of the third book. They read the same in all four manuscripts:

Ad mundum mitto mea iacula, dumque sagitto;
At ubi iustus erit, nulla sagitta ferit.
Sed male viventes hos vulnero transgredientes;
Conscius ergo sibi se speculetur ibi.

[I hurl my darts at the world and I shoot my arrows; yet where there is a just man, no arrow strikes. But I wound those transgressors who live evilly;

[20] Text and translation from R. F. Yeager, ed. and trans., *John Gower: The Minor Latin Works with In Praise of Peace,* ed. Michael Livingston (Kalamazoo: Medieval Institute Publications, 2005), 36–37.

[21] The two distiches occur in CEG in the above-mentioned place. In S and H, which likewise belong to the B-Text, they are missing: in S because two leaves with the end of the summary have disappeared after folio 5, in H because the manuscript is defective in the beginning, first starting with Book I, line 502. [They are reproduced in Macaulay, *Works*, 4:19. (Trans.)]

therefore, let him who is conscious of being in the wrong look to himself in that respect. (Trans. Stockton.)]

The verses are accompanied by a miniature that shows an archer, possibly representing the author himself, taking aim at a *mappa mundi* which, according to the customary scheme, appears in three parts.[22] This geographical division into thirds accords with familiar medieval notions about the division of society into three classes. If L should actually have preserved the original arrangement, the verses are admirably suited to the beginning of the third book, at which point the class critique begins with the old tripartite division of *clericus, miles, cultor.* The prologue of Book III also agrees with the motto, placing great emphasis upon the assurance that the author will attack no class as such, but only the evil-doers within a class.[23] Unfortunately, L is not to be trusted. Nevertheless, it is clear by the contents that the verses belong to the *VC*: their theme is so unlike that of the *Visio* that they cannot have been generated by the enlargement of the *VC* through the *Visio*. It is more comprehensible that a motto be shifted to the new beginning of a work upon a rewriting of its opening than that it should be shifted from the beginning to the third book without a cogent reason. The absence of the lines from the A-Text in no way proves that they were first written for the B-Text. Indeed, the B-Text is aligned with the political tendency of the *Cronica Tripertita* and is no longer as strongly interested in the class critique. Their absence in the A-Text is connected rather with the omission of the summary that precedes the motto. However, because the summary of the B-Text is clearly taken over from the Alpha Redaction—although in no preserved manuscript of the Alpha Redaction does a summary of contents exist—[24] it is likely that the accompanying verses which followed the summary also had their origin there, although they disappeared along with the summary from TH2.

---

[22] Macaulay gives the drawing opposite the title page of vol. 4 of his edition.

[23] See Book III, Prologue, esp. 23–26:

> *Novimus esse status tres, sub quibus omnis in orbe*
> *More suo vivit atque ministrat eis.*
> *Non status in culpa reus est, set transgredientes*
> *A virtute status, culpa repugnat eis.*

> [We recognize that there are three estates. In his own way, everyone in the world lives under them and serves them. No estate is accused of being at fault, but when estates transgress against virtue, their fault declares against them. (Trans. Stockton.)]

[24] Such a statement can be confidently maintained due to the wording of the summaries of Book III, Chapter 1 and Book VI, Chapters 7 and 18, which accord with the chapter headings of the A-Text and have been left untouched by the alterations of the B-Text. [See above, 19–20 for establishment of the Alpha Redaction. (Trans.)]

Whatever the fate of the accompanying verses in the successive development of the *Vox Clamantis*, this much is certain: according to their contents, and probably also according to manuscript evidence, they belonged to the *VC*. One must not overlook them when one seeks an explanation of the work's objective.

Two images underlie the verses: the archer (1–3) and the mirror (implicit in 4). The mirror metaphor is more hinted at than realized, but intelligible without more ado since it is in accordance with the taste of the times[25] and is used by Gower in his three major works.[26] The archer, however, does not appear elsewhere in his writing. In this passage he appears to be more important than the mirror, for three lines as well as the miniature are allotted to him. It must be asked what led Gower to the choice of precisely this role and how it is compatible with the concept *vox clamantis*.

At first glance the archer has two associations that have little enough to do with the voice of one crying in the wilderness. The archer is the embodiment of English national military strength around the turn of the fourteenth century, to whom the great victories in France were owed. Could Gower have chosen this emblem in order to emphasize the national character of his class critique? The likelihood is slim, since *ad mundum mitto* does not permit of a unilateral national interpretation. Besides, neither class critique nor *speculum principis* is nationally restricted in the late Middle Ages.[27] Nor is the archer's other association, which is based on the form of the statement, much more helpful. Did the author wish to emphasize that his critique would rain down upon its victim like a shower of arrows? Certainly he had something of that sort in mind; however, the core of the idea is derived from elsewhere.

The life of man is, according to good biblical tradition, a constant war against the world, the flesh, and the devil; *psychomachia* is, therefore, one of the

---

[25] See such titles as *Speculum Laici* (anonymous); *Speculum Christiani* (anonymous); *Speculum Morale, Speculum Historiale* (Vincent of Beauvais); *Speculum Ecclesiae* (the Dominican Cardinal Hugo); *Speculum Humanae Vitae* (Roderigo of Cagliari). A short study of the title *Speculum* occurs in Georgiana Lee Morrill, ed, *Speculum Gy de Warewyke: An English Poem,* EETS E.S. 75 (London: Kegan Paul, Trench, Trübner, 1898), xxii. See H. Grabes, *The Mutable Glass: Mirror-Imaging in Titles and Texts of the Middle Ages and the English Renaissance* (Cambridge: Cambridge University Press, 1982).

[26] The *Mirour de l'Omme,* or *Speculum Meditantis,* has the mirror already in the title. In the *Vox Clamantis* it appears once again in the Mirror for a Prince:

> *O bene si speculo, rex, te speculeris in isto,*
> *Quid magis expediens sit tibi scire potes.* 6.1051–1052.
>
> [If you should look, O king, into this mirror well,
> You'll learn how useful it can be for you.]

[27] W. Kleineke, *Englische Fürstenspiegel vom* Policraticus *Johanns von Salisbury bis zum* Basilikon Doron *König Jakobs I*, Studien zur englischen Philologie 90 (Halle: Niemeyer, 1937), 10.

chief forms of religious allegory from Prudentius to Bunyan. Mankind must be armed for this war, and again it is the Bible that describes the symbolic armor, most fully in the Epistle to the Ephesians (6:11–17). Although Paul has in mind the heavily armed Roman legionary rather than an archer, here nevertheless lies the point of departure from which the medieval fancy could develop unhindered.

There is attributed to Bonaventura a work entitled *Pharetra*,[28] the first book of which discusses the classes and the second the virtues and vices, which explains its title thus, that here as in a quiver may be found the arrows of ecclesiastical *auctoritates* (church fathers and biblical citations) with which the reader can overcome the archenemy.[29] The *Pharetra*, therefore, provides an analogous view of a subject closely related to that of the *VC*. One difference, to be sure, must not be overlooked: the book is considered an arsenal from which the warring Christian—who is the warrior, not the object of war—can withdraw for his own needs the *iacula*, the missiles of patristic maxims. However, I wish to emphasize the equation of *iacula* with *auctoritates*, with biblical and patristic passages, since we thereby enter into the broad tradition of ecclesiastical conceptions. The quiver, on the other hand, may be the anonymous author's individual development upon the general conceptual basis.

The image of the word of God as a sword or spear or arrow occurs in the Old as well as the New Testament,[30] from whence it is transmitted to the sermon. The preacher is thus assigned the role of soldier when, for example, in the *Homilies* Gregory the Great interprets the text (freely after Habakkuk 3:11) *In lumine jacula tua ibunt, in splendore fulguris armorum tuorum* [Your arrows will go in the light, in the splendid brightness of your arms] in the following manner: *Jacula Domini sunt verba Sanctorum, quae corda peccantium feriunt* [the arrows of the Lord are the words of the saints, which strike the hearts of sinners];[31] or when

[28] *Liber Salutaris Beati Bonaventure Cardinalis Ordinis Minorum Pharetra Vocatus* (Paris: Berthold Rembolt, 1518). See above, 30 n. 28.

[29] *Liber . . . Pharetra Vocatus*, prologue: *Opusculum autem istud Pharetram appellavi, quia sicut in pharetra iacula reponuntur, quibus hostem hostis ferit, vulnerat, et deiicit, sic et hic varie auctoritates fidedignorum quas si manu operationis tenemus, hostem antiquum deiiciemus.* [And I have called this little book *The Quiver*, because just as in a quiver arrows are stored with which foe strikes, wounds, and overcomes foe, so also here {are stored} variously the documents of those worthy of the faith, which we grasp with a sure hand if we wish to overcome the ancient enemy.]

[30] For example, Hebrews 4:12: *Vivus est sermo Dei, et efficax et penetrabilior omni gladio ancipiti* [For the word of God is living and efficient and keener than any two-edged sword]. In a similar manner are understood Psalm 44:6: *Sagittae tuae acutae, populi sub te cadent, in corda inimicorum regis* [Thine arrows are sharp, under Thee shall peoples fall, into the hearts of the king's enemies] and Psalm 119:4: *Sagittae potentis acutae cum carbonibus desolatoriis* [The sharp arrows of the mighty, with coals that lay waste].

[31] *Homilia in Ezechiel,* 1.5: *PL* 76:827; ed. M. Adriaen, CCSL 142 (Turnhout: Brepols, 1971), 64.

Honorius of Autun remarks: *Verba praedicationis per simile dicitur gladius vel ensis, quia sicut gladius animam a corpore separat* [the message of a sermon by analogy is called a sword or a blade, because like a sword it severs the soul from the body].[32] The object of the battle is the sinful man, or else the sins or the devil himself; the weapons are the words of God. Cardinal Humbert de Romanis depicts in his manual the military service of the preacher as follows:

> *Item praedicatores dicuntur milites Christi, propter quod dicitur 2. Tim. 2* [2:3]: *Labora sicut bonus miles Christi: Glossa praedicando, unde autem praedicando militare dicuntur? Quia sic errores tam infidelitatis quam morum regi suo contrarios, debellant.*
>
> [Likewise preachers are called soldiers of Christ, because it is said in 2 Timothy 2: Conduct thyself in work as a good soldier of Christ: Gloss for *praedicando*; but wherefore in preaching are they said to do battle? Because thus they vanquish the errors not only of faithlessness but also of customs hostile to their king.][33]

Bromyard writes (*s.v. praedicator*), concerning the manner in which such a champion should use his weapons:

> *Sermo namque domini quandoque in sacra scriptura sagittae comparatur, Sap. 5* [5:22]. *Sagitta emissa in locum destinatum. Sagittam vero ad hoc, quod feram occidat, sagittarius ita prope ad cor dirigere nititur, sicut potest, quia hoc est utilius pro eo: quia illo citius feram occidit. Sic volens vitam in peccatore destruere bestialem, utilius sagittas verborum ad cor quam ad aures dirigat . . . Patet ergo, quod sermo efficaciter ad cor directus est utilior: quia talia verba plures humiliant peccatores, de quibus dicit Psal. 43. Sagittae tuae acutae, populi sub te cadent, quia sc. diriguntur in corda inimicorum regis. Quod autem tales sagittae spirituales plures a statu superbiae et vacuitatis, quibus contra Deum eriguntur, ad gradum humilitatis cadere et colla sub iugo Christi humiliter submittere faciant, sequentibus ostenditur exemplis.*
>
> [For the word of the Lord in Sacred Scripture is sometimes likened to an arrow, Wisdom 5 {5:22}. An arrow discharged at a targeted place. So that it kill the wild beast, the archer endeavors to guide the arrow as near to the heart as he is able, since that is more beneficial to him, because by that he kills the beast more quickly. Thus wishing to destroy the bestial life in the sinner, let him direct the arrows of words more beneficially to the heart than to the ears. . . . It is obvious, therefore, that a sermon effectively

[32] *Expositio in Cantica Canticorum*, 3, on the text: *Uniuscuiusque ensis super femur suum* [every man's sword upon his thigh] (Canticles 3:8). *PL* 172:405.

[33] Humberti de Romanis *Liber de Eruditione Praedicatorum*, ed. J. J. Berthier, 2 vols. (Rome: n.p., 1889), 2:401.

> directed to the heart is more beneficial, because such words humble more sinners, concerning whom Psalm 43 {44:6} says, Thine arrows are sharp, under thee shall peoples fall, because of course they are shot into the hearts of the king's enemies. The following stories show that such spiritual arrows, moreover, cause many to fall from a state of pride and emptiness, by which they raise themselves against God, to a degree of humility and to submit their necks humbly beneath Christ's yoke.]

Six such *exempla* follow, to which Bromyard attaches the observation that simple sermons are most useful for this purpose:

> *et . . . sic praedicantibus, sicut dicitur in Ps. 67* [67:12], *Dominus dabit verbum evangelizantibus virtute multa, et . . . sub talibus sagittis plures cadunt et humiliantur peccatores.*
>
> [and . . . thus to those preaching, just as it is said in Psalm 67, the Lord shall give the word to them that preach good tidings with great power, and . . . many sinners shall be felled and humbled under such arrows.]

When Bromyard, the contemporary and countryman of Gower, speaks of the homilist as an archer, one can be certain that the image is common ecclesiastical property. The great advantage of the Bromyardian *Summa* for our purposes is that, by all standards of vivacious expression and presentation, it is so completely unoriginal and mediocre. It thus makes possible a glance into the spiritual public property of the time.

Gower's accompanying verses come remarkably close to a passage from the *De Modo Componendi Sermones* of Thomas Waleys. The English monk-preacher speaks of the priests' charges and complaints that their vices were ruthlessly denounced in public sermons by the mendicant friars, and recommends a careful choice of subject with regard to the composition of the audience. It is the old principle of the sermon *ad status*: one should preach about the transgressions of the clergy in the synod, about the sins of the secular classes in the parish church. Difficulties arise only with a mixed audience. In this case one should deal with those vices common to both parties, that is, with the universal human vices. Whoever should then feel attacked has only himself to blame; no reproach can attach to the preacher. For just as a soldier who practices archery in an authorized place cannot be blamed if he should wound someone who steps without authorization into the target area, so likewise is the preacher not to be blamed if he in a similarly appointed place should shoot his arrows toward his target—sin or the devil—and so wound someone who has toyed all too closely with them:

> *signum vero ad quod sagittat* [*sc. praedicator*] *est peccatum vel diabolus. Nullus igitur ibi aut prope stet, et nullus vulnerabitur aut laedetur.*

[The target at which he {that is, the preacher} shoots arrows is sin or the devil. Therefore no one should stand there or close by and no one will be wounded or killed.][34]

Here the notion of the religious archer is already formed even down to the particulars and, as in Gower, combined with a protest against the charge of character assassination.

The two conceptions of the preacher, as a *vox clamantis* on the one hand and as a s*agittarius* on the other, are therefore not only compatible with one another: they interlock. If the title *Vox Clamantis* suggests John the Baptist, it is because John is one of those of whom Gregory said:

Jacula Domini sunt verba Sanctorum, quae corda peccantium feriunt.

[The arrows of the Lord are the words of the saints, which strike the hearts of sinners.]

A baptismal sermon of St. Martin of León relates the words of Isaiah [29:12], *Posuit me sicut sagittam electam* [he hath made me as a chosen arrow], to John the Baptist: . . . *non immerito etiam et Joannes sagitta electa est* [. . . for I am unworthy and John is the chosen arrow].[35] The transference of the designation *sagitta* from the word of God to the preaching of His word and, further, to the herald of His word does not indicate a discrepancy between Gregory and Martin. The allegorical interpretation of the term *vox*, which points sometimes to the content of what has been said and sometimes to the speaker, undergoes a similar metonymical shift. The coexistence of several allegorical references disturbed no medieval reader.

The quotations cited do not have the purpose of suggesting Gower's dependence upon this or that author; they should convey only generally the conceptual milieu upon which he drew. He could, therefore, despite the brevity of reference, depend on his reader to understand the intention of his work, whereas the modern reader, not knowing the homiletic background, is apt to overlook the consciousness of and claim to divine mission upon which the seemingly secular lines are based. The *vox clamantis* and the *sagittarius* derive from the same tradition of the medieval sermon and testify to the poet's special task in this work.

---

[34] Thomas Waleys, *De Modo Componendi Sermones*, in Thomas M. Charland, *Artes Praedicandi: Contribution à l'histoire de la rhétorique au moyen âge* (Paris: J. Vrin, 1936), 338.

[35] *Sancti Martini Legionensis Sermo II Sancto Joanne Baptista*: *PL* 209:18.

B. The Topology of the Prologue

It is now time to return to a question which was left unanswered in the preceding section. We have seen that, with the formula *vox clamantis* and in the archer verses, Gower puts himself in the role of Christian homilist. Up to now we have not examined his qualifications for that role. The traditional places in which to obtain information about an author's own view of his function are prologue and epilogue. The *VC* contains two prologues, at the beginnings of Books II and III, and an epilogue, in Chapter 25 of Book VII.

An analysis of the prologues leads immediately to a dilemma. The late medieval reader looks in a prologue for a work's four *causae*, the modern reader for exordial *topoi*, both executed according to Matthew 7:7 [Ask, and it shall be given you; seek, and you shall find; knock, and it shall be opened to you]. There are, moreover, no certain criteria with which to distinguish *topos* from actual self-expression. Let us, to begin with, treat the prologue of the second book after the medieval method of interpretation.

The old *quis, quid, cur,* etc. formula of the rhetoricians appears to have found its way in the Middle Ages from the *narratio* to the *prooemium*. One required from a prologue information about the author, the subject, and the purpose of the work. The classical tradition—in this case the suasive—is still clearly perceptible in the twelfth century in Honorius of Autun, who begins his commentary on the Song of Solomon:

> *In principiis librorum tria requiruntur, sc. auctor, materia, intentio. Auctor, ut noveris nomen scriptoris, utrum ethnicus, an fidelis, utrum catholicus an haereticus fuerit. Materia, ut scias utrum de bellis an de nuptiis vel de quibus rebus tractat. Intentio, ut cognoscas utrum rem de qua tractet suadeat vel dissuadeat, vel liber lectus quid utilitatis conferat.*
>
> [Three things are required in the beginnings of books, namely author, subject, and purpose. The author, so that you will learn the name of the writer, whether he be pagan or faithful, catholic or heretic. The subject, so that you may know whether he discusses wars or weddings or whatsoever things. The purpose, so that you may learn whether he persuades or dissuades about what he discusses, or what profit comes from reading the book.][36]

Honorius employs no fixed terminology for these three prologue requisites, whereas by the thirteenth century there are employed the designations *causa efficiens, causa materialis, and causa finalis*—to which a fourth is added in case of need, the *causa formalis*. Thus, for example, Robert de Basevorn speaks in his sermon manual of the four *causae* as of something universally known:

[36] *Expositio in Cantica Canticorum, PL* 172:347.

> *. . . praesumpsi prosequi quod incepi, ab eadem nimirum judicans inchoandum, in qua quattuor hujus operis causae poterunt assignari quae in librorum principiis annotari solebant.*
>
> [I have presumed to pursue what I have begun, judging that one must certainly start from the very place in which the four causes of this work, of the sort usually designated in the beginnings of books, can be assigned.][37]

Honorius and Robert are ecclesiastical authors and occupy themselves with ecclesiastical subjects, the one with biblical exegesis, the other with sermon composition. However, their model is also appropriate for works of a secular character, for example, works of history. In an earlier chapter we had occasion to concern ourselves with the John of Bridlington prophecies.[38] These consist of an intentionally dark and oracular verse text from the 1370s accompanied by a prose commentary, both of which probably stemmed from the same author. The anonymous commentator occupies himself not only with the contentual difficulties of his text, but also enters with praiseworthy thoroughness upon stylistic and compositional questions. Thus in his first preamble he deals with the four *causae* of the work, at first concisely, and then explains them in his interpretation of the *prooemium* with the help of the text. For example, he explains the line *Jussit de bellis me metrificare novellis* [He commanded me to make verses about new wars] in the following manner:

> *. . . notandum est quod in isto versu notantur tres causae hujus prophetiae. Primo, causa efficiens, i. jussit me, i. Spiritus Sanctus jussit me factorem esse hujus libri; secundo, causa formalis, quando dicit metrificare, i. scribere per metrum quia est forma hujus libri; tertio, causa materialis, qui* [sic] *dicit de bellis novellis, de quibus tanquam de causa materiali in isto libro tractatur.*
>
> [. . . it should be noted that in this verse are noted the three causes of this prophecy. First, the efficient cause, that is "he commanded me," that is, the Holy Spirit commanded me to be the maker of this book; second, the formal cause, when he says "to make verses," that is to write in the measure that is the form of this book; third, the material cause, when he says "about new wars," about which, as it were about the material cause, this book discusses.][39]

In addition to the four *causae*, the commentator also uses the opportunity to provide four *regulae* according to which the text should be received and understood by the reader. They are not unimportant for an understanding of Gower's

[37] Robert de Basevorn, *Forma Praedicandi*, in *Artes Praedicandi*, 234. They are the *causae finalis, efficiens, materialis*, and *formalis*, as subsequent statements indicate.

[38] See above, 27–28.

[39] Charland, *Artes Praedicandi*, 130.

prologue, and generally for the evaluation of certain *topoi*, and should therefore be quickly glanced at. They are contained in the following awkward lines:

Si verum scribam, verum crede me fore scribam;
Scripsero si vanum, caput est quia non mihi sanum.
Non mihi detractes, sed falsa per omnia mactes.
Nullus deliro credit pro carmine miro.

[If I write the truth, believe that I will be a true writer;
If I have written a lie it is because my head is not sound.
You should not disparage me, but destroy the false throughout.
No one trusts to a crazy man for a miraculous song.][40]

The first line indicates that what is true in these prophecies should be attributed to the Holy Ghost, and not to the author: *. . . et in hoc vitat arrogantiam, quod sibi non attribuit quod deo est attribuendum* [. . . and in this he avoids arrogance, because he does not attribute to himself what must be attributed to God]. The first rule is thus obvious: avoid false presumption. The second line states that all falsehoods and errors are to be charged to the author, who lies sick in bed:

Et hic incurrit humilitatem, quia sibi assumit defectus eos a Deo removendo in quo nulla mala vel imperfecta inveniuntur.

[And here he incurs humility, because he takes upon himself the failings, removing them from God, in whom no evil or imperfect things are found.]

The second rule is thus the counterpart of the first: take responsibility for all errors. The third line is directed against the *detractores*, the slanderers, and solicits the correction of possible errors:

Et ibi excludit praesumptiones auditorum, qui proniores sunt ad detrahendum quam ad laudandum facta aliorum vel corrigendum.

[And thus he prevents the presumptions of the listeners, who are more prone to disparaging than to praising or correcting the works of others.]

The third rule is thus a rebuff of the slanderer and a request for correction. The fourth rule is especially tailored to the genre of the prophecy and is designed to protect the author against the *astutias sapientum mundi,*[41] who consider his account a delirium. The four *regulae* thus concern the moral posture of the author

---

[40] Charland, *Artes Praedicandi*, 129 (text), 131 (commentary).

[41] *. . . ubi sapientum mundi excludit astutias, qui capiunt verba sicut sonant secundum communem expositionem, et sic in proposito non sunt accipienda.* [Whereby he excludes the cunning of the world's philosophers, who take words just as they sound, according to

and his reader *vis-à-vis* the work.[42] The author's choice is between *arrogantia* and *humilitas;* the moral danger for the reader lies in *praesumptio, detractatio,* and *astutia.* Here ideas are brought together in a pattern which emerges again and again in medieval prologues and which we shall also encounter forthwith in Gower.

If one wishes to consider Gower's prologue in a contemporary sense, one must make clear its three or four *causae* and look for its *regulae.* The term *causa* occurs twice explicitly in the prologue of Book II, once as *causa materialis: Et visus varii sunt michi causa libri* (2.Prol.80) [And my several visions are the reason for the book], and again as *causa finalis:*

> *Quicquid ad interius morum scriptura propinat,*
> *Doctrine causa debet habere locum.* 2.Prol.43–44
>
> [Whatever morality a piece of writing supplies for your inner being ought to have its place, for the sake of its teachings. (Trans. Stockton.)][43]

If one wishes, one can analyze the entire prologue according to these categories: 1) *causa materialis* (1–2, 75–84), 2) *causa efficiens* (3–8, 65–74), 3) *causa finalis* (9–20,[44] 43–46), 4) *causa formalis* (21–30). The four *causae* are treated successively. Then follows a passage in which the rule concerning the author's *humilitas* frames the rule *contra detractores,* in the midst of which are inserted in their turn two distiches concerning the *causa finalis.* A kind of chiasmus arrangement thus emerges: A (*humilitas* 31–32), B (*contra detractores* 35–41), C (*causa finalis* 43–46),

their ordinary explanation, and thus they should not be received in this text]: Charland, *Artes Praedicandi,* 131.

[42] In Bonaventura there are, alongside the traditional four *causae* (which he always combines under the two headings of *causae extrinsecae—efficiens* and *finalis*—and *intrinsecae—materialis* and *formalis*), two more that he designates *insinuativum duplicis personae ad opus necessariae, scil. doctoris et auditoris* [the making known of the twofold persona necessary to the work, namely of the teacher and the listener], upon which he enlarges: *Primo igitur propositum verbum* [that is, the first clause of his Bible text] *secundum intellectum generalem indicat nobis, quis et qualis debeat esse doctor huius Scripturae evangelicae, adiungens nihilominus, qualem debeat habere auditorem* [Firstly, therefore, the word of the text discloses to us, according to general understanding, who and what kind of man should be the teacher of this Gospel, and no less the related issue, what kind of listener he should have]: *Commentarius in Evangelium Lucae,* 3 (*Prooemium*).

[43] In this line *causa* is, of course, used prepositionally.

[44] Lines 11–20 revolve, for no apparent reason, around the idea of *honestum.* However, the situation becomes more comprehensible if one refers to John of Bridlington. There the commentator distinguishes three *causae finales: utile, delectabile,* and *honestum.* The first two conform to the traditional *aut prodesse volunt aut delectare poetae* [poets wish either to be useful or to delight]. I cannot account for the separation of *honestum* from the stoic ethic (*de utile et honesto*).

B (*contra detractores* 47–52), A (*humilitas* 53–64). The *causa efficiens* and *causa materialis* are defined once again at the end, more fully than in the beginning.

When an author accommodates himself so completely to a traditional pattern as Gower has done here, it is to be expected that he will also follow traditional paths in the argument. Actually, the prologue of Book II is so crammed with Curtius' *topoi* that it creates the impression it is no more than a motley heap of conventional banalities. A quick survey reveals the following *topoi*:

1. Rejection of the appeal to the Muses and *invocatio* of the Christian God: 3–10.
2. Modesty *formulae*:
    A. *Res non persona:* 11–14
    B. Precious vein in base mineral: 15–18
    C. Ignorance: 21–30
    D. Balaam's ass: 45–46
3. *Torpor*: 31–32
4. Contrast between age and youth: 33–40
5. Knowledge is an obligation: 53–60
    A. Sparks beneath the ashes: 55–56
    B. The light under the bushel: 57–58
6. The work as an offering: 61–66
7. Prayer for divine assistance: 67–74.

The prologue of Book III enters more vigorously into the contents of the work and is thus less conventional. Its structure is based on a principle of doubling. The first paragraph (1–22) contains three themes:

1. The division of society into three estates;
2. The directing of the critique at issues, not people;
3. The establishment of the poet as spokesman.

The second paragraph (23–36) then handles the same themes in reverse order (3, 2, 1). After a connecting link that expresses in a mildly allegorical tone the poet's wish that God allow his seed to bear fruit (37–42), there occurs another, final doubling in the form of two prayers (49–70 and 83–104) that are interrupted by an interpolated apostrophe to the reader and a farewell to the book (71–82). Another *topos* then forms the conclusion: the poet puts to sea and begs the Holy Ghost to fill the sails.

Because a work employs *topoi* does not necessarily imply its inferiority. To be sure, they do have in times of literary sterility a tendency to be transmitted like an endless disease and thus fall easily into disrepute. However, it is only their misuse which discredits them. Here we must ask ourselves whether Gower's *topoi* are conventional forms whose content has already become torpid or traditional means of expression whose vigor was preserved in or perhaps even sprang anew from areas with which they historically had nothing in common. *Topoi*, as

Curtius has convincingly shown in the example of the aged boy, originate in a certain psychological situation.[45] Cannot a new psychology, of an individual or general sort, avail itself of an already rigidified *topos* and breathe new life into it? It would be good if one could pursue the inner history of a *topos* alongside its outer. One would at the same time have to feel its pulse and observe how its life surges and ebbs as it changes through the centuries. It may chance even with literary figures of the second order, like Gower, that traditional ballast is given a living function. I would like to demonstrate this with a few examples, especially of prayer and the modesty formula, from the *Vox Clamantis.*

The prayer and the modesty formula belong, according to their origins, to two different categories: the prayer, as a Christian variant of the appeal to the Muses, to the *stilus grandis* of the epic, the modesty formula to the means of *captatio benevolentiae* which Cicero recommends for the *prooemium* of an oration before a court of law. When Curtius, in his controversy with Schwietering about protestations of humility, warned against making the Middle Ages more Christian than they actually had been, he doubtless was historically correct.[46] It remains only to ask whether form and content are so inextricably bound together that in the course of development a newer and, in this case, specifically more Christian content could not have availed itself of the inherited form. For example, the wording of the first two *regulae* in John of Bridlington establishes the literary *humilitas* of the author in relation to God and not to the reader, thus indicating that Christian and literary humility are perhaps basically inseparable.

However, we shall begin with the beginning, with the *invocatio* which introduces the prologue of Book II of the *Vox Clamantis*, that is, the prologue of the *VC.* It reads:

> *Non tamen inceptis ego musas invoco, nec diis*
> *Immolo, set solo sacrificabo deo.*
> *Spiritus alme deus, accendens pectore sensus,*
> *Intima tu servi pectoris ure tui:*
> *Inque tuo, Criste, laxabo nomine rethe.*
> *Ut mea mens capiat que sibi grata petit.*
> *Inceptum per te perfecto fine fruatur*
> *Hoc opus ad laudem nominis, oro, tui.* 2.Prol.3–10

[I do not invoke the muses for my undertaking, however, nor do I make offering to the gods. But I shall sacrifice to God alone. Merciful God, Holy-Spirit, fire the innermost depths of Thy servant's breast, kindling the feel-

[45] Curtius, *European Literature and the Latin Middle Ages,* 98–101.

[46] Curtius, *European Literature and the Latin Middle Ages,* 412: "The foregoing remarks can supply a few guiding principles and furnish a warning against making the Middle Ages more Christian or more pious than it was. A constant literary formula must not be regarded as the expression of spontaneous sentiment."

> ings in his heart. In Thy name, O Christ, I shall spread my net, so that my mind may thankfully seize upon the things which it requires. I pray that this work, begun with Thy help for the praise of Thy name, may achieve a fitting conclusion. (Trans. Stockton.)]

The situation is perfectly clear from the standpoint of literary criticism. The rejection of the appeal to the Muses, together with the first distich's application to God in its stead, is a *topos*. The poet's *enthousiasmos* in the second distich is no less so. The third distich is based on a New Testament metaphor (John 21:6 and Matthew 4:19 are obviously combined), and the fourth represents yet another *topos*. Thus the *invocatio* is conventional, patched together from four *topoi*. What could be more devastating for the valuation of the author? The impression that the *invocatio* is little more than a cliché is reinforced by the recurrence of two invocations at the end of Book III's prologue, the specific value of which is hardly increased by the *verbatim* borrowing of an entire distich from Peter Riga's *Aurora*.[47]

And yet these prayers are something other than ornaments of an attempted high style. They also go beyond the common Christian view that the aid of God is necessary to the success of every human work. Rather, they receive their import from the tradition and the metaphysical mooring of the sermon.

The structure of the contemporary sermon provides for, in addition to the traditional opening and closing prayers, an *invocatio* at the end of the *prothema*. After the reading of the sermon text (the *thema*) follows a second, shorter Bible text (the *prothema*), which is loosely bound to the *thema* through the transference of a word or idea and whose usually brief treatment has the purpose of leading up to the prayer. The *thema* is repeated after the prayer, and the sermon proper, with its divisions and subdivisions, can then begin. In scope and function the *prothema* and its execution perform the part of a prologue.[48] The influence of the sermon may be indicated when, in addition to an opening and closing prayer, an *invocatio* appears at the end rather than at the beginning of Book III's prologue—where it can hardly be a substitute for an appeal to the Muses.[49]

Now there would obviously be little gained if one separated a *topos* such as the *invocatio* from one tradition only to enclose it in another. What is essential is the functional distinction between the literary prayer and the sermon prayer. The literary prayer became in the course of its development an arabesque affixed

[47] 3.Prol.101–102 and *Aurora*, Prologue, Bodleian Library MS. 822, fol. 4 b. Macaulay overlooked the parallel. Ed. P. E. Beichner (Notre Dame: University of Notre Dame Press, 1965), 1:xliv–xlv, 2: Appendix.

[48] On the structure of the sermon in the thirteenth and fourteenth centuries, see Gilson, *Les Idées et les Lettres*, 93–154; Charland, *Artes Praedicandi*, 107–36; Owst, *Preaching in Medieval England*, *passim*; Kienzle, *The Sermon*.

[49] It is all the same in this case whether one considers Book II as prologue to the class critique of Books III-VI or reckons with the possibility that it was belatedly placed before the class critique.

to a work, an embellishing ornament from which the existence of the poem is basically independent, that is, a *topos* in a mildly deprecative sense. The sermon prayer was spared such a degradation because it is not ornamentation, but prerequisite for and foundation of every sermon. An epic without an appeal to the Muses is conceivable; a sermon without prayer loses its import. According to the Christian view, no man can convert another: the words are the preacher's, but the work of salvation God's alone. According to Matthew 10:20, God is the *causa efficiens*, the preacher the *causa secundaria*: *Non enim vos estis, qui loquimini, sed spiritus patris vestri, qui loquitur in vobis* [For it is not you who are speaking, but the Spirit of your Father who speaks through you].[50]

The sermon presupposes two divine graces that must be requested anew upon each occasion: the *gratia sermonis* for the preacher, the *gratia auditus* for the listener. It is not enough if, with the help of the *gratia sermonis*, the preacher speaks well. Without the aid of the special *gratia auditus* the listener will be incapable of really absorbing what has been said. According to one of Gregory's remarks that was much quoted in the Middle Ages:

> *Formare vocem magistri exterius possunt, sed hanc imprimere interius non possunt. Nisi Spiritus Sanctus corda audientium repleat, ad aures corporum vox docentium incassum sonat.*
>
> [Teachers can shape the voice outwardly, but they are not able to imprint it inwardly. Unless the Holy Spirit fills the hearts of listeners, the voice of teachers sounds to no purpose to the ears of their bodies.][51]

When the *gratia auditus* is missing, the preacher finds himself in the position of the doctor who attains the object of his skill (*finis essentialis*) if he operates artfully. However, continues Alexander of Hales, from whom this simile derives, the healing of the patient (*finis accidens*) is in no way thus guaranteed. Likewise, the

[50] Resembling 2 Corinthians 2:17 and 1 Peter 4:10–11. See also Robert de Basevorn's interpretation of 2 Timothy 4:17 (*Dominus autem mihi astitit, et confortavit me, ut per me praedicatio impleatur* [But the Lord stood by me and strengthened me that through me the preaching of the Gospel might be completed]) in the prologue of his *Forma Praedicandi*. The author explains in respect to the phrase *per me* the sense in which God and the sense in which the preacher are the sermon's *causa efficiens*: *Licet enim Deus, qui et finis, sit causa principaliter efficiens tanquam universale influens . . . ego tamen instrumentum immediatius sum, istud executioni demandans. Quia tamen prima causa plus influit, non audeo mihi aliquid tanquam ex me attribuere.* [For although God, who is also the end, is from the outset the efficient cause, as if flowing into the whole . . . nevertheless I am more immediately the instrument bringing that about. However, because the first cause is much more influential, I do not dare attribute anything to myself as if from me.] In Charland, *Artes Praedicandi*, 234.

[51] Loosely after *Moralia in Job*, 27.38: *PL* 76:437.

preacher attains the *finis essentialis* of his skill if he preaches well; however, the goal of salvation requires an additional divine action, the *finis accidentalis*.[52] The relationship of these two *gratiae* to one another occupies Scholastic debate; however, it need not concern us here.[53] It is important for our context to establish that the sermon prayer distinguishes itself from the literary prayer in two essential points: 1) In its function, because it constitutes the essential prerequisite for the preaching of the Gospel; 2) In its form, because it appears as a double prayer[54] or in the form of two prayers;[55] divine assistance must be solicited for the preacher as well as for his public, and that is a notion far removed from the classical appeal to the Muses. Gower is soliciting the *gratia sermonis* in the first distich, the *gratia*

---

[52] *Summa Theologica*, 4 vols. (Ad Aquas Claras [Quaracchi]: Typographia Collegii S. Bonaventurae, 1924–1948), 3:1060.

[53] See Jean Leclercq, "Le Magistère du Prédicateur au XIIIe Siècle," *Archives d'histoire doctrinale et littéraire du Moyen Age* 15 (1946): 105–47, *passim*; and Alexander of Hales, *Summa Theologica*, 3:1060, especially the treatment of the question *utrum ad aedificationem auditorum sufficiat gratia sermonis* [whether the grace of the sermon is sufficient to the edification of the audience].

[54] Guibert de Nogent, *Liber quo Ordine Sermo Fieri Debeat*: . . . *sermonem praecedat oratio, ut animus fervens amore divino ardenter, quae de Deo sentit, enuntiet, et sicut apud se intrinsecus ardet, sic auditorum corda inflammet* [. . . let prayer precede the sermon, so that the soul [i.e., of the preacher], glowing with divine love, may zealously disclose what it perceives about God, and just as within him it glows internally, so may it inflame the hearts of the listeners]: *PL* 156:24.

[55] Bromyard, *Summa Praedicantium., s. v. praedicator:* . . . *sed quia nec tam excellentis praedicationis operatio, nec tam purae mentis intentio sine Dei possunt haberi adiutorio, praedicator ante omnem praedicationis actum, vel studium, orare habet ad impetrandum gratiam bene, et bona intentione verbum Dei seminandum, sicut agricola orat bonum tempus, et aeris amoenitatem seminandi terram suam, quod seminatum multipliciter. Sicut ergo agricola duo desiderat: unum, quod tempus aptum habeat seminandi: Aliud, quod seminatum semen bene cooperiatur et crescat: ita praedicator ante praedicationem, immo ante omne praedicationis studium orare debet, ut verbum Dei apte primo concipiatur, et postea bene seminetur. Post praedicationem ut bene crescat et fructificet* . . . [he quotes from Chrysostom]. *Orate ergo ante omne studium et praedicationem et post ne sit inanis praedicatio vestra.* [But because neither the effects of a distinguished sermon nor the intention of a pure mind can be realized to a sufficient degree without the assistance of God, the preacher has to pray well before every act or study of preaching in order to obtain grace and plant the Word of God with good intention, just as the farmer prays for good weather and a pleasant breeze in seeding his land, that it produce manyfold. Just as, therefore, the farmer desires two things (one, that the weather should be appropriate for seeding, the other that the sown seed be well covered and grow), thus the preacher should pray before preaching, nay rather before all study of preaching, first that the word of God be suitably grasped and afterwards well sown. After the sermon {he must also pray} that it {the seed} grow well and be fruitful . . . {he quotes from Chrysostom}. Pray therefore before all study and preaching and afterwards, lest your preaching be in vain.] The lines are reminiscent of 1 Corinthians 15:14.

auditus in the second, and is thus in the ecclesiastical tradition of the sermon, not in the literary tradition of the conventional appeal to the Muses when he writes in the prologue of Book III (39–41):

> *Si qua boni scriptura tenet, hoc fons bonitatis*
> *Stillet detque deus que bona scribat homo:*
> *Fructificet deus in famulo que scripta iuvabunt . . .*
>
> [If a piece of writing contains something good, may the fountain of goodness distil it and may God grant that a man write good things. May God make fruitful in his servant those writings which will be of use. Let man provide the proper seeds and God the grain. (Trans. Stockton.)]

Thus the beginning of Book II's prologue is in the tradition of the sermon, and the prayer which replaces the appeal to the Muses must be interpreted out of the spirit of the sermon.

We must return now to the two distiches which follow the thwarted appeal to the Muses.[56] The first places the author in the role of Old Testament prophet, with echoes of Isaiah and the Psalms,[57] the second in the role of New Testament apostle, with an allusion to the selection of the apostles.[58] Both notions are in harmony with Gower's claim to be the *vox clamantis*, the voice of one crying in

---

56 *Spiritus alme deus, accendens pectore sensus,*
Intima tu servi pectoris ure tui:
Inque tuo, Christe, laxabo nomine rethe,
Ut mea mens capiat que sibi grata petit. 2.Prol.5–8

[Merciful God, Holy Spirit, fire the innermost depths of thy servant's breast, kindling the feelings in his heart. In Thy name, O Christ, I shall spread my net, so that my mind may thankfully seize upon the things which it requires. Trans. Stockton,] Cf. above, 79.

57 See Isaiah 6:5–7; Psalm 16:1–4; Psalm 25:2.

58 See Matthew 4:19 (*Venite post me, et faciam vos piscatores hominum* [Come, follow me, and I will make you fishers of men]), combined with John 21:6. On the subject of the preacher as fisher of men, see Bromyard, *Summa Praedicantium, s. v. praedicator,* art. 1: *Tertio officium, et actus praedicatoris assimilari debet actui piscatoris . . .* [an allusion to Matthew 4:19]. *Executio vero eo modo fieri debet, quo plures capere possunt peccatores, quod ita fieri potest, si contra vicia praedicetur in speciali . . . Nam praedicatio generalis est quasi rete nimis latam* [sic] *habens foramina per quae multi pisces evadunt: specialis, quae nititur omnes tangere, est quasi rete arctum, quod omnes, quantum omnes* [sic], *quantum in se est, capit: propter hoc enim illi piscatores descendebant et reficiebant retia sua, ne aliqui evaderent. Lucae* 5. [Thirdly, the function and work of the preacher should be compared to the work of the fisherman . . . The performance should be carried out in a manner in which many sinners can be taken, which can be done if it {*i.e.*, the sermon} is preached against the sins in particular . . . For the general sermon is so to speak a net having too wide spaces through which many fish escape: the particular, which strives to touch everybody, is so to speak a tight net that

the wilderness, and lead us anew to the question of the terms according to which a layman could consider himself a homilist.

The sermon had the threefold task of fortifying the faith, teaching dogma, and encouraging moral conduct. The chief emphasis in the late Middle Ages was on its third function, that is, on the moral domain.[59] In this characteristic it turned into a *correctio.*

The *praedicatio* in the sense of a *correctio* is a precept of Christian charity and was never confined by orthodox medieval theologians to a professionally obligated priesthood. Gower speaks of the universal duty of *correctio fraterna* in the third book of the *Vox Clamantis*:

> *Ecclesie fratres in Christo nos sumus omnes,*
> *Semper et alterius indiget alter ope:*
> *Lex tamen hoc dicit, frater quod si tuus erret,*
> *Corripe, sic et eum fac revenire deo.* 3.1707–1710

> [We are all brothers of the Church in Christ, and one always stands in need of another's help. But the law says this, that if thy brother trespass, rebuke him, and thereby make him return unto God. (Trans. Stockton.)]

He is thus within a tradition that leads from the Bible through Augustine and Gregory to the vernacular devotional literature of the late fourteenth century. A passage in Gregory relates Gower's *vox* and *vocare* theme to this point of view:

> *Cui enim jam vox vocantis Dei efficitur in corde, necesse est ut proximis per praedicationis officium erumpat in voce; et idcirco alium vocet, quia jam ipse vocatus est.*

> [For whoever has been moved in his heart by the voice of God calling him must also burst forth in voice to his neighbors through the office of preach-

---

seizes everything whatsoever in it: because of this those fisherman were accustomed to go down and repair their nets, lest any escape. Luke 5.]

[59] See Guibert, *Liber quo Ordine Sermo Fieri Debeat, PL* 156:27: *Nulla enim praedicatio salubrior mihi videtur quam illa quae hominem sibimet ostendat, et foras extra se sparsum in interiori suo, hoc est in mente, restituat atque eum coarguens quodammodo depictum ante faciem suam statuat.* [For no sermon seems to me more beneficial than that one which shows a man to himself and restores him—scattered without and beside himself—within, that is, in his mind, and—rebuking him as it were—sets his depiction before his face.] That is precisely Gower's method, and calls to mind the last line of the accompanying verses: *Conscius ergo sibi se speculetur ibi* [Therefore let him who is conscious of himself look to himself]. The sermon *de vitiis et virtutibus* attained such an eminent position partly because Lent was the principal sermon time of the year and partly for reasons discussed below, 85–86.

ing; and therefore let him call another, because he has himself already been called.][60]

A passage which attempts to bring the duty of *clamare* home to the reader occurs in the *Speculum Christiani*, a compilation from around the turn of the fourteenth century:

> *Informare autem et docere potest unusquisque fratrem suum in omni loco et tempore opportuno, si videatur sibi expedire, quia hoc est elemosina, ad quam quilibet tenetur. Domino dicente: Quod gratis accepistis, gratis date. Unde Petrus Apostolus: Unusquisque sicut accipit graciam, illam administrare debet in alterutrum. Quomodo potest quis veraciter dicere se deum diligere et eius amorem appetere, si eius ymaginem videat denigrari et in sterquilinio peccatorum iacere, preciosissimum sanguinem Christi sub pedibus conculcari, spiritus sancti habitaculum pollui, sponsam Christi prostitui, fidem catholicam deici, preceptum dominicum et totam eius beatitudinem pro vilibus voluptatibus et viciis contempni, et ipse non curat, nec clamat, sed dissimulans solum suam quietem requirit?*
>
> [Moreover, each one is able to shape and teach his brother in every place and fit time if it seems to be advantageous to him, for this is charity, to which everyone is bound. The Lord having said: give freely what you have freely received (Matthew 10:8). Whence the apostle Peter: Just as each one receives grace, he ought to bestow it upon another (1 Peter 4:10). How may any man say truly that he loves God and hungers after His love if he see His image degraded and tossed onto the dung heap of sins, the most precious blood of Christ trampled under foot, the dwelling place of the Holy Ghost defouled, the bride of Christ prostituted, the universal faith cast down, the Lord's commandment and all his blessedness despised for vile lusts and sins, and not concern himself, nor cry out, but dissembling seek only his own quiet?][61]

The *Book of Vices and Virtues*, the English adaptation of the *Mirour des Pechiez*, likewise views the correction of sinners as a duty of Christian men that is restricted to no single class:

> The Braunches of Mercye. The first is to jeue good counseil to hem that han nede . . . But thilke that han God to-fore here eijen and reden the synful to leue synne, or thilke that ben out of synne and teche hem to kepe hem al-wey clene, as schrifte-fadres schulde do and prelates of holi chirche and

[60] *Homilia in Ezechiel, PL* 76:950–951; ed. M. Adriaen, CCSL 142 (Turnhout: Brepols, 1971), 227.

[61] *Speculum Christiani*, ed. Gustaf Holmstedt, EETS O.S. 182 (London: Oxford University Press, 1933), Prologue, 3.

> also othere good men, of what staat thei ben, thes don the first dede of mercye gostliche.[62]

In neither case are the words from a sermon. Formally there is a distinction between *praedicatio* and *doctrina*;[63] Gower's *Vox Clamantis* formally belongs to *doctrina*. However, the distinction is actually only of a technical-terminological kind. *Doctrina* and *praedicatio* both belong to the *ordo caritatis*. Both have the same goal: the glory of God and the betterment of man.[64] Both originate in the same moral duty and both have the same object: the *correctio* of sinful men. They approach each other even in form in the fourteenth century. Versified sermons were the order of the day and, according to Owst,[65] were appointed not only for private reading but for the pulpit. Thus the boundary between sermon and didactic literature of the kind of the *Vox Clamantis* was highly unstable. In service to the same cause, the preacher became poet, and the poet, preacher.

But now I would like to return once more to Guibert. He states his own thoughts on the problem in that passage from his preaching manual in which he renders Augustine's conception of the universal Christian duty of *correctio*:

---

[62] *The Book of Vices and Virtues*, ed. W. N. Francis, EETS O.S. 217 (London: Oxford University Press, 1942), 199.

[63] Alanus de Insulis distinguishes in his *Summa de Arte Praedicatoria* among *praedicatio, doctrina, prophetia,* and *concionatio*, defining them in the following manner: *Praedicatio enim est illa instructio quae pluribus fit, et in manifesto, et ad morum instructionem; doctrina vero est quae vel uni, vel pluribus fit, ad scientiae eruditionem; prophetia, est admonitio quae fit per revelationem futurorum; concionatio est civilis admonitio, quae fit ad reipublicae confirmationem* [For preaching is that instruction which is made for the many, in public and for moral training; doctrine is that which is made either for the individual or the many, for the advancement of learning; prophecy is admonition that is made through the revelation of future things; oratory is civil admonition, which is made for the upholding of the state]: *PL* 210:112.

[64] Bromyard, *Summa Praedicantium, s. v. praedicator, art. 5: Qui enim ad praedicandum mittitur duobus praeceptis geminae charitatis, sc., de dilectione Dei, et proximi debet esse munitus. Et est hic argumentum, quod nullus officium praedicandi debet assumere, nisi prius labia cordis igne charitatis habeat decocta, et post purgationem peccati, licite potest aliquis assumere officium praedicandi.* [He who is sent to preach should be armed with the two precepts of twinned charity, namely with the love of God and of his neighbor. And the argument here is that no one should assume the office of preaching unless first he shall have seared the lips of his heart with the fire of charity, and after the purgation of sin anyone can legitimately assume the office of preaching.] On the specific function of knowledge *in gloriam dei et utilitatem proximi* [to the glory of God and the benefit of one's neighbor], see below, 88–90. The expression survives until Francis Bacon, although he already gives the second element a more materialistic meaning: "for the glory of the Creator and the relief of man's estate."

[65] Owst, *Literature and Pulpit in Medieval England,* 90–91.

> *. . . sunt qui bene ac continenter vivunt, set quia pastoralem non habent in ecclesia locum, aestimant se non debere fratribus sanctae praedicationis verbum; quod valde absurdum est: si enim per subjugale mutum, id est per asinam, iuxta illud beati Petri* (2 Peter 2:16), *Deus corripi voluit prophetae insipientiam, quam multum et paene absque comparatione dignior est humana natura ad docendum et dandum coaequalibus disciplinam?*
>
> [There are those who live well and continently, but because they do not have a pastoral place in the church they think that they do not owe their brothers the word of sacred preachment; that is very absurd, for if through a beast accustomed to the yoke, that is, through an ass, as in St. Peter (2 Peter 2:16), God wished the foolishness of the prophet to be rebuked, then how much and almost without comparison more worthy is it to teach and provide instruction in human nature to equals?][66]

Here Balaam's Ass[67] appears as a significant element in the discussion of the duty of brotherly admonition. When God chooses even the dumb animal to bring human mistakes to light, to what greater extent does this duty pertain to men? Thus, when one reads in Gower: *Verba per os asini qui protulit, hic mea spes ist, / Eius ut ad laudem cercius ore loquar* (2.Prol.45–46*)* [He who brought forth words through the mouth of an ass is my hope that my lips may speak resolutely in praise of him], one dare not see the lines only as a curious specimen of the self-disparagement *topos*, but must endeavor to understand them, within the context of ecclesiastical trains of thought, as a legitimate expression of a divine duty.

Recent research has forcefully indicated how, after the middle of the thirteenth century, the moral problems and implications of preaching win out over the formal-technical in interest. Gilson, in his investigation of the structure of the sermon, came to the conclusion that "we are not in the presence of a literary work to be composed, but of a religious function to be fulfilled."[68] Leclerq demonstrated in a lengthy series of *quodlibet*s that the person of the preacher withdrew more and more behind his function and the moral problems connected with it.[69] The relatively large number of medieval *artes praedicandi* that seek to apply the formulae of rhetoric to the sermon should not obscure the fact that preaching never sank to *techne*. Cardinal Humbert de Romanis, for example, writes that the difficulty of preaching is that one could learn all other arts through persistent

66 *Liber quo Ordine Sermo Fieri Debeat, PL* 156: 22.

67 The story occurs in Numbers 22:20–35.

68 Gilson, *Les Idées et les Lettres*, 98.

69 Leclercq, "Le Magistère du Prédicateur au XIIIe Siècle," 108–9: "Preaching appears here to be a social function. The preacher fulfilled only an intermediary or interpretive role. It was his duty to assure the diffusion among men of the truth which he had received from Christ through the Apostles: he must therefore place himself in the service of the message which he had to transmit and take a back seat to his duties."

practice and many good teachers, while preaching is a special gift of God and its only teacher the Holy Ghost.[70] Of the two chief requisites of the preacher (*recta intentio* and *scientia*), *intentio*, according to this supposition, must be allotted by far the higher significance; that is, the ethical problem dominates the technical.[71]

According to Higden, the *rectitudo intentionis* is guaranteed if the sermon is preached for the glory of God, the edification of one's fellow man, and the manifestation of truth:

> . . . *quod tunc fit, quando praedicator ad Dei glorificationem, ad proximi aedificationem et ad veritatis insinuationem, non ad favorum aucupationem sicut faciunt adulatores . . . praedicat.*
>
> [. . . that occurs then when the preacher preaches for the glorification of God, the edification of his neighbor, and the manifestation of truth, not for the procurement of favors such as flatterers do.][72]

Gower employs the same three points in his prayer to Christ at the end of Book III's prologue:

> *In te qui es verus mea sit sentencia vera,*
> *Non ibi figmentum cernere possit homo.* 3.Prol.93–94

---

[70] *Liber de Eruditione Praedicatorum*, 6: . . . *Aliae enim artes acquiruntur per assuefactionem ex frequenti agere . . . Gratia vero praedicandi ex dono Dei speciali habetur. Unde Eccl. 10: In manu Dei potestas hominis; id est, praedicatoris, secundum Glossam. Quod ideo dicitur quia ex dono Dei est quod homo habeat potestativam praedicationem: quae autem homo ex opere suo non potest, sed aliunde oportet venire, difficilius est. Porro causae quare difficile est hujusmodi officium ad bene faciendum, sunt tres. Una est ex parte magistri: aliarum enim artium plures inveniuntur magistri, et qui facile possunt haberi: hujus vero artis unicus est magister, cujus copiam pauci habent, sc. Spiritus Sanctus.* [For some skills are acquired through practice from frequent performance . . . But the grace of preaching is had from God as a special gift. Whence Ecclesiasticus 10 {10:5}: the power over men, that is, according to the Gloss, over the preacher (*PL* 113:1198)—is in the hand of God. That is said because it is by the gift of God that a man should have the preaching power; which, moreover, a man cannot have by his own work, but needs to come from elsewhere, [and] this is rather difficult. In addition there are three causes why it is difficult to perform this office well. One has to do with the teacher. For of the other arts are found many teachers, who can be easily had, but the master of this art is unparalleled, whose abundance few men have, namely the Holy Ghost]: Humbert De Romanis, *Liber de Eruditione Praedicatorum*, 2:393.

[71] Leclercq, "Le Magistère du Prédicateur," 137: "Is it not admirable indeed that almost all the moral problems studied in the *Quodlibets* are problems of intention? We perceive here the extent to which spiritual preoccupations dominate the medieval clergy."

[72] *De Forma Praedicandi*, Bodleian Library MS. 316, Canon. Misc. 522, fol. 176v.

[Let my intent be true to Thee Who art true; let no man succeed in discerning any fabrication in it.]

Absit adulari, nec sit michi fabula blesa,
Nec michi laus meriti sit sine laude tua.
Da loquar ut vicium minuatur et ammodo virtus
Crescat, ut in mundo mundior extet homo. 3.Prol.97–100

[Let there be no flattery in my account, and let it not be hesitant. Let there be no praise for my accomplishment except Thine. Let me speak out so that henceforth vice will diminish and virtue flourish, in order that mankind may become purer in this world. (Trans. Stockton.)]

The order of appearance is altered, but they are clearly recognizable, one distich allotted to each. Even the protest against the charge of flattery is not forgotten. Now attacks against flatterers and protestations that flattery is far from the author's thoughts are so frequent in medieval literature that they have a *topos*-like character. They occur in great detail in John of Salisbury, and the article on *adulator* is one of the longest in Bromyard's compilation. They may be occasioned by the social structure of the time. The socially dependent position of the man of letters may have caused him to be bitter against more successful competitors. However, this aspect is of only secondary importance for the sermon and for sermon literature. And since Gower wrote here out of the ethos of the preacher, the *topos* has a specifically Christian coloring. In Gower, as in the medieval discussion of proper preaching, *adulatio* is contrary to that praise of God which is the sermon's goal, for it serves either the advancement of the author's material interests or the increase of his vainglory. *Adulatio* and *inanis gloria* are the two chief sins to which the preacher is exposed and which threaten the redemptive goal of his work. Here are a few examples from church fathers, sermon manuals, and *summae*:

Raymond of Pennaforte: *Non debet quoque praedicator adulationibus quaerere benevolentiam atque munuscula, set arguere peccata.*

[Likewise the preacher should not seek good will and favors by flattery, but should censure sins.][73]

Gerard d'Abbeville: . . . *tripliciter potest esse malum praedicare placentia: primo ex intentione adulandi principaliter . . . secundo intentione seducendi sicut haeretici . . . tertio intentione vanam gloriam extorquendi . . . Fraudulenter opus Dei agunt qui favorem humanum expectant, tales mundi favorem quaerunt et gloriam suam, non gloriam Dei, unde Glossa super illud: Si hominibus placerem* [*sc. Christi servus non essem.* (*PL* 113:1105) Gal. 1:10]*: cum hominibus, inquit,*

[73] *Summa Theologiae Moralis,* Bodleian Library MS. 316, Canon. Misc. 522, fol. 18v.

> *placere volumus, gloriam nostram quaerere non debemus sed illorum salutem, ut bene ambulantes imitando non errent et inde non nos sed Deum laudent qui tales nos fecit* [*Ordin.* VII, 79], *ut non appetatur favor humanus tamquam merces recte sanctorum.*
>
> [. . . in three ways it can be an evil to preach pleasing things: first, with the primary intention of flattering . . . second, with the intention of misleading like the heretics . . . third, with the intention of extorting vainglory . . . They do the work of God fraudulently who expect human applause; such seek the favor of the world and their own glory, not the glory of God, whence the Gloss upon that text: "If I were still trying to please men" [*sc.* "I should not be a servant of Christ." Gal. 1:10]: when we wish, he says, to please men we ought not to seek our glory but their well-being, so that walking rightly in imitation they do not go astray and thence they should praise not us but God who made us such [*Ordin.* VIII, 79], so that human favor should not be sought as if it were rightly the reward of holy men.][74]
>
> Nicolas Byard: . . . *non debet praedicator aliud intendere nisi salutem audientium, non gloriam, non commodum terrenum.*
>
> [. . . the preacher should not hold out anything but the salvation of the listeners, not glory, not earthly profit.][75]
>
> Thomas Waleys: . . . *statuat sibi rectum finem sermonis, ne videlicet ad sui ostentationem praedicet sed ad Dei laudem et proximi aedificationem. Declinet inanem gloriam, quae ex bonis operibus solet nasci, et maxime se ingerat importune hiis quae fiunt in publico in praesentia multorum. Propter quod praedicator contra motus inanis gloriae specialiter instat bellum.*
>
> [. . . let him set for himself the proper goal of the sermon, i. e. that he preach not to his own display but to the glory of God and the edification of his neighbor. Let him avoid empty glory, which should be born of good works, and especially let him in the presence of the many inveigh ruthlessly against things that happen in public. Because the preacher should wage war especially against the impulse of vainglory.][76]

Wyclif expresses his opinion on this question very forcefully in a sermon (*Sermones Quadraginta, Sermo XXXI*) from his orthodox period. His theme is *semen est verbum Dei* [the seed is the word of God] (Luke 8:11), and what he says applies especially to the preacher:

---

74 *Quodlibet* 10, *q.* 2; in Leclercq, "Le Magistère du Prédicateur," 122.

75 *Distinctiones*; in Leclercq, "Le Magistère du Prédicateur," 109.

76 *De Modo Componendi Sermones,* 1; in Charland, *Artes Praedicandi,* 330.

. . . Quam fatua ergo est intencio aptare labores bonos de genere ut vel principaliter vel mixtim captetur applausus populi. Idem est enim sic facere et commutare amiciciam Dei pro ficta et adulatoria fama mundi et per consequens bonum eterni gaudii perdere pro gaudio ypocrite quod est instar puncti breve, ymmo constituere unum talem vilem peccatorem Deum suum et sic (quantum in se est) pervertendo ordinem universi dum eius laudem prefert laudi Dei.

[How foolish therefore is the intention to prepare good works of this kind so that either principally or in part one should be desirous of the approval of the people. For it is the same thing thus to make and to barter the friendship of God for the false and flattering fame of the world, and as a consequence to lose the good of eternal joy for a feigned gaud that is the brief image of a moment, nay rather to establish one such vile sinner his God and thus (as far as he is able) perverting the order of the universe since he prefers his praise to the praise of God.][77]

The earnestness and vigor with which the sermon's moral prerequisites were pursued in the thirteenth and fourteenth centuries is shown by the constantly debated question of whether *adulatio* and *inanis gloria* are mortal or venial sins for the preacher. Robert de Basevorn is convinced that they are mortal.[78] An anonymous *quodlibet* distinguishes between the sermon which is preached with the intention of seeking vainglory and is therefore a mortal sin, and the sermon which is only the occasion of vainglory and therefore more gently judged.[79]

77 *Iohannis Wyclif Sermones*, ed. Johann Loserth, 4 vols. (London: Trübner, 1890), 4:217–78.

78 *Forma Praedicandi,* 5, in Charland, *Artes Praedicandi,* 242: *Videat autem praedicator prae omnibus quod finem bonum sibi faciat sui sermonis, puta laudem Dei vel sanctorum suorum, vel aedificationem proximi, vel aliquod tale meritorium ad vitam aeternam. Si etiam alium finem secundario convolvat, ut vel reputetur vel aliquod temporale lucretur vel aliquod tale, adulter est verbi Dei, quod reputatur mortale.* [Let the preacher see to it above all that he have a good purpose for his sermon—such as the praise of God, or His saints, or the edification of his neighbor, or some such object deserving eternal life. If, secondarily, he also includes another purpose—that he be famous, or that he gain something temporal, or the like—he is an adulterer of the Word of God, and this is considered a mortal sin.] Trans. Leopold Krul, in *Three Medieval Rhetorical Arts*, ed. James J. Murphy (Berkeley: University of California Press, 1971), 109–215.

79 *Si aliquis incipit praedicare bona voluntate et postea occasione praedicationis glorietur de hoc quod bene praedicavit, talis gloria non facit praedicationem peccatum, sive sit venialis sive mortalis, sed si vana gloria moveat hominem ad praedicandum, ut praedicatio referatur ad finem inanis gloriae, tunc praedicatio illa est peccatum mortale.* [If anyone begins to preach with a good will and after the occasion of the sermon should take pride in it because he preached well, such pride does not make the preaching a sin, be it either venial or mortal, but if vainglory should move a man to preaching, so that the sermon is delivered to the end of vainglory, then that sermon is a mortal sin]: Leclercq, "Le Magistère du Prédicateur," 118.

Seen against this background, Gower's plea of *absit adulare* is far more than a literary convention. Indeed, in many of the texts mentioned there appears alongside *adulatio,* when it is understood in the sense of illicit concession to the audience, a second item that is incompatible with *recta intentio* and that also occurs in Gower: the gratification of *curiositas*. When he writes in the prologue of Book III,

> *Non ego sidereas affecto tangere sedes,*
> *Scribere nec summi mistica quero poli;*
> *Set magis, humana que vox communis ad extra*
> *Plangit in hac terra, scribo moderna mala.* (3.Prol.53–56)
>
> [I do not aspire to reach the thrones of heaven, or seek to describe the mysteries of the lofty skies. Rather, I write of present-day evils which the common voice of mankind outwardly complains of in this country (Trans. Stockton)],

he calls to mind in a purely superficial way Curtius' *topos* of the rejection of trite material, by which the passage may have been formally influenced. The content, however, is a protest against the charge of *vana curiositas*. Thomas Waleys warns the preacher against admitting *vana, curiosa,* and *frivola* into the sermon in order to please the congregation. He should be intent upon the profit, not the praise or censure, of the listener. Otherwise it might befall him according to the words of the Psalm:

> *Deus dissipavit ossa eorum qui hominibus placent. Confusi sunt quia Dominus sprevit eos.*
>
> [For God hath scattered the bones of them that please men. They have been confounded, because God hath despised them] (Psalm 52:6).[80]

---

80 . . . *praedicator non conetur sic hominibus in praedicando placere ut sequatur aliquorum vanitatem qui frequentantes sermones ea quae sunt curiositatis commendant. Multi enim praedicantes talibus placere studuerunt, et ideo multa vana et frivola, et quae plus obsunt quam prosunt, introduxerunt;* . . . *Sed non expedit praedicatorem talium auditorum laudibus aut vituperiis commoveri. Quominus sic praedicet quo poterit auditoribus bonis prodesse, consideret illus Ps. Deus dissipavit ossa eorum qui hominibus placent* [. . . thus the preacher should not strive so to please men in preaching that he support the vanity of those who, frequenting sermons, praise those things which are curiosities. For many preachers take pains to please such men, and thus they have introduced both many empty and frivolous things and those which hinder more than they profit . . . But it does not avail the preacher to be concerned with the praises or condemnations of such listeners. Thus, lest he should preach in such a way that he can benefit {only} his "good" listeners, let him consider that Psalm: God hath scattered the bones of them that please men]. *De Modo Componendi Sermones*, in Charland, *Artes Praedicandi*, 336–37.

That is the same divine judgment that threatens the *adulator*: *Si adhuc hominibus placerem, Christi servus non essem* [If I were still trying to please men, I should not be a servant of Christ] (Galatians 1:10).

As Raymond explains in his *Summa*,[81] *vana, curiosa,* and *frivola* are theological sophistries, astronomy, secular poetry, and idle tales. That it is not a question of clerical bias against secular literature is shown by the coexistence of *fictiones poetarum* and *fabulae inutiles* on the one hand and *subtiles quaestiones theologiae* and *discursus astrorum* on the other, all of which are rejected. The cause is, rather, the sermon's consciousness of moral responsibility according to Ecclesiastes 7:1: *Quid necesse est homini maiora se quaerere, cum ignoret, quid conducat sibi in vita sua numero dierum peregrinationis suae* [What needeth a man to seek things that are above him, whereas he knoweth not what is profitable for him in his life, in all the days of his pilgrimage]? The Dominican Cardinal Hugh of St. Victor writes of the priority of morality above all other sermon themes:

> . . . *Et sic iustum et honestum esset praedicatoribus supradicta* [*sc. de peccatis, poenitentia, et bonis operibus*] *et similia, in quibus homines quotidie cadimus, praedicare et alia alta et subtilia et curiosa dimittere.*
>
> [And thus it would be right and honest for preachers to preach the aforesaid things {namely sins, penitence, and good works} and similar things into which we humans fall daily; and to leave aside any lofty, subtle, and quaint things.][82]

And a gloss in the manuscript of Raymond of Pennaforte's *Summa Theologiae Moralis* that I used remarks:

> *Non dicant, quid tamen praedicare: Scio quid dicturus est praedicator: Omnis enim sermo in hoc concluditur: Declina a malo et fac bonum.*
>
> [Let them not say, however, what to preach; I know what the preacher is going to say; For every sermon is composed to this end: turn away from evil and do good.][83]

The betterment of his fellow man also caused Gower to renounce *alta* and *curiosa*, as he does when he follows the cited lines with this statement:

---

81 *Non debet praedicare subtiles quaestiones theologiae, puta de esse et essentia, discursus astrorum, fictiones poetarum, fabulas inutiles, sed ea quae faciunt ad salutem.* [He should not preach the subtle questions of theology, about being and essence, the courses of the stars, the fictions of the poets, such as idle tales, but those things that make for salvation]: *Summa Theologiae Moralis,* Bodleian Library MS. 316, Canon. Misc. 522, fol. 19.

82 *Speculum Ecclesiae* (Seville: J. Kronberger, 1512), unpaginated.

83 Bodleian Library MS. 316, Canon. Misc. 522, fol. 19v.

Utilis adverso quia confert tempore sermo,
Promere tendo mala iam bona verba die. 3.Prol.57–58

[Since a useful discussion contributes something even though the times are hostile, I intend for my words of good to bring evil to light. (Trans. Stockton.)]

The antithesis of astronomy and that which is *utile* shows that the author was orienting himself not towards a didactic literary tradition, which would hardly have contrasted the two, but towards the moral problem of establishing the preacher's *rectitudo intentionis.*

Earlier we alluded to the two prerequisites of proper preaching, *recta intentio* and *recta scientia.* Most ecclesiastical authors discuss *utilitas* in the context of *recta intentio,* and some few consider it part of the *integritas sermonis*, that is, of the second prerequisite. In either case it is closely connected with *veritas* or *insinuatio veritatis.* For example, Raymond's *Summa Theologiae Moralis* defines the *integritas sermonis* thus: *quod fiet* [?], *si in eo* [*sc. sermone*] *fuerint veritas, utilitas, claritas* [what will result, if in it {sc. the sermon} there will have been truth, profit, clarity].[84] Now as we saw, Gower's prayer in Book III's Prologue includes—beyond the rejection of *adulatio* and the double purpose of *laus dei* (in this case *Christi*) and *utilitas proximi*—above all the *insinuatio veritatis.* When the Christian *invocatio* assumed the heritage of the classical appeal to the Muses, it usually directed itself, as Curtius noted,[85] to the Holy Ghost or to Christ as the word-become-flesh. The *Christus-veritas* theme, on the other hand, points—probably in itself and certainly by its proximity to the argument concerning the *recta intentio*—to the tradition of the sermon rather than to a literary cliché.

I wish now to quote in its entirety a passage that was only abstracted above:

O sapiens, sine quo nichil est sapiencia mundi,
Cuius in obsequium me mea vota ferunt.
Te precor instanti da tempore, Criste, misertus,
Ut metra que pecii prompta parare queam;
Turgida devitet, falsum mea penna recuset
Scribere, set scribat que modo vera videt.
In primis caveat ne fluctuet, immo decenter
Quod primo ponit carmine servet opus:
Hic nichil offendat lectorem, sit nisi verum
Aut veri simile, quod mea scripta dabunt.
In te qui es verus mea sit sentencia vera,
Non ibi figmentum cernere posit homo. 3.Prol.83–94

[84] Bodleian Library MS. 316, Canon. Misc. 522, fol. 18v.

[85] Curtius, *European Literature and the Latin Middle Ages,* 235–37.

[O Wise One, without Whom the wisdom of the world is as nothing, Thou into Whose service my devotions bring me, I pray Thee at this time, O merciful Christ, to grant that I can readily compose the verses I have striven for. Let my pen avoid what is turgid, let it refuse to write what is false; rather, let it now write what it sees to be true. Let it take care not to falter at the outset; instead, let what it puts in the very first line serve the whole work appropriately. Let nothing that my writings are to offer offend the reader, unless it is the truth or very like the truth. Let my intent be true to Thee Who art true; let no man succeed in discerning any fabrication in it. (Trans. Stockton.)]

The passage closely interweaves three themes: *Christus sapiens,* Christ as helper in the poem's composition, and *Christus veritas.* The direct invocation of *Christus sapiens* accords with sermon tradition. Thomas Waleys provides the reason:

Tertium documentum est ut praedicaturus verbum Dei consideret quod omnis sapientia a Domino Deo est. Et ideo cum in sermone specialiter requiritur donum sapientiae, convertat se per devotam orationem ad fontem Sapientiae, juxta illud Jacobi 1: Si quis indiget sapientia, postulet a Deo, qui dat omnibus affluenter, et non improperat . . . Ita et praedicator sapientiam postulet qua possit populum recte instruere.

[The third instruction is that a man about to preach God's word should consider that all wisdom is from the Lord God. And therefore when the gift of wisdom is especially required in a sermon, he should turn himself through devout prayer to the Fount of Wisdom, just like that passage in James 1 {James 1:5}: If any of you is wanting in wisdom, let him ask it of God, who gives abundantly to all men, and does not reproach . . . And thus let the preacher pray for wisdom, in which way he may correctly instruct the people.][86]

Thomas goes on to Gower's second point, Christ's help in the composition of the poem, when he continues:

. . . omnino expedit ut precetur ad auxilium divinitatis, plus confidens in divino auxilio quam in proprio ingenio, ne forte Deus subtrahat seu potius non tribuat sibi verbum.

[. . . altogether it is expedient that he should implore the aid of the Divinity, trusting more in divine aid than in his own cleverness, lest perhaps God take away or rather not grant him the word.]

The *artes praedicandi* also contain information about divine assistance in the concrete difficulties of composition. Robert de Basevorn interprets 2 Timothy 4:17

[86] *De Modo Componendi Sermones,* in Charland, *Artes Praedicandi,* 330.

(*Dominus mihi astitit et confortavit me, ut per me praedicatio impleatur* [But the Lord stood by me and strengthened me, that through me the preaching of the gospel might be completed]) in the following manner:

> *Tunc enim aliquid formaliter traditur et docetur quando ordinate quod principium operis promittit vel inquirendum praetendit continuatio prosequitur et finis concludit . . . Unde, Eccli. 24, de Deo qui istam impletionem formalem facit et a quo est principaliter quidquid a nobis fieri videtur, dicetur quod adimplet quasi Phison sapientiam . . . et iterum quod adimplet quasi Euphrates sensum, i. sicut illa duo flumina Phison et Tigris* [*sic*] *ordinate implent alveos suos, ita Deus in tractatoribus sapientiae suae facit, gratiam et sapientiam vel scientiam eis infundens ordinate et formaliter procedendi, ut sic aperiente eo manum suam omnia impleantur congrua bonitate.*
>
> [For then something is formally delivered and taught when the beginning of the work promises something arranged in order or puts forth a subject for inquiry, a continuation provides a detailed discussion, and a conclusion makes an end . . . Whence in Ecclesiasticus 24 {24:35–6} it is said about God, who effects this formal fulfillment and by whom is fundamentally done whatever seems to come from us, that He filleth up wisdom as the Phison and, again, that He maketh understanding to abound as the Euphrates. That is, just as those two rivers, Phison and Tigris [sic], fill their channels in an orderly way, so does God act for those who impart His wisdom, pouring into them grace and wisdom, or the knowledge of proceeding in an orderly and formal way, that thus, when he opens His hand to that end, all things may be filled with harmonious goodness.][87]

That calls to mind Gower's *Inceptum per te perfecto fine fruatur / Hoc opus . . .* (2.Prol.9–10) [Let this work, begun with Thy help . . . achieve a fitting conclusion] and apparently also has a bearing upon another distich:

> *Et si metra meis incongrua versibus errent,*
> *Que sibi vult animus congrua vota cape.* 2.Prol.25–26
>
> [And if the inharmonious meters in my verses go astray, receive the harmonious offerings my soul intends for you. (Trans. Stockton.)]

This view that divine assistance is more important than human artistry can lead to the depreciation of rhetoric, and I believe that herein lies the source of many *topoi* of self-deprecation which appear at first glance to fall under the rubric of "affected modesty." Thomas Waleys stresses in the prologue of his manual that the rules of rhetoric should not be unconditionally binding upon the preacher

[87] Charland, *Forma Praedicandi*, 233–34. The allusion at the end is to Psalm 103:28 (Vulg.).

and supports the argument with a verse from the second letter to Timothy (2 Timothy 2:9): *verbum Dei non est alligatum* [the word of God is not bound].[88] William of Auvergne advises:

> *Si vis habere modum praedicandi et copiam loquendi efficaciter et artificiose . . . curiosum sermonem et politum devita et, ne simplex et nuda veritas verborum fusco corrumpatur, in exordio sermonis auxilium Dei invocare debes et ad orandum pro te inducere auditores, ne prudentie tue, contra consilium Salomonis, initi videaris.*
>
> [If you wish to have an effective and skillful method of preaching and a rich supply of words . . . shun the ornate and embellished sermon and, lest the simple and naked truth be corrupted by the obscurity of words, you should invoke the aid of God in the introduction of the sermon and induce the listeners to prayer for you, lest against the counsel of Solomon you seem to depend on your own wisdom.][89]

Could Gower's emphasis on *simplicitas* and *ruditas* in the sense of deficient rhetorical schooling be superficially attuned to the tradition of affected modesty and yet at the same time reveal something of the Pauline self-esteem of the man who knows himself, as the instrument of God, to be above the tricks of rhetoric? His definite lack of embarrassment shows that Gower, rather than being seriously distressed by *simplicitas*, perceived it to be analogous with William of Auvergne's *simplex veritas*:[90]

---

[88] Obviously, he thinks he perceives in the Pauline verse the technical term *allegare*, which means a certain way of linking two Bible passages in the sermon: *Placeat autem diligenter advertere quod, sicut dicit Apostolus, ad Tim. 2: Verbum Dei non est alligatum. Et idcirco nullatenus est credendum quod verbum Dei praedicationis officio fidelibus ministrandum alligetur consuetudine alicui humanitus introductae seu regulis humano ingenio adinventis quae in hoc opere inseruntur, quasi contra eas praedicatori agere non liceat, aut, si praedicando illas servare omiserit, reputari debeat huiusmodi omissio vitiosa.* [Let it however be agreed to note carefully that, just as the Apostle says in Timothy 2, the word of God is not bound. And on that account it is by no means worthy of belief that the office of preaching the word of God ministered to the faithful should be bound by any custom brought in from daily life or by the rules invented by human ingenuity which are inserted into this work, as if it is not permitted the preacher to act contrary to them, or if he omit to observe them in preaching, it should on this account be thought a culpable omission.] *De Modo Componendi Sermones*, in Charland, *Forma Praedicandi*, 329.

[89] *Ars Praedicandi*, ed. Alphonse de Poorter (Bruges: n.p., 1927), 197.

[90] See also Humbert de Romanis, *De Eruditione Praedicatorum*, 2:403, in which *simplicitas sine curiositate ornatur rhetorici* [simplicity furnished without the curiosity of the rhetorician] is commended with reference to a passage from Seneca's letters: *Oratio quae veritati dat operam, incomposita esse debet et simplex. Aliae artes ad ingenium pertinent: hic negotium animarum agitur.* [The speech that pays attention to the truth should be unadorned

. . . absque rubore
Que mea simplicitas sufficit illa dabo. 2.Prol.31–32

[. . . I shall nevertheless render without any embarrassment the things for which my ingenuousness is adequate];

Ergo recede mee detractor simplicitati. 2.Prol.47

[Therefore, let my detractor yield to my ingenuousness. (Trans. Stockton.)]

The word *rudis*, which surfaces three times—*Et rudis ipse rude si quid tractavero . . . parce . . .* (2.Prol.23–24) [And if I who am unskillful treat of something unskillfully . . . take pity]; *Deque rudi dociles carmine sume notas* (2.Prol.42) [And single out the sweet notes from my harsh song]—is in a literary sense somewhat like the term *rusticus*,[91] and although the author here begs our indulgence, he may have done so conscious of the words of Jerome:

Multo quidem melius est ex duobus imperfectis rusticitatem habere sanctam quam eloquentiam peccatricem.

[Of two imperfect things, it is indeed much better to have a holy lack of sophistication than sinful eloquence.][92]

---

and plain. The other arts pertain to cleverness: here the business of souls is conducted.] *Moral Letters to Lucilius*, 41 and 75.

[91] Curtius, *European Literature and the Latin Middle Ages*, 411–12.

[92] Indirectly from *Pharetra* 1.15: *De Praedicatoribus Malis*; actually Jerome, *Ep.* 52.9, *PL* 22:535.

Chapter Four

The Mirror for a Prince

It does not pay for the literary historian to treat Gower's class critique in detail. The subject resists artistic shaping except in the form of satire, and satire in return resists the author's moral earnestness and edificational intention. The *Speculum Stultorum* of Nigellus Wireker and several branches of the French Reynard tales show what could be artistically accomplished in this area. The class critique of the *Vox Clamantis* is not their equal. Gower does not even achieve the vividness of a few descriptions of situations in his *Mirour.* One receives the impression that this man, whose power lies in the unassuming simplicity and liquid clarity of his English and, often, also his French style,[1] was possessed of the pernicious notion that solemnity and abstraction are the only suitable means of expression in Latin. Some few passages do raise themselves above the bleak, never-ending sterility of the elegiac distiches, and the reader breathes a sigh of relief. One such example is the portrait of the priest who forsakes his parish with the approval of his bishop in order to devote himself to theological studies at the university. He is inspired by the commendable zeal to put what he learns immediately into practice. Accordingly, his study of Genesis goes as follows:

"Ve soli," legimus ex scripturis Salomonis,
Namque virum solum nemo requirit eum:
Qua racione scole mos est, quod quisque studere
Debet cum socia doctus in arte sua.
Ipse deus sociam fecit per secula primam,
Ut iuvet hec hominem, sicque creavit eam:
Masculus in primo factus fuit, atque secundo
Femina, sic ut in hiis det deus esse genus:
Istaque principia discretus rector agenda
Perstudet, et vota prebet in arte pia.
Quis laterisque sui costam quam sentit abesse
Non cuperet, per quam perficeretur homo?

[1] R. F. Yeager, "John Gower's French," in *Companion*, ed. Echard, 137–51 provides a recent evaluation of Gower's French verse. Trans.

Prima viri costa mulier fuit ipsa creata,
Vult igitur costam rector habere suam.
Nam deus humanam precepit crescere gentem,
Cuius precepto multiplicabit homo:
Sic sibi multiplicat rector, dum semen habundat,
Ut sit mandati non reus ipse dei. 3.1417–1434

["Woe to him that is alone," we read in Solomon's writings, for no one looks after the man who is alone. For this reason it is the college's custom that everyone learned in his art ought to study with a female companion. God Himself made the first female companion in order that she might help man forever, and so He created her. Man was made first, and woman second, so that God might bring the human race into being through them. The discerning rector is very eager to carry out these precepts, and offers his devotions in a dutiful way. Who would not want the rib he feels missing from his side, the rib by which man is to be perfected? The first woman was created out of man's rib, and the rector accordingly wants to have his own rib. For God commanded the human race to be fruitful: by His command man is to multiply. Thus, since his seed is so copious, the rector does multiply, so that he will not be guilty in the light of God's mandate. (Trans. Stockton.)]

Such *lumina* are, however, so infrequent that one wonders whether this kind of sarcasm was really one of Gower's intellectual characteristics.

From a sociological point of view, the statements of the *Vox Clamantis* are to be evaluated with great caution. What Owst proved for *Piers Plowman* is certainly to a considerable extent also valid for Gower: he employs clichés inherited from the class sermon which in every single instance must be validated both for England and for the second half of the fourteenth century.[2]

I shall therefore not examine the class critique as a whole. Nevertheless, I wish to go into a few questions which result from its conclusion, the Mirror for a Prince.[3] This *speculum principis*, an open letter to the young Richard II, is by its position alone elevated superficially above the frame of the class critique. In the *Mirour* Gower had followed the traditional scheme of handling the religious and secular classes by degrees downward from the top. Thus he began the first section with the pope (or the *curia*),[4] the second with the emperor, followed by king, magnates, knights, lawyers, merchants, guildsmen, peasants, and serfs. In the *Vox Clamantis*, on the other hand, he organizes the class critique around the

[2] G. R. Owst, *Literature and Pulpit in Medieval England*, Chaps. 5–7, "The Preaching of Satire and Complaint." On Gower see 230.

[3] For Gower's overall view of the king's role, see R. A. Peck, "The Politics and Psychology of Governance in Gower: Ideas of Kingship and Real Kings," in *Companion*, ed. Echard, 215–38. Trans.

[4] The pope appears to have been interpolated belatedly; see above, 14–16.

principle of the three estates, which was already becoming antiquated.[5] They are discussed from Book III, Chapter 1 to Book V, Chapter 10. To the third estate is attached the urban populace, which occupies the rest of Book V. Emperor, king, and advocate of the law were not to be accommodated in this three-class frame. The emperor is not mentioned in the *Vox Clamantis*, perhaps because a successor had not yet been crowned following the death of Charles IV, perhaps because the special character of the Mirror for a Prince left no room for him. The guardians of the law receive their own book, the sixth, and unlike the other classes are presented not in descending but in ascending order of rank, until one passes beyond the royal advisor to the king himself as the highest representative of justice. This sixth book is not mentioned in the plan of the class critique that Gower outlines in the prologue to Book III.[6] Its absence and the altered arrangement *vis-à-vis* Books III-V create the impression that either the Mirror for a Prince is a belated rounding-off of the class critique or the class critique is a kind of prelude to the Mirror for a Prince. In any case, Gower abandoned in the *Vox Clamantis* the customary scheme that he had accepted without any modifications in the *Mirour.* He isolated the section concerning the king and thus raised it to a special prominence.

In addition to the superficial factor of the arrangement, form and content determine the special character of the Mirror for a Prince within the class critique. According to its form, it is an open letter to the young king. Now personal address as a means of enlivening the subject matter occurs so frequently in the *Vox Clamantis* that in itself it is not very noteworthy. The letter form also appears, at least in rudiment, in another place.[7] However, nowhere does there occur an open letter of the Mirror's extent, so entirely complete in itself and so clearly detached from its context. Its beginning and end are carefully set off from the surrounding text. The introduction is a distich that establishes motivation and from which the direct address to the king follows:

Hinc est, quod normam scriptis de pluribus ortam
Regis ego laudi scribere tendo mei. 6.587–588

[5] These are the *clerus, miles,* and *cultor*; see 3.1–2 and Book III, Prologue.

[6] Book III, Prologue *passim*; see esp. lines 103–104, which possibly allude, in the phrase *trina series*, to three projected books (III-V?).

[7] Compare the prose summary of Book VI, Chapter 5: *Hic loquitur quasi per epistolam Iudicibus illis directam, qui in caduca suarum diviciarum multitudine sperantes, deum adiutorem suum ponere nullatenus dignantur.* [He speaks as if in a letter directed to those judges who, trusting in their perishable heap of riches, are in no way worthy that God make them His deputy.] See also the end of the chapter, 413–414: *Iudicibus populi vanum tamen est quod in ista / Materia scripsi; perdita verba dedi.* [But I have written in vain about these matters / To the people's judges; I waste my words.]

[That's why in honor of my king I mean to write
A rule of conduct drawn from many texts.]

The end, however, is marked differently in the two redactions of the text. Only in the A-Text does Chapter 18 have the character of an epilogue. It contains a closing prayer, a benediction for the young monarch, the presentation of the letter,[8] and a formula of valediction. There is no transition from the close of the letter to the following chapter. As to the development of the *Vox Clamantis*, one can hardly derive a reliable conclusion from this state of affairs. Yet one may with some certainty consider the later version an attempt to bridge an old gap between sections.[9]

The special position which the Mirror for a Prince occupies is due to the fundamentally dissimilar character, despite all their overlappings, of class critique and *speculum principis*. The didactic interest of the latter is of a pedagogical nature and posits not only an optimistic view of human educational capacity and willingness, but also a positive, or at least neutral, human educational substance. The class critique, on the other hand, while it, too, cannot manage without the belief that mankind is educable to a certain degree, proceeds from the negative assumption that human nature is powerfully corrupt and perverse. Gower sees himself readily in the likeness of the doctor; one would call his objective in the class critique therapy and his goal in the Mirror for a Prince prophylaxis.

We come now to the Mirror for a Prince itself. It is no systematic treatise, but a random file of current themes, among which the first and most important is the theme of justice. Any attempt to ascertain its precise sources would be a waste of time. Gower did not follow directly the two basic models for the medieval *speculum principis*, Deuteronomy 17:14–20 and the pseudo-Cyprian's *De XII Abusionibus Saeculi*. His acquaintance with the pseudo-Aristotelian *Secretum Secretorum* has been proven for the *Confessio Amantis*,[10] and may be considered equally certain for the *Vox Clamantis*.[11] His ideas were in a general way influenced by the pseudo-Plutarch's *Institutio Traiani* and its interpretation of the state as an image of the human organism; however, he did not, unlike the authors of many other medieval mirrors for princes, take it over *in toto*.[12] He no-

[8] It is designated *metra* in 6.1191, *scripta* in 1194, *epistola* in the prose summary of Chapter 8.

[9] See below, 161–63.

[10] See George L. Hamilton, "Some Sources of the Seventh Book of Gower's *Confessio Amantis*," *MP* 9 (1911/12): 323–45.

[11] See below, 126–28.

[12] It appears in a free adaptation in John of Salisbury's *Policraticus*, Books 5 and 6, in a more concise form in the first chapter of Roger of Waltenham's *speculum principis*, and also in Vincent of Beauvais' *Speculum Historiale*, Book 7, Chapter 24. The extraordinary popularity of the *Institutio* in the High and Late Middle Ages is probably due to the fact that the organic conception of the state—which was in itself not new and which was

where refers directly to John of Salisbury and seems not to have known Giraldus Cambrensis. His field of vision does not extend to Thomas Aquinas and Albertus Magnus. Gower probably did not draw his knowledge at all from specialized studies. Every major *summa* transmitted knowledge of the pertinent passages from the church fathers. The convenient compilations of Vincent of Beauvais, Roger of Waltenham, and John Bromyard provide the best insight into the sort and extent of the knowledge which in this province may be considered representative of the second half of the fourteenth century.[13]

For Gower the central problem of the Mirror for a Prince, as well as of the entire sixth book, is the question of law and justice in the state. In the transition to the Mirror he defines the function of the laws in the following manner:

> *Pro transgressore fuerant leges situate,*
> *Quilibet ut merita posset habere sua.* 6.469–70
>
> [The laws have been established for the transgressor,
> That every man can have his just deserts.]

Here law is understood primarily as criminal law. It conforms to the usual medieval view of statute law as an arrangement of force which became necessary through man's moral degeneration in the Fall. One could interpret Gower through Wyclif, obviously without suggesting a dependency:

> *Jus autem civile est jus occasione peccati humanitus adinventum ad justificandam rempublicam coactive quoad bona corporis et fortune.*
>
> [Civil law, however, is law devised upon the occasion of human sin in order to justify the use of authority in public affairs for the good and the fortune of the state.][14]

This introductory chapter of the Mirror for a Prince also discusses justice as a constituent and preserving principle of the state. Because it is Gower's chief concern, he devotes to justice a lengthy passage which, despite the fact that it lacks conceptual clarity and is to a considerable extent permeated with biblical ideas, can be traced to Cicero's definition of the state:

---

related to the New Testament conception of the nature of the church—offered so many possibilities for arranging details and toying with proportions.

[13] See, respectively, *Speculum Historiale*, ed. D. Bernardi (Venice: D. Nicolinus, 1591); *Compendium Morale de Virtuosis Dictis et Factis Exemplaribus Antiquorum*, Bodleian Library MS. Fairfax 4; *Summa Praedicantium* (Venice: D. Nicolinus, 1586), *s.v. regimen*.

[14] *Ioannis Wycliffe Tractatus de Civili Dominio*, ed. Reginald Lane Poole (London: Trübner, 1885), 125.

Gens sine lege quid est, aut lex sine iudice quid nam,
Aut quid si iudex sit sine iusticia?
In patria nostra si quis circumspicit acta,
Hec tria cernet ibi sepe timenda michi.
Omnia dampna gravant, set nulla tamen graviora,
Quam cum iusticiam iustus habere nequit.
Ex iniusticia discordia crescit, et inde
Cessat amor solitus, murmurat atque domus:
Murmur si veniat, venit et divisio secum,
Terraque divisa non bene stabit ea;
Et quodcumque sit hoc per se quod stare nequibit,
Ve sibi, nam subito corruet absque modo.
Testis enim deus est, dicens quod regna peribunt
In se divisa, credoque dicta sua. 6.481–494

[What is a nation without law, a law without
A judge, or then a judge without justice?
If anyone surveys the doings in our homeland,
He'll see these three that often make me fear.
All evils are oppressive but none is more grave
Than when a good man cannot have justice.
From injustice waxes discord, and thence ceases
Charity, and so the homeland murmurs.
If murmur comes, division also comes with it,
And that land divided will not stand well;
And woe to whatever cannot stand by itself,
For it will come to grief without measure.
For God is my witness, noting kingdoms perish
Divided against themselves, which I believe.]

Does Cicero's *populus est coetus multitudinis iuris consensu . . . sociatus* [a people is . . . a joining together of a multitude associated in a common agreement about the law] in the *De Republica* (1.25.39) become *gens sine lege quid est* in Gower's uncertain terminology?[15] When Gower maintains in imitation of the Bible[16] that *ex iniusticia discordia crescit . . . venit et divisio . . . regna peribunt in se divisa* [strife

[15] A similar passage occurs in the *Confessio Amantis* 7.2695–2701, where the same stylistic device of a series of questions is employed for the same train of thought:

What is a lond wher men ben none?
What ben the men whiche are al one
Withoute a kinges governance?
What is a king in his ligance,
Wher that ther is no lawe in londe?
What is to take lawe on honde,
Bot if the jugges weren trewe?

[16] Matthew 12:25–26, Mark 3:24–26, Luke 11:17–18.

grows out of injustice . . . dividedness comes with it . . . kingdoms divided against themselves shall not stand], he stands in a classical tradition, transmitted by the church fathers, that regards the state above all as an arrangement for the maintenance of justice among men.[17] On this concept of the state depends the remark about the ruler's function with which Gower begins the Mirror for a Prince:

Regis et est proprium, commissam quod sibi plebem
Dirigat, et iusta lege gubernet eam. 6.585–586

[The king should guide the people given to his care,
And also govern them with proper law.]

The phrase *commissa plebs* implies the view that kingship is a divine institution.[18] The phrase *iusta lege gubernare* describes, in the metaphor customary since antiquity, the king's function as executor of the law. From this twofold statement results the necessity of a more precise definition of what should be the king's relationship to God as the origin of his kingship and to the law as its norm and means. In the beginning of the Mirror for a Prince Gower therefore furnishes guidelines that tell the king how he should exercise his authority in harmony with the demands of the law and of God:

O pie rex, audi que sit tua regula regni,
Concordans legi mixtaque iure dei. 6.589–590

[O pious king, hear what should be your rule of realm,

---

[17] See R. W. and A. J. Carlyle, *A History of Medieval Political Theory in the West*, 6 vols. (Edinburgh: William Blackwood and Sons, 1903–1936), 1:161. I have gratefully used the rich collection of materials from these volumes over and over in this chapter.

[18] The problem of the legal basis of the monarchy is not yet acute for Gower at the time of Richard II and is therefore only slightly touched on in the *Vox Clamantis*. After the accession of Henry IV, Gower treats the question in more detail, designating three claims for Henry's kingship: the right of the conqueror, the claim of legitimacy, and the choice of the people:

Unde coronatur trino de iure probatur,
Regnum conquestat, que per hoc sibi ius manifestat;
Regno succedit heres, nec ab inde recedit;
Insuper eligitur a plebe que sic stabilitur:
Ut sit compactum, iuris nil defuit actum. Cronica Tripertita 3.332–336

[His right to take the crown is triply justified:
First, by martial conquest his right was clarified;
Next, by inheritance, a claim he did not cede,
And third, by people's choice, and thus he could accede.
No point of law was missed to make it quite secure. (Trans. Rigg.)]

Suiting to law and to God's justice joined.]

The word "guidelines" is perhaps an unfortunate choice [Wickert uses *Richtlinien*, which also means "directives"], since no official authority stands behind Gower's statements. And yet he claims for his Mirror a degree of binding force that is not inherent in his modest collection of advisements to the king. The term *regula*, with which he designates his compilation in the lines cited,[19] must have expressed an authoritative importance in an age that knew a "regulated" life not only in the ecclesiastical orders but also in other religious and lay communities.[20] It can be found applied to the prince in Bromyard, whose article on *regimen* in the *Summa Praedicantium* begins in a manner similar to Gower's Mirror for a Prince:

> *Primo ostenditur regula per quam seipsos et alios regere deberent atque regularent [*sc. *regentes].*
>
> [First there is presented a rule by which they {*sc.* rulers} should rule themselves and govern others.]

For Bromyard this rule is of twofold derivation: it stems on the one hand directly from God, on the other from Cyprian—a somewhat surprising combination.[21] His *regula* is therefore a summary of Deuteronomy 17:14–20 and the *De XII Abusionibus*, that is, of the Bible and the wisdom of the church fathers. Gower's *regula* makes reference to a large number of unnamed sources, that is, to the mass of *auctores*. However, it derives its real claim to authority less from these references than from its accord with the *lex* and the *ius dei*. Of course, I am not taking *dei* in connection with both *lex* and *ius*; rather, I am of the opinion that Gower is talking about statute law and God's commandments. It would certainly be rash to infer from the joining of these two concepts that the ruler should be subject to the law in the same way as to God's commandments, perhaps in the manner demanded by the most important English lawyer of the thirteenth century: *ipse autem rex . . . debet esse . . . sub deo et sub lege* [the king himself . . . should be . . .

---

19 In 587 he styles it *normam scriptis de pluribus ortam* [a rule of conduct taken from many writings].

20 According to scholars of the Romance languages, the term has an innate, definite meaning. The definition of the *Digest* reads: *Regula est quae rem quae est breviter enarrat* [a rule is that which briefly expounds a matter], and . . . *non ut ex regula ius sumatur, sed ut ex iure quod est regula fiat* [not that the law be derived from a rule, but that what is a rule should come from the law]. Paul. *Dig.* 50.17.1. Cited after R. Leonhard, "*regula iuris,*" in Pauly-Wissowa, *Realenzyklopädie der klassischen Altertumswissenschaft*, 1A.1:510–11.

21 *S.v. regimen*, art. I: . . . *Quantum ad primum illorum [*sc. *regnantium] regula est duplex: una que a deo datur, alia que a Cypriano, que a priori non discordat, sed magis illam explanat* [. . . As far as the first of these {*sc.* rulers} the rule is twofold: one which is given by God, the other by Cyprian—which is not at odds with the first, but rather explains it].

subject to God and to the law].[22] Gower makes several other complementary statements about the relationship of the ruler to statute law, but without being very systematic:

1. *Tu super es iura, iustus set vive sub illis* (6.613);
   [You are atop the law but just within it live];

2. *Legum frena tenens freno te forcius arce* (6.591);
   [Laws' reins in hand, I hitch you firmly to the Ark];

3. *Iuraque dans plebi, des ita iura tibi* (6.604);
   [The law to commons given give yourself].

Naturally, Gower knew the Roman principle *princeps legibus solutus* [the prince is above the law], which was understood in the Middle Ages to mean he was exempt from the law.[23] And, like most medieval authors, he acknowledges it[24] although it in no way accorded with the position of the English king in the second half of the fourteenth century. The acknowledgement is academic, however, not only because of its practical meaninglessness, but above all because of its incompatibility with the principle that justice is the foundation of the state.

From this point the royal exemption from the law experiences its first limitation, which is connected with the ideal of the *rex iustus*. When Gower admonishes the ruler, *Tu super es iura, iustus set viue sub illis* (1), we are reminded of Isidore, who set down in the *Sententiae* the subordination of the ruler to the law

[22] Henricus de Bracton, *De Legibus et Consuetudinibus Angliae*, ed. George E. Woodbine, 4 vols. (New Haven: Yale University Press, 1915–42), 2:33: *Ipse autem rex non debet esse sub homine sed sub deo et sub lege, quia lex facit regem. Attribuat ergo rex legi, quod lex attribuit ei, videlicet dominationem et potestatem. Non est enim rex ubi dominatur voluntas et non lex. Et quod sub lege esse debeat, cum sit dei vicarius, evidenter apparet ad similitudinem Ihesu Christi, cuius vices gerit in terra.* [The king himself, however, should not be subject to men, but to God and the law, because the law creates the king. Let the king therefore allot to the law what the law allots to him, namely domain and might. For he is not king when his will rules and not law. And that he should be subject to the law, since he is God's substitute, appears clearly according to the likeness of Jesus Christ, whose role he carries out on earth.]

[23] It is unimportant for our purposes how it is actually to be understood; see Theodor Mommsen, *Römisches Staatsrecht*, 3rd ed., 3 vols. (Leipzig: S. Hirzel, 1887–1888), 2:751–52.

[24] See also the *Confessio Amantis* 7.2718–19:

And natheles upon som side,
His [the king's] pouer stant aboue the lawe.

Of contemporary English poets, Chaucer did not take a position on this question. Langland's interpretation is similar to Gower's; see below, 118–19.

as a requisite for law and justice.[25] Gower does not follow Isidore's argument in all the details and is very frugal with his proofs. On the most important point, however, he agrees vigorously with the *Sententiae*, namely that the ruler as *rex iustus* is obligated by inner necessity, even though not by external forces, to keep the *lex iusta* if he does not wish to carry *ad absurdum* the principle that he embodies *iustitia*. Isidore's thesis that *principes teneri legibus suis, neque in se posse damnare iura quae in subiectis constituunt* [princes should be held to their own laws, and not be able to condemn for themselves the laws which they decree for their subjects] is reflected in Gower's demand (3) that *iuraque dans plebi, des ita iura tibi.*[26] Isidore expands on the term *licere* in his proof; Gower discusses at length the relationship of *licere* and *posse*, of *licitum* and *probum*.[27] Because he employs *licere*

---

[25] *Sent.* 3.51: *Justum est principem legibus obtemperare suis. Tunc enim jura sua ab omnibus custodienda existimet, quando et ipse illis reverentiam praebet. Principes legibus teneri suis, neque in se posse damnare jura quae in subjectis constituunt. Justa est enim vocis eorum auctoritas, si quod populis prohibent, sibi licere non patiantur.* [It is just that the prince obey his own laws. For then let him suppose his laws should be observed by all when he himself renders them reverence. Princes can be held to their own laws, nor can they by themselves condemn the laws which they decree among their subjects. For the authority of their voices is just only if they do not allow to themselves what they deny to the people.] *PL* 83:723; ed. P. Cazier, CCSL 111 (Turnhout: Brepols, 1998), 303.

[26] Gower appends some related considerations to the catalogue of lawgivers in Book VII of the *Confessio Amantis*:

And so ferforth it is befalle
That lawe is come among ous alle:
God lieve it mote wel ben holde,
As every king therto is holde;
For thing which is of kinges set,
With kinges oghte it noght be let.
What king of lawe taketh no kepe,
Be lawe he mai no regne kepe.
Do lawe away, what is a king? 7.3067–3075

[27] 6.611–620:

Dum tibi cuncta licent, ne queras cuncta licere,
Res etenim licite noxia sepe ferunt:
Tu super es iura, iustus set vive sub illis,
Spesque tui nobis causa salutis erit.
Est mors ira tua, potes id quod non licet, et te
Prestita vota tamen ducere iuris habent:
Quod licet illesa mentis precordia servat,
Omne tamen licitum non probat esse probum:
Quod licet est tutum, set que potes illa sub arto
Discute iudicio fultus honore tuo.

[Though all to you permitted, seek not all to do,
Permitted things bring often grievous harm.

indiscriminately, now in the sense of what is legally, now in the sense of what is morally permissible, the clarity of his presentation suffers.[28] However, the train of thought, which was plainly influenced by a remembrance of Cassiodorus, can be supplemented with the help of the *Variae*.[29] His regard for the welfare of the state (611–614) and his own honor (617–620), which is probably to be understood here as moral integrity, keep the king from exploiting that immunity which is his by law. The result is that the royal autonomy suffers its first limitation from *honestum* and *utile*.

There is also another and, for Gower, a more important limitation, which originates in the divine world order. With it we come to the second point, the relationship of the ruler to God, the source of his authority. The principle of the *ordo* manifests itself not only in the hierarchical gradation of created beings, but in a chain of dependent relationships which links the individual elements of the creation. Thus the ruler's obligation to obey God matches that of the subjects to obey him:

You are atop the law but just within it live,
Because of you there's hope of weal for us.
Your wrath is death, you are allowed illicit acts,
Yet custom's vows by law hold you in check.
Though something lawful may preserve your peace of mind
Unharmed, yet may it not be upright too.
Granted something prudent is, examine yet what
You can do, judging firm with honor's aid.]

[28] *Licere* in the juridical sense appears in 611, 612, and 618; in a moral sense in 615 and 619. In 617, it is simply the impersonal *licet*, 'although'.

[29] Gower's acquaintance with the writings of Cassiodorus, be it direct or indirect, is evident from the *Mirour*, where he is cited under the name Cassodre in 11770, 13920, 23059, and 24592. Here Gower appears to have had in mind the following passage from the *Variae*: . . . *Imperiosa nimium res est, patres conscripti, pietas nostra, quando propria voluntate vincimur, qui alienis condicionibus non tenemur. Nam cum deo praestante possimus omnia, sola nobis credimus licere laudanda.* [. . . O Senators, our piety is a matter of extreme importance, since we are bound only by our own wills, we who are not held in check by any other considerations. For whereas we are able to do all things, God granting, we believe that only praiseworthy things are permitted us.] *Variae* 10.16, in *Cassiodori Senatoris Variae*, ed. Theodor Mommsen, MGH Auctores Antiquissimi 12 (Berlin: Weidmann, 1894). The antithesis of *posse* and *licere* is not the only point of contact between Gower and Cassiodorus. The use of such measures of value as *laudanda* in Cassiodorus and *honor tuus* in Gower links the two with reference to Isidore's argument, which concentrates more on the aspects of utility and equity. A third point of contact lies in the importance which Cassiodorus attributes to the ruler's *pietas*. In Gower's Mirror for a Prince, the epithet *pius* is more frequent than any other in the apostrophe to the king. In the *Confessio*, "pite" as the moderator of an inflexible justice is discussed in great detail.

Est propter mundum tibi subdita sors aliorum,
Tu propter celum subditus esto deo.
Ut tibi deservit populus de lege subactus,
Christi serviciis temet ad instar habe. 6.597–600

[Your peoples' lot subject to you for worldly sake,
For heavenly sake be subject to the Lord.
So that the people docile serve you by the law,
For your servants in Christ's likeness persevere.]

In both instances, the relationship is characterized through *subiectio* and *servitus.*[30] Elsewhere in the *Vox Clamantis* and the *Mirour*, as well as in the *Confessio Amantis*, the equation is of course not Subject:Ruler::Ruler:God, but Creature:Man::Man:God.[31] Since, according to Genesis 1:28–29, all creatures are subject to man and obligated to obey him, so man is subject to God and placed at his service. Thus there is not only a parallelism, but a causal nexus between the two obedience equations. The revolt of man against God inevitably brings about the revolt of creation against man.[32] This general human situation becomes specifically political when the citizenry are substituted for the creation. The analogy between the political cosmos and the created cosmos is so far-reaching for Gower that elsewhere he allows it right up to the point of rebellion.[33] However, there is no trace in Gower of the finer distinctions of these two orders, such as occupy the church fathers when they perceive the political-social cosmos with its authority of man over men as a consequence of the Fall and contrast it to

[30] The duty of subjects is similarly enjoined in the introduction to the Mirror for a Prince:

Cumque sui Regis legi sit legius omnis
Subditus, et toto corpore servit ei . . . 6.581–582
[Since every liege is subject to his king's own law
And does him service with all his body.]

[31] See *Mirour* 26789–26805; *Confessio Amantis* 7.511–514; *Vox Clamantis* 7.561–564, and esp. 573–76:

Auctor enim rerum sic res decrevit, ut orbis
*Queque creatura consequeretur eum [*sc. *hominem];*
Ut serviret ei factura, suumque vicissim
Factorem solum consequeretur homo.

[For the author of things has so decreed it that every creature of the world should wait upon man; that the creation should serve him and that he in turn should therefore wait upon only his creator. (Trans. Stockton.)]

[32] See below, 144–49, 153–55.

[33] See 6.1005–1006 and 6.1197–1198 (B-Text).

the original, God-intended condition of equality for all men that allowed only a mastery of men over the creation.[34]

We have spoken of justice as the foundation of the state, of the duty of the king to realize justice in the state, of his relationship to the law, and of the duality of his place within the divine *ordo*. But we have not yet inquired about Gower's definition of the prince. The usual medieval attempts in this direction are variations on the formula which Isidore handed down in the *Etymologies*. He derives *rex* from *recte facere*:

> *Reges a regendo vocati; . . . Non autem regit, qui non corrigit. Recte igitur faciendo regis nomen tenetur, peccando amittitur. Unde apud veteres tale erat proverbium: Rex eris si recte facies, si non facies, non eris.*
>
> [Kings are so called from ruling; . . . but he does not rule who does not correct. Therefore by acting rightly the name of king is maintained, by sinning is lost. Whence among the ancients there was a certain proverb: You will be king if you act rightly, if you do not, you will not.][35]

This formula provides not a constitutional but an ethical definition of the ruler. If it is a flaw that Western medieval mirrors for princes so frequently degenerate into catalogues of virtues, the source may lie here. Certainly, this kind of definition is the only one suitable within the compass of a view of history that regarded the fate of individuals and of peoples as the result of moral conduct. And there is yet another factor. The notion that political science is a branch of ethics quite naturally gained force in a time that barely knew the abstract idea of the state and that identified it largely with the person of the ruler.

The formula *rex a recte faciendo* occurs in Gower in the context of individual ethics as well as of political science. It appears in its general meaning in the sev-

[34] Thus, for example, St. Augustine says in the *De Civitate Dei* 19.15: . . . *Rationalem factum ad imaginem suam noluit nisi irrationabilibus dominare [*sc. *Deus]; non hominem homini, sed hominem pecori. Inde primi iusti pastores pecorum magis quam reges hominum constituti sunt, ut etiam sic insinuaret Deus, quid postulet ordo creaturarum, quid exigat meritum peccatorum. Condicio quippe servitutis iure intellegitur inposita peccatori.* [. . . He {*sc.* God} did not intend that His rational creature, who was made in His image, should have dominion over anything but the irrational creation, not man over man but man over the beasts. And hence the righteous men in primitive times were made shepherds of cattle rather than kings of men, God intending thus to teach us what the relative position of the creatures is, and what the desert of sin; for it is with justice, we believe, that the condition of slavery is the result of sin]. Quoted from *De Civitate Dei*, ed. B. Dombert (Leipzig: Teubner, 1905–1909), trans. Marcus Dods, *The City of God* (New York: Random House, 1950), 693.

[35] On the origin and tradition of this monarchic formula, see Jozsef Balogh, "*Rex a recte regendo*," *Speculum* 3 (1928): 580–82.

enth book—*Rex est quisque sui, bene qui regit acta, beatus* (7.927) [Every saintly man who governs his actions well is king over himself]—and is applied to the king in the Mirror for a Prince:

> *Si rex esse velis, te rege, rex et eris.*
> *Qua fore se regem poterit racione fateri,*
> *Mentis qui proprie non regit acta sue?* 6.606–608
>
> [Self-ruled be king, if king you wish to be.
> By what reason does one proclaim he can be king
> Who cannot rule the urgings of his mind?]

It is used yet again in a later part of the Mirror to distinguish the king from the tyrant:

> *Qui bene regis agit regimen, rex est, set inique*
> *Qui regit in viciis, ipse tirannus erit.* 6.1003–1004
>
> [A king is he who well performs the ruling task,
> A tyrant, he who rules unjust by crimes.]

Because Gower creates out of the common property of his time, he does not require a systematic foundation. The relationships between the general and political aspects of the formula remain unexplained. If one uses as an aid the article *regimen* from Bromyard's approximately contemporary *summa*, then one obtains detailed information on this question. Bromyard divides ethics in the customary fashion into individual, social, and political ethics (*monastica, iconomica,* and *politica philosophia*).[36] These are not independent branches, but stages which are

[36] Bromyard, *Summa Praedicantium, s.v. regimen: Sic ergo qui regis Israel intende* [Psalm 79:2] *ut per istas tres perfectiones tres partes compleas et perficias que in ethica continentur, vid. monasticam que docet de regimine sui ipsius, iconomicam que docet de regimine domus et familie, et politicam que docet de regimine civitatis seu communitatis* [Therefore strive, you who rule Israel, that through these three fulfillments {i.e., neglecting none?} you complete and master the three parts that comprise ethics: namely monastics, which teaches about self-rule; economics, which teaches about the rule of house and family; and politics, which teaches about the rule of the city or the community]. This is the old Aristotelian classification as one also encounters it, for example, in Bonaventura: *Postremo, quia regimen virtutis motivae tripliciter habet attendi, scilicet respectu vitae propriae, respectu familiae et respectu multitudinis subiectae; ideo moralis philosophia triplicatur, scilicet in monasticam, oeconomicam et politicam* [Finally, because the reign of virtue has to be regarded in three ways, namely in consideration of the individual life, in consideration of the family, and in consideration of the ruled multitude, therefore moral philosophy is divided into three parts, namely into monastics, economics, and politics]. *De Reductione Artium ad Theologiam, Opera Omnia,* 5:321. Gower knows this classification himself and uses it

successively attained. It would be absurd if someone who had not mastered the task of the most basic stage would presume to advance to the following or even to the ultimate stage. Whoever does not know how to govern himself is unsuited to rule over a larger community, be it of an ecclesiastical or political kind: *gradatim ascendendum es, quia absurdum est quod qui seipsum regere nescit, accipere presumat regimen animarum vel cuiuscunque communitatis* [one should rise step by step, because it is absurd that he who does not know how to govern himself should presume to undertake the governance of souls or of whatsoever community].[37] That is exactly what Gower expresses in the verses cited above (6.606–608) and what recurs with a slight shift of emphasis in the distich:

> *Est tibi, rex, melius quod te de lege gubernes,*
> *Subdere quam mundi singula regna tibi.* 6.595–596
>
> [Far better, king, that you should rule yourself by law
> Than subject to yourself all worldly realms.]

Here—depending, indeed, on two biblical passages—[38] the Christian element is stressed more strongly than in the other variants of the *rex a recte faciendo* formula. Yet one may in no way deduce from the lines a renunciation of the world. They are part of the context of the Stoic-Christian monarchic ideal. It necessarily follows from them that instruction in the virtues and vices is more important as royal propaedeutic than any specific political, military, or diplomatic schooling. A catalogue of virtues is necessarily the central piece of any *speculum principis*, for all other things will of their own accord fall to the lot of the virtuous ruler:

> *Rex, ita si fugias viciorum pondera, mores*
> *Et teneas, poteris quicquid habere velis.* 6.915–916
>
> [Thus flee the sins' impediments and custom keep,
> And you will have whatever you desire.]

---

in the seventh book of the *Confessio Amantis* (1641–1710) with a minor variation in the nomenclature: he inserts the general notion "etique" in place of *monastica*. In doing so he refers to Aristotle, that is, in this case to the *Secretum Secretorum*—incorrectly, as Hamilton, "Some Sources of the Seventh Book of Gower's *Confessio Amantis*," 326–27, first remarked. Hamilton is of the opinion that Gower followed Brunetto Latini in the passage in question.

[37] Bromyard, *Summa Praedicantium, s. v. regimen.*

[38] Proverbs 16:32: *Melior est . . . qui dominabitur animo suo expugnatore urbium* [He that ruleth his spirit is better than he that taketh cities]; Matthew 16:26: *Quid enim prodest homini, si mundum universum lucretur, animae vero suae detrimentum patiatur* [For what does it profit a man, if he gain the whole world, but suffer the loss of his own soul]?

In this his characteristic feature, the *rex iustus* gains simultaneously the earthly and the divine kingdom and need have no fears about the stability of his kingship:

> *Lucratur populum que deum rex iustus utrumque,*
> *Statque per hoc regni firma corona sui.* 6.1007–1008
>
> [A just king gains the people both and God, the crown
> Of his kingdom accordingly stands firm.]

Perhaps it is permissible at this point to cast a side glance at Langland and at the relationship of the king to the law and justice in *Piers Plowman*.[39] The question is treated in detail in B, XIX, 462–473 (C, XXII, 467–478):

> Then cam ther a kynge and by hus corone seide,
> "Ich am a kyng with corone the comune to reule,
> And holychurch and clergie fro corsede men to defenden.
> And yf me lacketh to lyue by the lawe wol that ich take
> Ther ich may haue hit hastelokest for ich am hefd of lawe,
> And ye ben bote membrys and ich a-boue alle.
> Sitthen ich am youre alre hefd ich am youre alre hele,
> And holychurches chef help and chefteyn of the commune.
> And what ich take of yow two ich take hit at techynge
> Of *spiritus iusticie* for ich Iugge you alle;
> So ich may baldely beo housled for ich borwe neuere,
> Ne craue of my comune bote as my kynde asketh."

Langland proceeds more intensely than Gower from the then acute problem of royal taxation, which he ties to the king's threefold duty to be guardian of justice, defender of the realm, and protector of the church. In every other respect his formulations match those of Gower. The king is the head (hefd, *caput*) and the health (hele, *salus*) of the political *organismus*, just as in the first chapter of Gower's Mirror for a Prince. The monarch's designation of himself as the "hefd of lawe" (C, XX, 471) is not entirely clear. It appears as if the king here claims for himself a position above the law like that expressed by Gower in 6.613 (*Tu supra es leges*).[40] However, Langland continues, "And ye ben bote membrys and ich a-boue alle." In the following line, in the statement "Sitthen ich am youre alre hefd," the matter is taken up again. Obviously the discussion is not about the head and members of the law but of the political community, and "give" and

[39] I used the *editio maior* of W. W. Skeat, *The Vision of William Concerning Piers the Plowman*, 2 vols. (Oxford: Oxford University Press, 1886).

[40] Thus E. T. Donaldson, *Piers Plowman* (New Haven: Yale University Press, 1949), 91 understands the phrase.

"take" in the sense of taxation are to be understood according to the analogy of the story of Menenius Agrippa or the *Institutio Traiani*. Accordingly, the genitive "of lawe" (in the half-line "for ich am hefd of lawe") must be understood adverbially ("by law, legally") which is grammatically possible. Be that as it may, it clearly follows from the subsequent lines that the king regards himself only as a functionary of law and justice (470: "The lawe wol that ich take"; 476: "ich take hit at techynge of *spiritus iusticie*") and that the execution of justice does not cease before the person of the king:

> *Spiritus iusticie* spareth nat to spille
> Hem that beoth gulty and for to corecte
> Thy kyng, and the kyng falle in eny thynge gulty.[41]

If the relationship is reversed and justice bows to royal caprice, then perversion sets in and the stability of the state founded in law is endangered:

> And *spiritus iusticie* shal Iugen, wol he, nul he,
> After the kynges counsaile and the commune lyke.[42]

Thus Langland's monarchic ideal is also determined by the concept of the *rex iustus*.

When Gower implores the young king to strive after virtue as the highest value, he distinguishes it from other, lesser values, raising the question of what role these other values play in his portrait of the ruler:

> *O bone rex iuvenis, fac quod bonitate iuventus*
> *Sit tua morigeris dedita rite modis.*
> *Quid tibi forma iuvat vel nobile nomen avorum,*
> *Si viciis servus factus es ipse tuis?* 6.627–630
>
> [O good young king, act that your youth benevolently
> Be given to accommodating ways.
> What avails beauty or ancestral noble name
> If slave to your own vices you've become?]

Medieval doctrine about possessions distinguishes three *dona: naturae, fortunae, gratiae*. Of the *dona naturae*, Gower mentions in the lines cited the noble body (*forma*), of the *dona fortunae*, noble lineage (*nobilitas*).[43] His attitude toward the

[41] *Piers Plowman, C*-Text, XXII, 303–305.

[42] *Piers Plowman,* C-Text, XXIII, 29–30.

[43] I employ the customary terminology, although Gower himself—at the point in the second book where he denies the existence of *Fortuna*—allows only *dona naturae* and *dona gratiae*; see 2.298–302.

beauty of the noble body is not at all original, but yet apparently not clear enough to preclude misunderstandings. Thus Kleineke writes in his short section on the *Vox Clamantis'* Mirror for a Prince: "The eye for noble physical forms and the related demand that a beautiful soul and spirit should be harmoniously suited with a well-shaped body belong to a world newly discovered by chivalry."[44] Kleineke refers to 6.1081–1084:

> *Nobile corpus habes et singula membra decora,*
> *Sit virtus animi sic magis illa tibi:*
> *Ut foris est forma tibi splendida, splendeat intra*
> *Mens tua, quod tibi, rex, sit decor ille duplex.*
>
> [You have a noble body, handsome every limb,
> Let thus your spirit's strength be greater yet.
> As splendid as your outer form, let shine within
> Your soul, so that your beauty twofold be.]

To begin with, the triad body, soul, and spirit in Kleineke's statement is not entirely correct. Gower sees mankind dualistically. The entire *psychomachia* of the *Mirour* is based on the duality of *corps* and *alme*, of *passiouns* and *raisoun*, and the conception is not altered in his later works. It is expressed in the distiches cited by the word *duplex*, which clearly shows that the second distich is to be understood as a variation upon the first, and that *mens* must be understood as a synonym for *animus*, not as a third new quantity alongside *corpus* and *animus*. However, more important than the question of trinity or duality is the question of "harmonious suiting." Kleineke was obviously correct insofar as concerns the thought that the soul shapes the body, but one can hardly call that a new discovery of chivalry. However, if the use of the term should postulate an equation of the two quantities of body and soul, such a thought is very far from Gower. Even the context of the cited verses urges caution. Lines 1077–1080[45] state that all mankind's possessions stem from God and that nothing belongs to man as his own. Thus from the outset the noble body is deprived of inherent value. The passage referred to is

---

[44] Kleineke, *Englische Fürstenspiegel*, 131.

[45] *O rex, quicquid habes dedit hos deus, et nichil a te*
Est quod habes proprium, vel quod habere potes:
Esse creaturam te nosce dei, nec ab eius
Tu discede viis, si bene stare velis.
[God has given all that you have, O king; nothing
You have or ever will is from yourself.
Know that you are God's creature, do not forsake
His ways if you should wish to stand secure.]

followed by a section that, borrowing from Neckam, indicates the transitoriness and questionable nature of physical beauty.[46] It ends with the distich:

> *Non tibi forma deum set mens sincera meretur,*
> *Iusticie soli vita beata datur.* 6.1089–1090
>
> [A spirit pure and not good looks earns God for you,
> The just alone receive the blessed life.]

This clear and plain appraisal of relative values precludes harmonious suiting as a balance of physical and ethical values. It is the same ratio of values that Gower employs for nobility of origin and nobility of virtue:

> *Mores namque bonos veneratur curia celi,*
> *Et celum iustus, non generosus, habet.* 6.1023–1024
>
> [For heaven's court good customs venerates, the just
> And not the noble will God's heaven have.][47]

With that we come to the second point: the value of noble lineage.

With it Gower touches on a theme that had acquired topical political significance in the 1370s. In the waning Middle Ages the demand for a thorough social reform appeared occasionally in connection with the thought that men had originally been social equals. The thought in itself is neither new nor revolutionary.[48] It receives a politically aggressive turn in England in the years before the Peasants' Revolt in the "Song of Adam and Eve":

> When Adam delved and Eve span,
> Who was then a gentleman?

The programme expressed in the song was probably understood communistically only by radical leaders, and even with regard to them one must reckon with the

---

[46] *Labile forma bonum, species inimica pudoris*
Utile virtutum sepe retardat iter:
Forma dei munus, etc. 6.1085–1087.
[Good looks, a fleeting gift hostile to modesty,
Often impede the virtues' useful path.
Beauty, the gift of God, etc.]

[47] Adopted from Neckam, *De Vita Monachorum*; see Macaulay's Notes ad loc.

[48] See Carlyle and Carlyle, *A History of Medieval Political Theory in the West,* 1, Chaps. 10 and 11; Bede Jarrett, *Social Theories of the Middle Ages, 1200–1500* (London: Benn, 1926), 122. The church, without causing revolutions, constantly preached the equality of men in the sight of death and God.

possibility that a biased writing of history has distorted their image for us.[49] At any rate, the nobility's right to exist was then for the first time doubted in principle, and the divinely-ordained Christian class arrangement assailed through a shibboleth likewise sprung from a Christian source. Of the poets of the time, Chaucer, as might be expected, did not take a position on the problem. Supposing that he was at the time working on *Troilus and Criseyde*, he did not in any case find it necessary to include a "degree speech." Langland singled out a part of the problem when he turned against the doctrine of the common ownership of property (in the B-Text of *Piers Plowman*, composed *ca.* 1378–1379):

> Enuye herd this and heet freres to go to scole,
> And lerne logyk and lawe and eke contemplacioun,
> And preche men of Plato and preue it by Seneca,
> That alle thinges vnder heuene oughte to ben in comune.
> And yit he lyeth, as I leue that to the lewed so precheth,
> For god made to men a lawe and Moyses it taughte,
> *Non concupisces rem proximi tui.* B, XX, 271–276

Of course, Langland oversimplifies when he contrasts the communism of pagan philosophers with the Ten Commandments' protection of property (cf. Deuteronomy 5:21). It was not a question of a discrepancy between antiquity and Christianity. The Stoic doctrine that there is no private property according to natural law was domesticated early by Christianity and transmitted to the Middle Ages by Isidore.[50] It was, rather, a question of interpretation. One usually distinguished between communism before the Fall and its curtailment by private ownership after that event, and thus escaped the dilemma. Of course, when Gower writes *Sunt nam communes omnibus orbis opes* (6.360) [For the treasures of the earth are common to all], he is thinking about neither a paradisal state of affairs nor a communistic programme. Rather, he is thinking of the indiscriminate

[49] See Trevelyan, *England in the Age of Wycliffe*, 196 concerning Froissart's account.

[50] *Ius naturale commune est omnium nationum; . . . hoc iure communis est omnis possessio, et omnium una libertas* [*Etymologiae* 5.4]. [Natural law is shared among all peoples; according to this law, all property is common and there is a single freedom for everybody.] See, for example, Alexander of Hales on the passage from Isidore: . . . *dicendum quod iure naturali essent omnia communia et omnium una libertas, hoc fuit ante peccatum, et post peccatum quaedam sunt quibusdam propria et haec duo sunt per legem naturalem* [. . . it is said that by natural law all things are common and there is a single freedom for all; that was before sin, and since sin certain things belong to certain people and these are both according to natural law]. *Summa* III, *Q.* 27, *M.* 3, *Art.* 2, *Resolutio.* Cited, along with other instances, by Carlyle and Carlyle, *A History of Medieval Political Theory in the West,* 5:14.

distribution of earthly possessions that makes their value seem dubious and their ownership hardly worth the effort.[51]

Langland does not discuss the more significant aspect of the question of human equality insofar as it concerns not property but class. Gower, however, discusses this problem in detail. The chief passage in the Mirror for a Prince is a series of verses that he appropriated from Peter Riga:[52]

> *Disceque cunctorum quod sit communis origo,*
> *Ortus et occasus unus, et una caro. ...*
> *Nobilis est mentis quisquis virtute refulget,*
> *Degener est solus cui mala vita placet; ...*
> *Mores namque bonos veneratur curia celi,*
> *Et celum iustus, non generosus, habet.* 6.1019–1024[53]
>
> [And learn there is one common origin of all,
> One beginning, one ending, and one flesh.
> The one who shines with virtue has nobility
> Of mind, base he who likes an evil life.
> For heaven's court good customs venerates, the just
> And not the noble will God's heaven have.]

There are added Gower's own words to Richard, with which he challenges the royal youth to double his hereditary nobility with the nobility of virtue, that is, to harmonize in his person the principles of inheritance and accomplishment:

> *Si te nobilitas generosaque nomina tangunt,*

---

51 *Quid petis argentum tibi? spem quid ponis in aurum?*
Sunt nam communes omnibus orbis opes.
Sepis ista dei data conspicis hostibus esse,
Ante deum nulla laus et habetur eis:
Ista paganus habet, Iudeus, latro cruentus;
Crede quod iratus sepe dat ista deus. 6.359–364

[Why seek silver for yourself? Why place hope in gold?
The treasures of the earth belong to all.
Often you see God's things given His enemies,
There is no merit in them before God.
A pagan has them, a Jew, a savage bandit;
Be sure, an angry God often gives them.]
The valuation of earthly possessions is fundamentally different in the *Mirour;* see below, 121 n. 56.

52 On 6.1019, see Macaulay, Notes ad loc.; P. E. Beichner, "Gower's Use of *Aurora* in *Vox Clamantis,*" *Speculum* 30 (1955): 582–95.

53 *PL* 158:695B (under the name of Anselm) (variant text).

In genus exemplum fer magis ipse tuum:
Nomine perspicuo cum sis generosus avorum,
Equipares stirpis moribus acta tuis.
Hoc in honore dei communi voce precamur,
Ut gemines animi nobilitate genus. 6.1011–1016

[If nobleness and noble name influence you,
Take your own familial example.
Noble ancestrally and with a famous name,
To family custom you should match your deeds.
This by the grace of God implore we with one voice:
Join family with nobleness of mind.]

That true nobility is based on virtue, not birth, is a Stoic-Christian commonplace. In the *Aurora* citation Gower proves to be in accord with patristic tradition as it was particularly nurtured in the monastic orders, whose internal peace could be easily destroyed through emphasis on social distinctions.[54] The second passage, which immediately follows the panegyric to the Black Prince, has a more courtly character,[55] since on this question the Mirror for a Prince is generally much more

[54] Bromyard, *s.v. nobilitas*, gives the following citation supposedly from Bernard of Clairvaux: *Quid gloriaris de parentela, ubi Christus non invenitur? Si Christus cum parentibus suis iustissimis in Hierusalem non inveniebatur, quando Maria et Joseph eum requirebant, Luc. 2, quomodo tu cum parentibus tuis usurariis vel raptoribus illum invenies? De qua parentela dici potest illud, Ezech 22, Sordida nobilis, grandis interitu. Sordida quo ad animam, nobilis quo ad mundum.* [Why do you boast about your ancestors, among whom Christ is not found? If Christ was not found with his most just parents in Jerusalem when Mary and Joseph sought him (Luke 2{2:41–50}), how will you, with your usurious or even rapacious parents, find him? About such ancestors it can be said (Ezechiel 22{22:5}), thou filthy one, infamous, great in destruction. Wherefore filthy in respect to the soul, therefore infamous in respect to the world.] [Actually not found in the works of Bernard. The valuation of *nobilis* in this passage from the Vulgate, as translated in the Douay version, is unusual and must be taken ironically for *ignobilis*. Trans.]

[55] It appears to have been influenced by a passage from Seneca that found its way into Waltenham's mirror for a prince, a passage which, however, I have been unable to identify among the fragments of the work cited, the *De Moribus*. The same passage seems to me to be present in Thomas More's *Discourse Concerning the Way of True Nobility*, which he inserted in his translation of the *Vita* of Pico della Mirandola. The Senecan passage in Waltenham reads as follows: *Nobilitatis tue ad hoc memineris ut cum claritate generis morum sanctitate vel honestate contendas et cum nobilitate corporis seu generis animi nobilitatem assequaris. Pulcrum est enim nobilitati generis moribus contendisse* [?], *pulcrius genus humiliter* [sic] *moribus illustrasse* [You should be mindful of your nobility in that you should match behavior in holiness and integrity with the fame of family, and rival nobility of soul with nobility of body or family. For it is a handsome thing to have matched nobility of family with behavior, but more admirable to have glorified a humble family by behavior]. Roger

moderate than the *Mirour.*[56] Gower holds fast to the principle of the nobility of virtue, yet is very benevolently disposed towards nobility of birth and attempts a

---

de Waltenham, *Compendium Morale de Virtuosis Dictis et Factis Exemplaribus Antiquorum.* Bodleian Library MS. Fairfax 4, fol. 10v.

[56] See *Mirour* 23377 ff., esp. 23401–23412:

Seigneur de halt parage plain,
Ne t'en dois faire plus haltain,
Ne l'autre gent tenir au vil;
Tous suismes fils de dame Evain.
Seigneur, tu qui me dis vilain,
Comment voes dire q'es gentil?
Si tu le dis, je dy nenil:
Car certes tout le flom de Nil
Ne puet hoster le sanc prochain
De toy, qui te fais tant nobil,
Et du vilein q'en son cortil
Labourt pour sa vesture et pain.

[Lord of such a lofty lineage,
You should not act so superior,
Nor hold other people so base;
We are all sons of the lady Eve.
Lord, you who call me base,
How can I say to you that you are gentle?
If you say you are I shall say not at all:
For surely all the waters of the Nile
Cannot deny that the blood is the same
In you, who are so noble,
As in the peasant who in his garden
Labors for his clothes and bread.]

Or 23426–23433:

He, quel orguil te monteroit,
Seigneur, si dieus fourmé t'avoit
D'argent ou d'orr ou de perrie,
Sique ton corps ne purriroit:
Mais certes n'est de tiel endroit,
Ainz est du vile tay purrie,
Sicome la gent q'est enpovrie.

[Well, what pride would have elevated you,
Lord, if God had made you
Of silver or gold or precious stones,
So that your body would not decay:
But it certainly is not of such kind,
Rather from vile clay it is rotten
As the people by their poverty.]

synthesis of the two. Kleineke regarded such cases as overlappings of the Christian-Stoic and the courtly-chivalric ideals of the prince.[57] Gower would hardly have been conscious of them. To harmonize the *nobilitas generis* with the *nobilitas animi* was the natural endeavor of a courtly-oriented poet who, unlike members of the monastic orders—especially the mendicants—had a quasi-professional attitude towards inherited nobility.[58] The tradition of the Latin panegyrists had paved the way for him there. These had also, in their attempt to portray the ideal ruler, confronted the dilemma of inherited and virtuous nobility. The influence of antiquity is wholly sufficient to explain the many layers exhibited in courtly literature by the theme of *nobilitas*. Among Gower's contemporaries, for example, Walter of Peterborough—in a poem about Prince Edward's Spanish campaign composed after 1367—linked hereditary nobility and the performance principle in the following model portrait:

Magnus avis, major animis, modo maximus armis,
Nomen quodcunque magnificare potest.
. . . .
Quis dux, quis dominus majores progenitores
Aut habet, aut habuit? saecula longa lege.
. . . .
Lumen conventu, leo conflictu, lyra cantu;
Ergo prudens, ergo probus, ergo pius.
Per tot signa sacra probat Edwardus genitores,
Et plus quo senior praedicat ipse patrem.
Semper enim sanguis vester, de semine divo,
Narrat si quid habet, notificatque patres.[59]

[Great in ancestry, greater in courage, greatest in arms,
He is able to glorify whatsoever name.

The aggressive tone is probably made possible because the addressee is unspecified, whereas the personal direct address to the king would demand another style.

[57] Kleineke, *Englische Fürstenspiegel,* 129–30.

[58] An aggressive undertone is quite noticeable already in Bernard of Clairvaux. The Dominican Bromyard, however, expresses his opinion much more sharply: *Nobilitas est duplex: una quantum ad Deum et animam, alia quantum ad mundum et carnem. Una vera, et existens, et approbata in curia Dei; alia falsa, apparens, et non existens, in curia quidem mundi approbata, sed in curia Dei reprobata et damnata, et peior quacunque corporali servitute.* [There are two kinds of nobility: the one as far as concerns God and the soul, the other as far as concerns the world and the flesh. The one true and existing and approved in the court of God; the other false, apparent and non-existing, approved indeed in the court of the world, but in the court of God reproved and damned and worse than any bodily servitude.] *Summa Praedicantium, s.v. nobilitas.*

[59] "Prince Edward's Expedition into Spain," ed. Thomas Wright, *Political Poems and Songs*, 1:98–99.

. . . .
What leader, what lord either has or has had
Greater progenitors? Read through the long ages.
. . . .
A light in the assembly, a lion in the conflict, a lyre in the melody;
Therefore prudent, therefore upright, therefore virtuous.
Through so many holy signs Edward proves his ancestors,
And as he grows in years proclaims his father more.
For always your blood, from divine seed,
Tells if it has something, and makes its fathers known.]

Had Claudian written these lines, the Latin would doubtless have been more classical; the content, however, would not have been essentially different. The juxtaposition of a demand for nobility of virtue and a positive estimation of noble derivation, therefore, probably has its beginnings in a literary genre rather than in Gower's inability to keep separate cultural values of different origin.

One could rather fault Gower's indiscriminate syncretism with the ideas that derive from the *Secretum Secretorum*. They surface frequently in Chapters 13 and 14, which have just been discussed. If medieval complexes of ideas could be interpreted clearly in the sense of their origins, one might conclude that here the oriental-despotic portrait of the ruler is combined with the Christian-Stoic and courtly-chivalric ideals. The valuation of *fama, laus,* and *gloria*, for example, inclines sometimes to the Stoic-Christian side, and sometimes conforms to the *Secretum* or to chivalric views. The Christian view is prominent at the point where, in connection with the theme *ubi sunt qui ante nos*, the transience of earthly glory is discussed:[60]

Ecce diu res nulla manet mortalibus, ecce
Nullus honor prohibit, gloria nulla mori:
Non prosunt quicquam preconia vana sepultis,
Torquent famosos tartara sepe reos. 6.1113–1116

[Behold! for mortals nothing stays for long, behold!
No fame, no honor, keeps them from their deaths.
To those in tombs vain praises bring no benefit,
Hell often torments famous guilty souls.]

---

[60] The preceding lines read:
Magnus erat Cesar totoque potencior orbe,
Nunc quem nec mundus ceperat, urna capit. 6.1107–1108
[Great Caesar was more powerful than all the world,
An urn now holds whom earth did not contain.]
On the *ubi sunt* theme, see E. Gilson, *Les Idees et les Lettres*, Chap. 1.

It is also prominent a little later: *Gloria nulla potest in mundi rebus haberi* (6.1129) [No fame in worldly concerns can be retained].[61] The chivalric view appears to me to prevail especially where thoughts of fame and *agon* are combined, particularly in the chapter concerning the Black Prince:

> *Acta patris vince, maiorque vocaberis ille,*
> *Totaque vox clamet laudis honore tue.* 6.977–978
>
> [Surpass your father's deeds, greater you will be called,
> And every voice will shout your glory's praise.]

In other places the more utilitarian conception of the *Secretum* shines through, especially in the interesting passage at 6.811–832. Here Gower handles the theme of *largitas* or *liberalitas*, and interprets it in the Christian sense as almsgiving. He begins with the word *larga*, which proves in the course of the first verse to be an epithet for *elemosina*: *Larga tuis meritis inopes elemosina curet* [Through your merits, let your generous alms take care of the poor]. And he ends on a purely Christian note:

> *Est ancilla dei simplex elemosina, mortis*
> *Antidotum, venie porta, salutis iter:*
> *Disputat adversus dantis peccata, perorat*
> *Auctori, redimit probra, precatur opem.* 6.827–830
>
> [The plain handmaid of God is alms, the antidote
> To death, the gate of grace, salvation's way.
> It disputes the giver's sins, for its author pleads,
> Atones disgrace, and for the rich man prays.]

In between, however, are the *Secretum*'s reflections upon the cautions with which *largitas* or *liberalitas* should be exercised. They are the same reflections that Gower repeats with reference to Aristotle, without any of the Christian trimming, in Book 7 of the *Confessio Amantis*.[62] In this context *largitas* does not serve the goal of redemption, but is a means of acquiring fame, and, according to the view of the *Secretum*, fame is the proper goal of any lordship:

> . . . *fama ergo est quod principaliter et per se ipsum appetitur in regimine, quia regimen non appetitur propter se, set propter bonam famam.*

---

[61] *Gloria nulla, precor, te, rex, extollat inanis* (6.789) [Extol, O king I pray you, empty glory not] does not belong in this context. *Inanis gloria* is a form of *superbia*.

[62] See *Confessio Amantis* 7.1–6. Generosity as the second point of political ethics is discussed at 7.1685–1694 and illustrated with exemplary tales.

[. . . therefore it is fame that principally and for itself is sought in ruling, because rule is not desired for itself, but for great fame.][63]

The *Confessio Amantis* combines the two points, the end and the means of *largitas*, in a Latin distich in a chapter superscription:[64]

Fama colit largum volitans per secula Regem,
Dona tamen licitis sunt moderanda modis.

[Fame flying through the ages honors a generous King;
His gifts, however, are guided by lawful rules.]

The verses are then explained in detail in the text (*Confessio* 7.2014–2176). No doubt the like formulations of the Mirror for a Prince also derive from the *Secretum*:

Da tua non parce, cui des tamen aspice caute;
Crede, satis res est ingeniosa dare:
Non perit hec probitas que dona rependit honeste,
Namque piam laudem res data dantis habet. 6.815–818

[Give generously, but cautious be to whom you give;
Believe it is inborn to give enough.
Goodness that weighs out worthy gifts goes not to waste,
For donor's grant a godly merit has.]

The extent to which Gower departs from the Christian point of view is made clear by such sententious remarks as *Munera tempus habent, fama perhennis erit* [Gifts endure for a time, but fame will be everlasting], which recalls the *Secretum*'s . . . *acquisitio largitatis est gloria regis et perhennitas regnorum* [the acquisition of liberality is the glory of the king and the perpetuity of kingdoms].[65] And yet the borrowings from the *Secretum* do not appear as intrusive elements from an alien value system. They are, even though awkwardly, so etched into the portrait of the Christian ruler that they can be understood as an expression of the double

---

63 Roger Bacon, *Secretum Secretorum*, in *Opera Hactenus Inedita*, ed. Robert Steele (Oxford: Clarendon Press, 1920), 5:45.

64 Macaulay, *Works*, 3:287.

65 Bacon, *Secretum*, 44. Gower's text of the *Secretum* appears to have been the French version of Jofroi de Watreforde or its Latin prototype, since it uses an extended interpolation concerning the cardinal virtues that occurs only there. Jofroi is available to us in Yonge's English version, dating from a generation after Gower. It is printed as the last of three English texts of the *Secretum* in Robert Steele, *Three Prose Versions of the Secreta Secretorum*, EETS E.S. 74 (London: Kegan Paul, 1898). I cite Bacon's text only to show how the Latin *termini* agree.

nature of the royal position with regard to this world and the next. *Largitas* secures the prince fame in this world and forgiveness of sin in the next, just as *iustitia* similarly secures him the earthly and the heavenly kingdoms.[66]

Gower does not adopt the *Secretum*'s characteristic views on methods of conducting brutal warfare, crafty diplomacy, and methodical intimidation of subjects, in which the oriental element is prominent. In the question of conducting war, he instead develops the theory of the *bellum iustum* with the customary Christian modifications;[67] in the question of how best to insure the obedience of subjects, he decides emphatically in favor of *amor* against *terror.*[68] One must in general bear in mind that the version of the *Secretum* Gower used already had strong Christian impulses,[69] and was sanctioned by the name of Aristotle. The medieval user had no suspicion of its oriental extraction.

---

[66] See 6.1007: *Lucratur populum que deum rex iustus utrumque* [A just king gains both the people and God].

[67] See 6.971–974; above all, however, see 4.3–18 and 481–496.

[68] See Book VI, Chapter 14, esp. 1025 following. That *fratris amor* appears in lines 1025, 1026, and 1027—instead of the expected *plebis amor,* which is demanded by the establishment of the problem in the beginning of the chapter—I would attribute to the influence of the biblical *speculum principis,* Deuteronomy 17. It stresses in the beginning that the king should be elected from a circle of *fratres,* and at the end enjoins the king not to elevate himself above his brothers (*Nec elevetur cor eius in superbiam super fratres suos* [Deut. 17:20]).

[69] One example, unimportant in itself but philosophically attractive, which shows that Gower derived a biblical train of thought directly from the *Secretum,* occurs in Book VI, Chapter 17 of the *Vox Clamantis.* There the Mirror for a Prince discusses the theme of *memento mori.* In these surroundings is accommodated a view of human life as an unending battle:

Est hominis vita quasi milicies reputata,
Bella super terram nam tria semper agit:
Rex qui per medium belli transibit inermis,
Sepius incaute stulcior ipse cadit. 6.1135–1138

[The life of man is thought of as a long campaign,
For on earth he always wages three wars.
The king who will oppress through war defenseless men
Will foolishly incautious often fall.]

The passage begins with a quote from Job to the effect that all human life is a struggle (1135); the struggle is threefold in nature (1136); the king who goes rushing off unarmed to war pays for his folly with death (1137–1138). Everything is clear up to line 1136's *tria bella,* which are not even explained. It appears as though a distich has been lost here. However, the triad is easily restored from the Bible, the liturgy, or from Latin hymns. They are the world, the flesh, and the devil. In order to give an approximately contemporary example, I wish to cite from a rimed English version of the sayings of Bernard of Clairvaux in the commonplace book of the Vernon MS. (Furnivall and Horstmann, *Minor Poems of the Vernon Manuscript,* 1:515):

The last chapters of the Mirror for a Prince (from the end of Chapter 14 through Chapter 17) are tightly connected thematically and as far removed from the *Secretum's* king as they are from chivalry's ideal life. They proceed from the proposition that God has set self-understanding and love of his creator as rules of life for the king:

> *Noscere te studeas et amare deum, duo namque*
> *Hec sunt, que tibi, rex, scire necesse iubet.*
> *Hec est condicio sub qua tibi contulit esse*
> *Vivendique modum conditor ipse tuus.* 6.1035–1038

> Man, thou hast threo luther fon
> Heore nomes con I wel vchon
> Gif I schal touchen alle:
> Thyn oune flesch, the world, the fend . . .

What makes the *Secretum* seem to be Gower's direct prototype is the similar course of the argument, the only minor exception being that in the *Secretum* Job appears at the end of the section rather than at the beginning. The *Secretum*'s design is also tripartite. Sentences coincide with thoughts and occasionally match one of Gower's distiches:

a. Gower: *Est hominis vita quasi milicies reputata,*
Bella super terram nam tria semper agit.

Secretum: Al the day of oure lyfe in grete Perill we byth, for thre enemys vs werryth, dayes and nyghtes in vs hare assautes makynge.

b. Gower: - - - - - - - - - -

Secretum: The worlde that vs drawyth to cowetyse, the fleshe vs chasyth to lecheri; the Deuyl vs assaylyth by Pryde and envy.

c. Gower: *Rex qui per medium belli transibit inermis,*
Sepius incaute stulcior ipse cadit.

Secretum: Moche is he a fole and vncunnynge that in so cruel a battaill noght dreddyth ne helpe sechyth. There—for sayth Jope, that chyualrie is manys lyfe in erthe. (Steele, *Three Prose Versions*, 156.)

Another image that may go back to the *Secretum* is the comparison of the people to a garden which bears the king fruit or thorns according to how he tends it. Shakespeare is familiar with this metaphor and develops it with great art in *Richard II.* I have encountered it in the Middle Ages only in the *Secretum* and in Gower's Mirror for a Prince. Thus it appears to me more plausible to posit a direct dependence rather than a *topos.* In Gower the image goes as follows:

> *Plebs est regis ager, rex cultor qui colit agrum;*
> *Si male, fert tribulos, si bene, grana parit.* 6.1001–1002

In the *Secretum* (Roger Bacon, *Secretum Secretorum*, in *Opera Hactenus Inedita*, 5:213), one reads: "Thou shalt leve well that thy subiectis bene lyke a gardyn, in wych bene dyuers maneres of trees, and thou shalt noght holde ham as londe berrynge thornes wythout frute." Whether Gower's advice to the young king (*reminiscere facta paterna* [remember your father's deeds], 6.919) is related to the *Secretum*'s demand, "Alexandre, remembyr the of the dedis and werkis of thyne auncestres" (Bacon, *Secretum*, 5:143), can hardly be determined.

> [Desirous be to know yourself and God to love,
> For these two things He orders you to learn.
> Such are the terms by which your creator assigned
> Existence and your mode of life to you.]

This divine goal-setting has nothing to do with the ethic of rule *per se*, but is, as Gower describes it in Book VII with reference to the creation of man, the life task of every man.[70] It has to do with monarchic ethics only insofar as they are a more important form of individual ethics, and because the consequences of the king's moral failures threaten the entire people.

Now knowledge includes *sapientia*, which is a gift from God and which is furthered by sustained contemplation of the vanity of earthly life. The Mirror for a Prince illustrates the first point with the story of Solomon's successful prayer for wisdom,[71] a narrative of paradigmatic significance for every ruler that appears in all three of Gower's major works. The second point is treated in Chapters 16 and 17. According to the medieval view, any moral philosophy without a thorough discussion of the vanity of worldly goods and the transitoriness of all things lacks importance and makes impossible the first step towards self-knowledge. Thus Pseudo-Vincent of Beauvais begins his *Speculum Morale* with the biblical text, *In omnibus operibus tuis memorare novissima tua, et in aeternum non peccabis* (Ecclesiasticus 7:40) [In all thy works remember thy last end, and thou shalt never sin]. Thus Lorenz, the Dominican royal father confessor, prefaces with an *ars moriendi* the section of his *Somme le Roi* that discusses the virtues.[72] Thus Gower also begins the general observations that frame his class critique with the Solomon-like *vanitas* theme (Book II, Chapter 1), and concludes them with a detailed contemplation of death (Book VII, Chapters 9–19). It appears to me that the medieval predilection for the theme of death differs from similar manifestations of the baroque in that the didactic intent remains most important even in the most realistic description, and in that there is inherent within it a tendency that is completely positive and directed towards this life. The keynote is optimistic rather than macabre when, for example, the theme is stated in the anonymous *Myrour of Synners*:[73]

> Biholde now frende how profitable a myrrour it is for synners inwardly biholdyng of this hije sentence [*sc.* Ecclesiasticus 7:40]: that is wolde god that men sauereden and understonden and purueiden for the laste thingis; for jif thou ofte biholde thiself in this myrrour and jif thou bisily studye to set

[70] See below, 149–54.

[71] Book VI, Chapter 15, in imitation of the *Aurora*; the story occurs in 1 Kings 2.

[72] There are two English versions of the work in the fourteenth century: the *Ayenbite of Inwyt* of Dan Michel of Northgate (*ca.* 1340), and the anonymous *Book of Vices and Virtues* (*ca.* 1375).

[73] Bodleian Library MS. Laud 174, fol. 93.

> thus thi self bifor thi silf, douteles thou schalt be strengere than sampson, more war than dauith, and wiser thanne salomon.

Meditations on death of this kind appear rather infrequently in mirrors for princes. The only examples I know of are Waltenham and Gower.[74] It is not readily conceivable in Gower's case that such observations were occasioned by the person of the addressee. Richard II was fifteen in 1381; he was, therefore, eleven to fifteen years of age during the time of composition of the *VC*'s Mirror for a Prince. And yet these last chapters may have seemed to Gower most fitting, for they lead to the true self-knowledge that the ruler cannot acquire early enough in order to choose the right way between virtue and vice. His free will and his free choice then determine the weal and woe not only of his own person but of the state entrusted to him:

> *Fac ea que tibi vis, bona vel mala, sic et habebis,*
> *Te tamen in melius dirigat oro deus.* 6.1157–1158
>
> [Do what you wish, or good or bad, and that you'll have,
> But God I pray may to the better point.]

With that the Mirror for a Prince ends. The epilogue (Chapter 18) shall be treated in the next chapter in the context of the *VC*'s history of origin, or better, history of development.

When one attempts to evaluate Gower's Mirror for a Prince as a whole, it becomes evident that its value does not lie in a rational philosophy of government. Gower had neither practical political experience to employ nor systematic studies to utilize. However, he did have a strongly pronounced perception of the ethical foundation of the state. With passionate emphasis he discusses the problem of *iustitia* and the ideal of the *rex iustus*. Certainly his Mirror for a Prince is a mirror of virtue; however, it is virtue far removed from moral narrow-mindedness. It portends welfare and prosperity for the ruler as well as his subjects.

---

[74] The material is treated in Waltenham's last chapter. For Gower, see also the *Confessio Amantis* 7.4469–4477:

> That every worthi Prince is holde
> Withinne himself himself beholde,
> To se the stat of his persone,
> And thenke hou ther be joies none
> Upon this Erthe mad to laste,
> And hou the fleissh schal ate laste
> The lustes of this lif forsake,
> Him oghte a gret ensample take
> Of Salomon . . .

Chapter Five

Gower's Sense of Order

A class critique springs from diverse roots and comprehends diverse, or at least greatly differing, areas of human existence. It can either attack the class organization of the state as such or censure the lapses of individual classes. It can be oriented nationally or internationally, terrestrially or transcendentally.

As far as the first alternative is concerned, the class-organized state surmounted by the monarch is, for Gower as well as for the most of his contemporaries, a divinely-ordained reality toward which no criticism is directed. It is in its essence an image of the hierarchical order of the cosmos, and according to its history a divine arrangement of force and an institution of salvation for bringing about law and justice among a mankind morally weakened by the Fall.[1] The unequal distribution of earthly goods likewise rests upon a divine arrangement and is therefore unassailable. But it has to be understood correctly in its moral function. When God subjugated the newly created world to the rule of man, he thus established a kind of communal property. The church fathers speak of it, although traces of it are hardly ever to be found in Gower.[2] He is interested in conditions after the Fall and the inequality of possessions that then prevailed. Earthly possessions have been lent their owners ever since the exile from Paradise, not as an expression of a divine favoritism, but as a test and trial of their sense of moral duty.[3] They have, on the other hand, been withheld from the

---

[1] See above, 31–32.

[2] See above, 117–19.

[3] See *Mirour* 23221–23232:

N'est pas pour ce que dieus n'avoit
Assetz du quoy dont il porroit
Avoir fait riche chascuny,
Q'il les gens povres ordinoit;
Ainz fuist pour ce que dieus voloit
Essaier les seignours ensi,
S'ils ussent leur corage en luy:
Car qui q'est riche et joust auci,
Laissant le tort pour faire droit,

possessionless, not out of prejudice, but in order to facilitate for them, through earthly difficulties, the way to heavenly bliss. Therefore, Gower criticizes not the principle underlying the political or social order, but the deviation from this principle of which the individual classes are guilty.

The question of whether Gower's class critique is nationally or internationally oriented is difficult to answer. After we separated the *Visio* from the original plan of the *Vox Clamantis*, we saw that the passages with a distinct national imprint are confined to Books II and VII, that is, to the frame of the class critique. If one ignores the Mirror for a Prince, which according to its genre belongs only conditionally to the class critique, Books II-VII nowhere claim to describe specific English conditions in the second half of the fourteenth century. There is absent any allusion to the topical questions of contemporary politics, to taxation and its apportionment, to the relationship of *consuetudines* to *leges* that one would expect in the sixth book (which treats of justice and its functionaries). Not England but the world furnishes the material for Gower's class critique. Thus the prologue of the third book speaks of *mundus* and *orbis*, but not of *mea tellus*:

> *Fit mundique status in tres divisio partes,*
> *Omnibus unde viris stat quasi sortis opus,*
> *Et modo per vicia quia sors magis astat iniqua,*
> *Ponderet in causis quilibet acta suis:*
> *In quocumque gradu sit homo, videatur in orbe*
> *Que sibi sunt facta, sors cadit unde rea.* 3.Prol.3–8

> [And since the state of the world is divided into three parts, so that it seems like the work of fate to all men; and since our fate nowadays is quite adverse because of our vices, everyone ought to consider happenings in the light of their causes. No matter what rank a man is in, it would seem that fate turns

---

Il ad grant grace deservi,
Qant pour les biens q'il fait yci
Les biens sanz fin puis avoir doit.

[It is not because God hadn't
Enough of that of which he could
Have made each one rich,
That He ordained people poor;
Rather it was because God wished
To test lords in this way,
To see if they had their trust in Him:
For whoever is rich and just also,
Leaving wrong in order to do right,
He deserves great grace,
For as many good things as he does here
He ought to have good things without end.]

out to be responsible for the things which happen to him in this world. (Trans. Stockton.)]

Likewise, the goal of the work is the moral renewal of all mankind, not just the English:

Da loquar ut vicium minuatur et ammodo virtus
Crescat, ut in mundo mundior extet homo. 3.99–100

[Let me speak out so that henceforth vice will diminish and virtue flourish,
in order that mankind may become purer in this world. (Trans. Stockton.)]

Nor does the summary of the first chapter of the class critique proper formulate a national question, naming as its theme the *status et ordo mundi.*[4] Therefore the national issue is at first only peripheral, yet intensified so much under pressure of the events of 1381 that, after the addition of the *Visio*, the final version gave the overall impression, and was intended to as one may infer from colophon A, that it was nationally oriented.[5]

According to its line of sight, Gower's class critique is transcendental. He has no conception of the historical character and true nature of the state, and one could hardly expect otherwise. The responsibility of individuals as well as of classes is not to the state but directly to God, with whom originates the principle of *ordo* and *status.*[6] Therefore the restoration of the relationships between God and mankind (affiliated by classes) is the prerequisite for political regeneration. Thus the transcendentally determined class critique develops necessarily into a homily. Its scope is the entire cosmos, which is implicated in the consequences of the conflict between man and God. Thus there results a breadth and depth of questioning that is impressive even though absolutely unoriginal in its whole and in its parts. It is a complete world picture in which all the parts are related to each other and in the midst of which stands man:

Hoc fateor vere, quicquid contingit in orbe,
Nos sumus in causa, sint bona sive mala. 2.629–630

[4] *Hic tractat qualiter status et ordo mundi in tribus consistit gradibus, sunt enim, ut dicit, Clerus, Milicies, et Agricultores, de quorum errore mundi infortunia nobis contingunt.* [Here he discusses how the state and order of the world consists in three degrees. They are, as he says, the clerics, knights, and peasants, by whose lapses the misfortunes of the world befall us. (Trans. Stockton.)]

[5] See above, 5–6.

[6] That the classes are responsible for each other is self-evident; thus, for example, the people have to suffer the consequences of the king's sins (see 6.609–610). For all that, the people may not call the ruler directly to account.

[I truly acknowledge that whatever happens in the world, whether it be good or evil, we ourselves are the cause of it. (Trans. Stockton.)]

The basic questions concerning the essence and destiny of man are discussed in Books II and VII of the *Vox Clamantis*. Book II deals with the problem of fate and responsibility. The common view holds that *Fortuna* is to blame for the change of times and, therefore, is responsible for all present hardships. Here, from the periphery, Gower begins the thrust towards his true theme. He starts with Solomon's judgment regarding the vanity of earthly life and endows it with the traditional *topoi* of *contemptus mundi* literature (2.3–16). One distich ("if it is possible that one may be happy")[7] forms a transition to the contrasting pictures of a blissful national past and a gloomy present (2.19–36). Here the theme of the decline of the times is applied to a concrete historical situation and is therefore more than a *topos*. Of course, Gower does not achieve a detailed comparison of two historical epochs; however, he locates his golden age neither in the beginning of human history nor in the misty distance of an Arthurian antiquity, but in the immediate past, and thus attains a certain degree of realism.[8] Then, under the impress of the subject of *mutatio rerum*, he poses the question of blame. The common view holds that *Fortuna* is responsible for everything, while everyone considers himself individually blameless:

Se tamen inmunes cause communiter omnes
Dicunt, ut si quis non foret inde reus;
Accusant etenim fortunam iam variatam,
Dicentes quod ea stat magis inde rea. 2.43–46

[Nevertheless, all men commonly say that they have nothing to do with cause, as if no one were responsible for things; in fact, they now blame fickle Fortune, saying that she is responsible for them. (Trans. Stockton.)]

If one considers *Fortuna* the cause of decay, one thus acknowledges a limitation by external forces upon the freedom of human will and action. What sort of external forces these are is unimportant to Gower. He reduces them to the common denominator *Fortuna*, probably because that conforms to the literary mode

---

[7] *Si tamen esse potest quod felix esset in orbe,*
Dudum felices nos dedit esse deus. 2.17–18

[Long ago, God granted that we be happy, if it is possible that one may be happy on earth. (Trans. Stockton.)]

[8] One would probably not be wrong in assuming that the brilliant period of Edward III and the Black Prince is intended. It appears to lie just in the past (line 26, *nuper*) and to have been of short duration (19–36). The enthusiastic tone matches that of the eulogy to the Black Prince (Book VI, Chap. 13). The same kind of historical view occurs in the song "Seldom Seen is Soon Forgot" (see above, 37–38).

and evokes in the reader familiar notions. In addition to fortune, he also refers to *sors, fatum,* and *astra*, without clearly distinguishing them.[9] We shall investigate them together as to whether and to what extent they limit man's freedom of self-determination.

Behind Gower's superficial, slightly dramatizing treatment of the question, one occasionally notices the formulations of the theologians. It cannot, however, be said that Gower had his knowledge at first hand. He could have consulted the entries under *fatum* or *liberum arbitrium, fortuna,* or *providentia* in anyone's theological *summa*, and was sure to hit upon the relevant passages from Boethius, Augustine, and Gregory. Of course, on the question of *fatum* a considerable contradiction between Boethius on the one hand and Augustine and his spokesman Gregory on the other would have become immediately apparent. Boethius affirms the existence of *fatum* and defines it as an arrangement inherent in all moveable (that is, changeable) things, by means of which divine providence binds all that is individual with its eternal laws of order.[10] *Fatum* and *providentia* are two aspects of one and the same thing, namely the divine control of the world. From God's point of view as the undivided whole implicit in the unity of the divine *ratio*, the control is *providentia*; from the point of view of the world, dispersed in time and space and with reference to individual phenomena, it is *fatum*.[11] Augustine and his disciple Gregory, on the other hand, deny the existence of *fatum*. Gregory states clearly, *sed a fidelium cordibus absit ut aliquid esse fatam dicant* [but let it be far from the hearts of the faithful that they should assert that fate is a particular thing],[12] and, as the surrounding text makes clear, identifies *fatum* with the influence of the stars. Augustine allows the word *fatum* if by it nothing other than divine providence is understood, although he considers such

[9] The approximation of *fatum, fortuna,* and *casus* may go back to Boethius, *De Consolatione Philosophiae* IV, *prosa* 6–8. I have used the edition of Adrian Fortescue (London: Burns, Oates, and Washburne, 1925).

[10] *De Consolatione*, IV, *prosa* 6: . . . *fatum vero inhaerens rebus mobilibus dispositio per quam providentia suis quaeque nectit ordinibus* [. . . but Fate is a disposition inherent in changeable things, by which Providence connecteth all things in their due order. Trans. "I.T.," rev. H. F. Stewart (Cambridge, MA: Harvard University Press, 1918), 341].

[11] *De Consolatione,* ibid.: *Providentia namque cuncta pariter, quamvis diversa, quamvis infinita, complectitur; fatum vero singula digerit in motum, locis, formis ac temporibus distributa; ut haec temporalis ordinis explicatio in divinae mentis adunata prospectum providentia sit, eadem vero adunatio, digesta atque explicata temporibus, fatum vocetur* [For Providence embraceth all things together, though diverse, though infinite; but Fate putteth every particular thing into motion being distributed by places, forms, and time; so that this unfolding of temporal order being united into the foresight of God's mind is Providence, and the same uniting, being digested and unfolded in time, is called Fate (Trans. "I.T.," 341)].

[12] *Homilia in Evangelia*, Book I, Homily 10. *PL* 76:1112.

careless usage reprehensible.[13] Now, when Gower says of *Fortuna*, *Attamen ore meo te nichil esse puto* (2.86–87) [In my opinion I still reckon you as nothing], he aligns himself with Gregory, whose Homily I.10—from which the *fatum* citation derives—he also uses elsewhere. That theological discussion is not entirely foreign to him is apparent from such formulations as:

> *Cum solo causante deo sint cuncta creata,*
> *Num fortuna dei solvere possit opus?* 2.595–596
>
> [Since all things were created solely through the agency of God, Fortune could not undo the work of God, could she? (Trans. Stockton.)]

After the account of creation, he points out that

> *Fortune nichil attribuit, set solus ut ipse* [sc. *deus*]
> *Cuncta creat, solus cuncta creata regit.* 2.623–624
>
> [He allowed nothing to Fortune, but because He alone creates everything, He alone rules all creation. (Trans. Stockton.)]

The second distich, with its *Fortune nichil attribuit*, provides a proof of *Fortuna*'s non-existence similar to that which Francis of Hales adduces for the non-existence of *fatum: Providentia divina . . . nihil relinquit in rebus futuris* [Divine providence . . . forsakes nothing in future matters].[14]

It may be an influence of late antiquity that the problem of fate and free will almost invariably becomes critical on the question of the extent to which men are subject to the influence of the stars. In Augustine and Gregory the star of Bethle-

---

13 *De Civitate Dei* 5.1: *Prorsus divina providentia regna constituuntur humana. Quae si propterea quisquam fato tribuit, quia ipsam Dei voluntatem vel potestatem fati nomine appellat, sententiam teneat, linguam corrigat.* [In a word, human kingdoms are established by divine providence. And if any one attributes their existence to fate, because he calls the will or the power of God itself by the name of fate, let him keep his opinion, but correct his language. Trans. Dods, *The City of God*, 142–43.]

14 *Summa Theologica*, pars 1, inq. 1, tract. 5, sect. 2, quaest. 3, tit. 1: *De Fato*, cap. 1: *. . . providentia divina est cognoscitiva eorum quae sunt futurae. Praecognitio autem Dei nihil relinquit in rebus futuris . . . quare si fatum, sicut dicit Boetius, est "dispositio in mobilibus" relicta ex divina providentia, cum nihil aliud a providentia relinquatur in rebus futuris: aut fatum simplicter nihil erit vel non erit aliud a divina providentia.* [. . . divine providence is aware of those things which belong to the future. However, God's foreknowledge forsakes nothing in future matters . . . wherefore if fate, just as Boethius says, is "a disposition in changeable matters" apart from divine providence, since nothing other is apart from providence in future matters, then fate will either be simply nothing or it will be nothing other than divine providence.] Francis of Hales, *Summa Theologica* (Ad Claras Aquas [Quaracchi]: Typographia Collegii S. Bonaventurae, 1924–1948), 4:304.

hem is a prime instance in showing that the stars are subject to man and not *vice versa.*[15] Gower is not content with that. He constructs around the star of Bethlehem a systematic catalogue of all creation and shows how everything—from angels down to fish—exists to serve the *vir iustus.*[16]

The examples that Gower cites are all of a miraculous nature: Moses's passage through the Red Sea, Daniel in the lions' den, Jonah in the belly of the whale. Consequently he goes so far as to maintain the extreme thesis that the *homo iustus* is not only free of the influence of *Fortuna, fatum,* or the stars, but that he also stands above the law of nature:

> *Ac elementorum celestia corpora iustum*
> *Subdita iure colunt, et sua vota ferunt.*
> *In virtute dei sapiens dominabitur astra,*[17]
> *Totaque consequitur vis orizontis eum.* 2.237–240
>
> [And subject to the law of the elements, the celestial bodies favor the just man and carry out his prayers. The man who is knowing in the virtue of God will dominate the stars, and all the power of heaven attends him. (Trans. Stockton.)]

---

15 Gregory, *Homilia in Evangelia* I.10: *Sed inter haec sciendum quod Priscillianistae haeretici nasci unumquemque hominem sub constitutionibus stellarum putant; et hoc in adjutorium sui erroris assumunt, quod nova stella exiit cum Dominus in carne apparuit, cuius fuisse fatum eamdem quae apparuit stellam putant. Sed si Evangelii verba pensamus, quibus de eadem stella dicitur: Usque dum veniens staret supra ubi erat puer, dum non puer ad stellam sed stella ad puerum cucurrit, si dici liceat, non stella fatum pueri, sed fatum stellae is qui apparuit puer fuit. Sed a fidelium cordibus absit ut aliquid esse fatum dicant. Vitam quippe hominum solus hanc conditor qui creavit administrat. Neque enim propter stellas homo, sed stellae propter hominem factae sunt.* [But among these things it should be understood that the Priscillianist heretics thought each man is born under the dispositions of the stars; and this they supposed in support of their error, that a new star became visible when the Lord appeared in the flesh, whose fate they thought was the very star that appeared. But if we consider the words of the Gospels, in which it is said about the same star, "until it came and stood over the place where the child was {Matthew 2.9}," since the boy did not hasten to the star but the star to the boy, the star, if one may say so, was not the boy's fate but he, the boy who appeared, was the star's fate. But let it be far from the hearts of the faithful that they should say fate is anything. Certainly the founder who created human life alone directs it. For man was not made because of the stars, but the stars because of man.] *PL* 76:1111–12.

16 2.237–274. The same catalogue appears with slight variations in the *Mirour* 26989–27072. However, the *Mirour* speaks for the most part simply of *homme*—once of *prodhomme*—while the *VC* seeks to develop, with great emphasis, the idea of the *homo iustus.*

17 For an earlier treatment of this proverb, the origin of which is still disputed, see G. G. Fox, *The Medieval Sciences in the Works of John Gower* (New York: Haskell, 1931, repr. 1966), 61–62.

Here, obviously, the assertion is overstated for the sake of the effect.[18] In other passages in the *Vox Clamantis*, as well as in the *Confessio Amantis*, the laws of nature are considered incontestable, and not the *homo iustus* but only the saintly man has the power, in prayer, to breach them:

> *Contra naturam fiunt miracula, vires*
> *Nature deitas frangere sola potest.* 5.625–626
>
> [Miracles happen only contrary to nature; only the divinity of nature can go against its own powers. (Trans. Stockton.)]
>
> Bot yit the lawe original,
> Which he [*sc.* God] hath set in the natures,
> Mot worchen in the creatures,
> That thereof mai be non obstacle,
> Bot if it stonde upon miracle
> Thurgh preiere of som holy man. *Confessio* 7.658–663

It is not only polemical zeal against a blind fatalism or fervid joy that motivates Gower to elevate the *homo iustus* to the absolute ruler of creation; it is above all an active conviction of man's majesty. One may not be immediately prepared for observations such as the following in a medieval moralist and homilist:

> *O quam dives homo, quam magno munere felix,*
> *Cui totus soli subditur orbis honor!*
> *Felix pre cunctis, cui quicquid fabrica mundi*
> *Continet, assurgit et sua iussa facit.* 2.275–278
>
> [O how rich, how happy is man in his great reward! All the honor of the world is granted to him alone. He is happy above all others. Everything the fabric of the world contains arises for him and performs his bidding. (Trans. Stockton.)]

One has become too much accustomed to associating quite the opposite picture with medieval thought, as if the consciousness of the *miseria humanae condicionis* had led to a narrow, pessimistic interpretation of the human situation. However, *dignitas* and *miseria* are by their very nature not to be divorced from one another. They complement each other and are in their duality the perfect expression for

18 The *Confessio* handles the question of free will and belief in the stars with more reserve. 7.633–663 contrasts the views of the "naturien" and the "divin" and ends with a compromise. In a later passage (1281–1438), the influence of the stars is categorically accepted: ["the sterres] . . . worchen manye sondri thinges / To ous, that ben here underlinges" (1293–1294). [It should be noted that Genius is the speaker in these passages. Trans.]

the disunity of human existence. When one consults Bromyard, one thus encounters both aspects:

> *Hominis conditio est duplex. Una nobilis, quam cogitare debet, ne peccatis vilescat. Alia fragilis, quam cogitare debet, ne superbiat.*
>
> [The nature of man is twofold. The one aspect is noble, which he should ponder lest he be debased by sins. The other is weak, which he should ponder lest he be proud.][19]

The first chapter of the pseudo-Bernardine *Meditationes Piissimae de Cognitione Humanae Conditionis* is *De Dignitate Hominis*, the second *De Miseria Hominis.*[20] Examples could be multiplied endlessly. Gower therefore follows familiar ideas when he first draws the majesty of man, that is, of the *homo iustus*, in its full splendor and then contrasts it to the misery of man, that is, of the *homo peccator.*[21] Thus Chapter 5's catalogue of men whom the entire creation serves with joy is matched by a second catalogue in Chapter 6 that describes the misery of fallen sinners. And just as emphatically as man's *dignitas* was made independent of *Fortuna*, *fatum*, and the stars, his *miseria* is now removed from the influence of fateful and natural powers and traced unmistakably back to moral causes:

> *Non sors fortune poterat sibi talia ferre,*
> *Set pro peccatis contigit illud eis.* 2.331–332
>
> [The lot of Fortune could not have brought such things upon them, but it happened to them because of their sins. (Trans. Stockton.)]

Bromyard gives this line of thought an especially attractive and less fervid expression, which may be inserted here as an illustration contemporary with Gower:

> *Ratione primi est sciendum, quod aliqui tribulationes pluvie et siccitatis huiusmodi attribuebant planetis et causis naturalibus. Unde diligenter inquirunt, quis planeta tunc regnet, et quamdiu regnabit, et huiusmodi questiones vanas et frivolas faciunt, quorum dictum videtur esse contra rationem et contra sacram scripturam et contra legem canonum . . . Potius ergo videntur tales pestilentie ortum habere et causari a causa voluntaria, i.e. a peccato quod ex mala oritur voluntate quam a causa naturali. Huic etiam videtur concordare sacra scriptura. Querendum est enim ab illis qui dicunt quod planeta hoc facit, quis planeta regnavit tempore diluvii . . . Quis autem planeta vel constellatio illius pluvie occasio fuit nisi peccatum? Illa enim planeta videlicet peccatum tunc regnavit et pluvias*

19 *Summa Praedicantium*, *s.v. homo.*

20 *PL* 184:485–489.

21 2.281–348.

> *illas occasionaliter causavit. Optimus namque astrologus deus illam assignavit causam . . .*
>
> *Qua in re pensandum est quod illi qui peccando deum derelinquunt et diabolo adherent, terram tempestatibus et vindictis et fame turbant. Et quod peccatum est planeta regnans qui nos conturbat.*[22]
>
> [In regards to the first point, it is known that some men were accustomed to attribute afflictions such as rain and drought to the planets and to natural causes. Whence they inquire diligently what planet then might govern, and how it will govern, and pose all manner of empty and silly questions, the content of which is seen to be contrary to reason, to Sacred Scripture, and to canon law . . . Rather, then, such plagues are seen to have their beginning in and to be caused by a willing cause, that is, by sin that arises from evil will rather than by natural cause. For this is seen to agree with Sacred Scripture. It should be asked of those who say that a planet did it, what planet governed at the time of the flood? . . . Yet what planet or constellation but sin was the occasion of that rain? For that planet, namely sin, governed then and on that occasion was the cause of those rains. The very best astrologer, God, assigned that cause . . .
>
> In any such matter it must be concluded that those who forsake God by sinning and follow the devil roil the earth with tempests and punishments and famine. And that sin is the governing planet that confounds us.]

The passage shows its kinship with Book II of the *Vox Clamantis* in its emphasis on human free will and the resultant responsibility of man not only for his own fate but also for events in nature.[23] It agrees with the *Vox Clamantis* in its way of thinking insofar as it holds that *tribulatio*—worldly misfortune—must be explained on moral grounds and be relieved by a moral regeneration; mankind's earthly welfare is the focus of interest. That is characteristic of the second book of the *Vox Clamantis*, but not at all pertinent for the analogous parts of the *Mirour*. The *Vox Clamantis* states:

> *Ex meritis vel demeritis sic contigit omne,*
> *Humano generi quicquid adesse solet:*
> *Sic vario casu versabitur alea mundi,*
> *Dum solet in rebus ludere summa manus.* 2.345–348
>
> [So whatever happens to the human race, everything is wontedly due to merit or lack of merit. Thus the die of the world will be cast with varying

[22] *Summa Praedicantium, s.v. tribulatio.*

[23] Gower leaves this second part of the problem unexplained at this point, since it does not pertain directly to his theme, the national misfortune. He returns to it in the seventh book of the *Vox Clamantis* and in the *Confessio*; see below, 145–46, 148, 154–55.

luck, as long as the hand of the Most High is wont to sport with our affairs. (Trans. Stockton.)]

The focus is primarily concentrated on this world, even with the very strong emphasis upon human free will and self-determination.[24] The *Mirour*, on the other hand, is permeated by the idea of the close tie between human existence in this world and in that to come, and in the end does not make manifest its kinship with confessional *speculum* literature. It sees its main concern as the adjustment of man's relationship to his creator and considers the betterment of the world a by-product:

Pour ce chascuns qui le mal fait
S'amende, et ce serra bien fait,
Car deux biens en puet rescevoir:
L'un est q'il puet de son bienfait
Le siècle, q'est sicomme desfait,
Refourmer tout a son voloir;
L'autre est que nous savons du voir,
Cil qui bien fait du ciel est hoir;
Dont m'est avis, puisq'ensi vait,
Qe l'omme ad propre le povoir
De l'un et l'autre siècle avoir;
Fols est s'il l'un ne l'autre en ait. Mirour 27205–27215

[For each one who does wrong
And makes amends, that will be well done,
For two good things he can receive:
The one is that by his good deed he can
Reform to his liking
The world, which is almost undone.
The other is that we know as truth
That he who does good is heaven's heir:
Therefore, I think since things are so,

---

[24] See 2.201–206:

Set fortuna tamen nichil est, neque sors, neque fatum,
Rebus in humanis nil quoque casus habet:
Set sibi quisque suam sortem facit, et sibi casum
Ut libet incurrit, et sibi facta creat;
Atque voluntatis mens libera quod facit actum
Pro variis meritis nomine sortis habet.

[But in spite of this, Fortune is nothing, and neither destiny nor fate nor chance has anything to do with human affairs. But each man fashions his own destiny and opposes chance as he pleases and creates his own fate. And indeed, a free mind considers what it voluntarily does for its own benefit as done in the name of fate. (Trans. Stockton.)]

That man has the power
In the one world and the other;
He is a fool who has neither the one nor the other.]

The close relationship of, but also the difference in rank between, the earthly and heavenly *siècles* appears even more clearly in another part of the *Mirour.*[25] Both aspects of human life are taken into account, although the focus is primarily on the world to come.

One may consider the *Mirour* unoriginal, pedantic, and tedious for long stretches, but it is all of a piece, a perfect whole. It shows man the vices and virtues in their *proprietates*, that he might choose correctly. It shows him the duality of his own nature in the antithesis of body and soul, will and reason, that he might know his place and his duty. Here man stands for the *genus humanum*, caught in the conflict between the forces of light and darkness.

This general section is followed by the application of concrete instances. Individual impressions of the different classes are presented in a *psychomachia* that reveals human deficiency all along the line. For the individual, the classes, the *genus humanum*, there is but one possibility: to follow the way of the prodigal son. Then from the restoration of his relationship with the Father follows reinstatement in that step of the cosmic hierarchy that God designed for man. The fatted calf was not the prodigal son's goal when he began his journey to his father from the *regio longinqua*, the place far from God: it was a sign of reconciliation. And thus the *Mirour* also assesses worldly prosperity.

---

[25] *Mirour* 27121–27129:

He, homme, molt es benuré,
Sur toutes bestes honeuré,
Que dieus t'ad fait lour capitain,
Et si bien fais ta dueté,
Apres la mort t'ad ottrié
Du ciel la joye plus haltain:
Du double bien tu es certain,
Si bien governes le mondain,
Le ciel avras enherité.

[Ah, man, you are most blessed,
Honored above all animals,
For God has made you their captain,
And if you do your duty well,
After death there will be bestowed on you
The highest joy of heaven:
You are certain of a double good:
If you govern well the earthly,
You will inherit heaven.]

In the *Vox Clamantis*, on the other hand, Gower begins with the decline of the times and searches for a remedy to a specific historical situation; he shows the prodigal son the fatted calf, which he can attain only through reconciliation with the heavenly father. The difficulty is that the author himself, approaching from the literature of edification, does not take the fatted calf altogether seriously and wants to lead the reader now to earthly prosperity, now to renunciation, a renunciation that regards the goods of this world in the same manner it does the misfortunes. Thus there result inconsistencies such as the juxtaposition at the beginning of Book II of the *vanitas* theme and the melancholy glorification of a golden national past. Similar contradictions occur elsewhere. At the same time, however, therein also lies the charm of the *Vox Clamantis*. It was comparatively simple in the fourteenth century to establish a complete theological/philosophical system that discussed the relations of man to his creator as an individual and as a genus, and that illustrated these relationships in its discussion. It was substantially more difficult, but also incomparably more attractive, to disclose this relationship and its consequences in a concrete historical situation; it was, as it were, the proof of the pudding. Gower attempted this task in vain to the end of his life. That does not mean that the task was incorrectly posed. It had to be put thus and not otherwise as long as it was held self-evident that the God of history was a living God, that the justice of history was a moral justice, and that the prosperity of the citizens, at which the state aims, lies in a moral mode of life.

We must return now to the seventh chapter of Book II. Just as in the preceding chapters *Fortuna*'s power over man was contested because his fate springs purely and simply from his moral behavior, so now she is doubted because of divine omnipotence. *Est deus omnipotens,* begins Chapter 7 (2.349–360). There follows a summary of the doctrine of the Trinity (2.361–378), a passage on Christ (2.379–436), another about belief and the thirst for knowledge (2.437–494), and a last about idolatry, the cult of the saints, and the adoration of the cross (2.495–580). These sections are often not uninteresting as cultural and religious history; yet one cannot escape the impression that Gower lost sight of his theme proper from time to time and inadvertently fell into the customary exposition of the *Credo* and the Decalogue. The intellectual connection is clearly that the true ruler of human destiny must be discussed after *Fortuna*'s false claims have been rejected.

With Chapter 11, Gower returns to his original concern and demonstrates that the creation allows *Fortuna* no scope. Because God has created all, all is directly dependent upon His will.[26] There is attached a short description of the Hexaemeron, half-biblical, half-Ovidian, which ends with this rather neo-Platonic distich:

[26] 2.581–620.

Ars operi dictat formas, opifexque figurat,
Artificis sequitur fabrica tota manum. 2.621–622

[The Maker's skill lent form to the work and He fashioned it. The whole framework resulted from the Author's hand. (Trans. Stockton.)]

With that *Fortuna* can be abandoned and the way is clear for a critique of man, who bears unlimited responsibility for his fate:

Est nichil infelix, nichil aut de sorte beatum,
Immo viri meritis dat sua dona deus.
Quicquid adest igitur, sapiens qui scripta revolvit
Dicet fortunam non habuisse ream:
Hoc fateor vere, quicquid contingit in orbe,
Nos sumus in causa, sint bona sive mala. 2.625–630

[Nothing is fortunate or unfortunate because of fate; rather, God bestows his gifts according to man's deserts. The wise man who ponders the scriptures will therefore say that, whatever happens, he does not hold Fortune responsible. I truly acknowledge that whatever happens in the world, whether it be good or evil, we ourselves are the cause of it. (Trans. Stockton.)]

If one skips the class critique of Books III-VI, the Mirror for a Prince of Book VI, the discussion of the cardinal vices *luxuria* and *avaricia* and the historical/philosophical essay concerning Nebuchadnezzar's dream at the beginning of Book VII, one returns with Book VII, Chapter 4 to the theme of Book II, the question of who is to blame for the present *miseria humanae condicionis*. The only difference lies in the terminology. Just as popular opinion blamed *Fortuna* in Book II, so now it accuses Lady World (*Mundus*):

"*O mundus, mundus,*" *dicunt,* "*O ve tibi, mundus,*
Qui magis atque magis deteriora paris!" 7.361–362

["O world, world," people say. "O woe unto you, world, you who spawn baser and baser things!" (Trans. Stockton.)]

And again the author sees himself obligated to investigate the nature of this supposed force:

Quid sibi sit mundus igitur, que forma vel eius,
Que vel condicio, singula scire volo. 7.363–364

[I therefore wish to know everything—what the world is in itself, or what the essential nature is, or what its condition. (Trans. Stockton.)]

Can Book VII be nothing more than a repetition of Book II with different terminology? Or does Gower borrow generously from his own *Mirour*? In the *Mirour*, *Fortuna* plays a subordinate role: *Siècle*, the equivalent of *Mundus*, is allegedly to blame for the ruin of man.[27] However, the *Siècle* passages of the *Mirour*, according to their form (a predilection for *increpatio*) and content, are more like the *Fortuna* than the *Mundus* sections of the *Vox Clamantis*. Are we therefore to conclude that in the *Vox Clamantis* Gower allowed for reasons of symmetry a double appearance, with slightly altered name, of that power to which man generally attributed the responsibility for all hardship and which he himself had introduced in the *Mirour* under the name *Siècle?* Or did he divide it into two aspects, which he examined as *Fortuna* in the introduction and as *Mundus* in the conclusion? One would think that the elimination of *Fortuna* and the concomitant demonstration of man's responsibility for his fate had once and for all cleared the way for Gower's class critique. But that is obviously not so. The question of responsibility is probed once more, as if Book II had never been written. Men wish to hold *Mundus* responsible.[28] Why?

To anticipate somewhat, the result of the investigation is the acquittal of World. Just as it was demonstrated in Book II that the nature of fate depends on the moral conduct of man,[29] so it is now shown that the nature of the world is dependent upon the moral nature of man.[30] The posing of the same question with

[27] The word "world" originally had a temporal character and served as a translation of *mundus* as well as *saeculum*; in this second sense it is still contained today in the liturgy: "world without end"—*in saeculum saeculorum*. An exchange of the terms was thus possible.

[28] A charming illustration of Gower's lines occurs in Bromyard, *s.v. tribulatio*. He speaks of how David ended the tribulations of his people by admitting his guilt (1 Kings 24), while today each pushes guilt off upon the other: *Sed heu in modernis tribulationibus omnino contrarium est, quia illi qui sunt causa tribulationis peccata propria non confitentur nec facta iudicant nec sibi ipsis cum David tribulationis causam imponunt sed aliis . . . Adam culpam imponit Evae et Eva Adae ad excusandas excusationes in peccatis, quod neuter sine culpa est . . . Si in aliquo recognoscant tales tribulationes propter peccata incidere, dicunt: mundus est malus et falsus vel illi sunt tales; mundum et alios accusant et aliena confitentur delicta.* [But, alas, it is altogether opposite in today's tribulations, because those who are the cause of the tribulations do not confess their own sins nor judge their deeds, nor do they with David place the cause upon themselves for tribulations, but instead upon others . . . Adam places the blame on Eve and Eve on Adam in seeking excuses in their sins, because neither is without blame . . . If they should recognize in someone that such tribulations occur on account of sin, they say: "the world is evil and false, and there are such people"; they accuse the world and others and they disclose another's faults.]

[29] *Debet enim semper sors esse pedisseca mentis* [For fate ought always to be the handmaiden of the mind (Trans. Stockton)] (2.207).

[30] See 7.646–660:

Est homo qui mundus de iure suo sibi mundum

the same conclusion twice within the same work is suspicious, especially when to all intents and purposes the question occurs the second time *post festum*. A class critique of the *VC*'s sort presupposes man's responsibility; it must therefore be discussed in the introduction, not in a postscript. And thus we come again to the problem of the genesis of the work. Before we take this up for the last time, however, we will occupy ourselves with the content of the seventh book.

The fifth chapter contains a long and penetrating discussion of the transitoriness of all earthly things. It does not concern itself with *mutatio rerum* in that narrow, sentimentally-colored sense of a depraved present contrasted to the good old days, but with a fundamental cosmic principle that is binding on man as well as the entire creation. The insight in this principle leads to two results: a depreciation of earthly existence and a query about the originator of such changes.

The individual themes that Gower employs here are traditional; however, they are presented with great urgency and genuine concern. It is hardly worthwhile in every instance to ask about the *topoi* and their origin. Without effort one can hear Horace, Ovid, Seneca, and Boethius; one could with even greater justification point to the Bible and the church fathers. However, what appears important to me is not so much the fact that Gower here, as elsewhere, employs ready-made forms of expression and commonplace lines of thought, but the in-

---

Subdit, et in melius dirigit inde status:
Si tamen inmundus est, que sunt singula mundi
Ledit, et in peius omne refundit opus:
Ut vult ipse suum proprio regit ordine mundum.
Si bonus ipse, bonum, si malus ipse, malum.
Qui minor est mundus, fert mundo maxima dampna,
Ex inmundiciis si cadat ipse reus:
Qui minor est mundus, si non inmunda recidat,
Cuncta suo mundi crimine lesa gravat:
Qui minor est mundus homo, si colat omnipotentem,
Rebus in humanis singula munda parit:
Qui minor est mundus, si iura dei meditetur,
Grande sibi regnum possidet ipse poli.

[The man who is pure in his own right subjects the world to himself, and accordingly guides its circumstances for the better. If he is impure, however, he is injurious to everything which pertains to the world, and redirects its whole fabric for the worse. He rules his world by his own command as he wishes: if he is good, it is good; if he is evil, it is evil. One who is a microcosm brings the greatest misfortunes upon the world, if he falls because guilty of impurities. If one who is a microcosm does not check his impurities, he weighs heavily upon everything in the world, which is impaired by his wickedness. {But} if one who is a microcosm worships the Omnipotent, he is the source of everything pure in human affairs. If one who is a microcosm meditates upon the laws of God, he will possess the great kingdom of heaven for himself. (Trans. Stockton.)]

tensity with which he expresses the perplexed awareness that everything slips away from man, that nothing truly belongs to him. It is familiar as dogma to the Christian from youth on. Yet the dogma, or the fact, can be considered from two sides. It can increase gratitude to God, the giver of all gifts, or it can produce the bitterness of material and spiritual poverty. It is this second aspect, in which man perceives himself as deprived, not divinely bestowed, which Gower works out with full force. He is very deeply affected by it and repeats the theme over and over in different variations. In Chapter 5 he analyzes it in component images: the changing of the times, the ages of man, the transitoriness of spiritual and material possessions, the transfiguration of the earth, dread. Everything is not only in flux, but drives toward destruction:

> *Discite quam prope sit et quam vicina ruina,*
> *Talis enim nullum que relevamen habet:*
> *Discite quam nichil est quicquid peritura voluptas*
> *Possidet et false vendicat esse suum.* 7.371–374

> [Learn how close and near destruction is, such destruction, indeed, as has no remedy. Learn that whatever a fleeting pleasure embraces and falsely claims to be its own, it is as nothing. (Trans. Stockton.)]

The two forces that govern the life of man are sorrow and dread, *dolor* and *metus.*[31] For Gower they are one and the same: *metus* governs the future, *dolor* the present. Sorrow is the reaction to present hardship, dread the reaction to present prosperity, behind which lurk transitoriness and imminent destruction. Thus fortune and misfortune alike are cause for sorrow. Gower parades an entire series of material and spiritual goods before the eyes of the reader, only to belittle and dismiss them again at once with the refrain *hinc doleas*:

> *Si te nobilium provexit sanguis avorum,*
> *Hinc est quod doleas, degenerare potes.* 7.431–432

> [If the blood of noble ancestors has exalted you, you should therefore lament the fact that you can degenerate.]

> *Si tibi persuadet uxorem fama pudicam,*
> *Hinc eciam doleas, fallere queque solet.* 7.435–436

[31] See 7.497–498:
Quo se vertit homo, dolor aut metus incutit ipsum;
Excipitur nullus qui sit in orbe gradus.
[Wherever a man turns, grief or fear strikes him; no rank on earth is exempt. (Trans. Stockton.)]

[If fame persuades you that your wife is chaste, you should also lament accordingly that every woman is accustomed to deceive.]

Si tibi perspicue pollet sapiencia mentis,
Ut merito doleas, in Salomone vide.
Si facies nivea rubicundo spersa colore
Splendeat, hinc doleas, curva senecta venit. 7.449–452

[If you possess the forceful wisdom of a keen mind, look upon Solomon so that you may grieve for your worth. If your complexion, tinged with a rosy hue, gleams white as snow, you should accordingly grieve that crooked old age is approaching. (Trans. Stockton.)]

Thus all the world's offerings are vanities, tarnished by *dolor* and *metus*:

Sic inmunda suis de fraudibus omnia mundus
Polluit, et nullo tempore munda facit:
Iste per antifrasim nomen sibi vendicat unum,
Quo nullo pacto participare potest. 7.505–508

[Thus the world corrupts everything through its wrongdoings, and at no time makes everything pure. Through a contradiction it claims for itself the name {of being pure}, in which it by no means can share. (Trans. Stockton.)]

Thus the essence of the world is recognized and revealed, and Gower turns anew to the question of blame.

Book II discusses the problem of mankind's responsibility from the point of view of the possible infringement upon human free will by the external forces that were combined in the notion of *Fortuna*. Book VII investigates the origin, nature, and scope of this responsibility:

O si vera loquar, quicquid sibi mundus iniquum
Gestat, homo solus est magis inde reus. 7.509–510

[O, if I were to speak the truth, whatever wickedness the world contains, man alone is guilty of it. (Trans. Stockton.)]

Responsibility arises for man out of the role that God had originally intended for him when He created man in His own image.[32] The Genesis account expresses

---

[32] 7.513–520:

*"Nos faciamus," ait [*sc. *deus] "hominem, qui nos imitari*
Possit; et ut nobis serviat atque colat,
Inspiremus ei sensum racionis, amorem,
Vim discretivam, quid sit et unde venit:

this likeness by means of *imago* and *similitudo*,[33] which were distinguished in medieval theology in that *imago* was associated with knowledge, *similitudo* with love.[34] *Imago* and *similitudo* do not appear in Gower, although the two faculties of *cognitio* and *amor*, which are based upon them, and the duty of man to know and love God, do: *Unde creatorem noscat ametque suum* [Whence he may come to know and love his creator] (7.518). Man's *dignitas* consists in his likeness to God, which is also the reason why the creation is subject to him: *Mundus eum sequitur et famulatur ei* [The world serves and waits upon him] (7.520).

There follows an account of the creation of man,[35] the climax of which is the moment when the newest and noblest part of creation awakens wondering to a consciousness of himself. The section is unusually good and impressively shaped. Here Gower, who in this part of his work usually employed the artistic only as a means to enliven the purely didactic content a little and to preserve the reader from monotony, knew how to describe convincingly something of the first man's wonder in the beginning of the world.

Stat formatus homo, miratur seque suosque
Gestus, et nescit quid sit et ad quid homo:
Corporis officium miratur, membra moveri,
Artificesque manus articulosque pedum.
Artus distendit, dissolvit brachia, palmis
Corporis attractat singula membra sui:
In se quid cernit sese miratur, et ipsam
Quam gerit effigiem non videt esse suam:

Inspiremus ei factoris cognicionem,
Unde creatorem noscat ametque suum,
Quis suus est auctor, quis ei dedit esse vel unde:
Mundus eum sequitur et famulatur ei.

[Let us make man, who can be like us. And in order that he may serve and worship us, let us breathe into him the sense of reason, love, the power to distinguish what he is and whence he is come. Let us breathe into him the knowledge of his maker, whence he may come to know and love his creator, and may come to know Who his author is, Who gave him essence, or for what reason the world serves and waits upon him. (Trans. Stockton.)]

33 Genesis 1:26: *Et ait: Faciamus hominem ad imaginem et similitudinem nostrum* [And he said: Let us make man to our image and likeness].

34 Hugh of St. Victor summarizes the evidence quite concisely: *Factus est homo ad imaginem et similitudinem Dei, quia in anima . . . fuit imago et similitudo Dei. Imago secundum rationem, similitudo secundum dilectionem; imago secundum cognitionem veritatis, similitudo secundum amorem virtutis.* [Man was made to the image and likeness of God since in his soul . . . he was the image and likeness of God. Image with respect to reason, likeness with respect to love; image with respect to the recognition of the truth, likeness with respect to love of virtue.] *De Sacramentis Christianae Fidei, PL* 76:264.

35 7.525–566.

Miratur faciem terre variasque figuras,
Et quia non novit nomina, nescit eas.
Erexit vultus, os sublimavit in altum,
Se rapit ad superos, spiritus unde fuit:
Miratur celi speciem formamque rotundam,
Sidereos motus stelliferasque domos:
Stat novus attonitus hospes secumque revolvit,
Quid sibi que cernit corpora tanta velint.
Noticiamque tamen illi natura ministrat;
Quod sit homo, quod sunt ista creata videt:
Quod sit ad humanos usus hic conditus orbis,
Quod sit ei proprius mundus, et ipse dei.
Ardet in auctoris illius sensus amorem,
Iamque recognovit quid sit amare deum. 7.545–566

[Man stands created and marvels at himself and his movements, and does not know what he is and for what purpose he exists. He marvels at the role of his body, that his limbs have motion, at the skills of his hand, and at the joints of his feet. He stretches his limbs, relaxes his arms, and touches every limb of his body with his hands. He marvels at whatever he beholds in himself, yet he does not see that the likeness which he bears is his very own. He marvels at the face of the earth and at the various shapes, and does not recognize them, since he does not know their names. He lifts his face, he raises his voice to the heights, he transports himself to the heavenly hosts, whence his spirit came. He marvels at the beauty and rounded shape of the sky, at the sidereal movements and the starry mansions. His new friend stands astonished, and ponders with him what the many [heavenly] bodies he observes may intend for them. Nature, however, serves notice to him that he is man, that these are created things which he sees, that this earth is established for human use, that the world belongs to him and to God. His feelings flame into love for the author of it, and he now has recognized what it is to love God. (Trans. Stockton.)]

His astonishment proceeds from the things nearest at hand, his own body and its functions, and forges ahead in a wider and wider circle—in an astonished and incessant expansion of the horizon. The gaze of man, awakened from the sleep of creation, passes from his own person to the yet virgin, yet unnamed earth,[36]

[36] One is reminded slightly of the old magical theory about language, according to which the bestowing of a name amounts to acquisition of the object named, in 553–554 and its complement in the following chapter:

Te caput esse dedit rerum, rebusque locatis
Nomina te cunctis queque vocare dedit [sc. *deus*]. 7.605–606

[The author of things caused you to exist, and once things were set in order, He caused you to summon up names for everything. (Trans. Stockton.)]

and finally to heaven. The three stages of the perceptual occupancy are indicated each time by an expression of astonishment or bewilderment (7.545–546; 551–552; 554; 559–560). The underlying notions are *mirari* (545, 547, 551, 557) and *nescire* (546, 554), which are varied and subsumed in the last line (559): *Stat novus attonitus hospes secumque revolvit* [His new friend stands astonished and ponders with him].

The conclusion is at the same time a new beginning, marked by the anaphora *stat novus . . .* (corresponding to *stat formatus homo*, 545). After man has assimilated the three domains of the universe and passed from admiration to bewildered questions about their meaning, he has progressed far enough that Nature can help him along to understanding. Nature, that is, the innate *ratio* of man, is sufficient in this instance.[37] Then, from an understanding of the creation and his own creatureliness, springs man's love of the creator. Again the development is in three stages: *admiratio—cognitio—amor*, forming an intentional crescendo that ends in the distich:

> *Ardet in auctoris illius sensus amorem,*
> *Iamque recognovit quid sit amare deum.* 7.565–566
>
> [His feelings flame into love for the author of it, and he now has recognized what it is to love God. (Trans. Stockton.)]

The argument is traditional.[38] Gower's achievement is that he shapes a personal experience of the first human out of a doctrinaire abstraction.

The notion was readily employed in the exegesis of Genesis 2:20–21; see Hugh of St. Victor: *Nam idcirco ipse creator non a se . . . singulis quibusque animalibus, sed ab homine nomina formari voluit, ut manifeste ostenderet quod singulorum naturam et usum et officia ex insita sibi ratione homo agnovit. Quae enim propter illum creata erant, ab illo regenda et disponenda erant, et idcirco horum omnium Deus illi scientiam tribuit et providentiam reliquit.* [For on that account the Creator Himself wished the names for each and every living thing to be formed not by Himself but by man, so that He might clearly show that man perceived by the reason implanted in him the nature and use and office of each one. For those things were created on account of him, were meant to be governed and administered by him, and for that reason God granted him the knowledge of them all and bequeathed their providence.] *De Sacramentis Christianae Fidei, PL* 76:271.

[37] See lines 129–132 of "Merci Passeth Alle Thing," a poem from the Vernon MS. (Furnivall and Horstmann, *The Minor Poems of the Vernon Manuscript*):

> And whonne we breken Godes heste,
> Ajeynes kuynde we ben un-trewe:
> Ffor kuynde wolde that we him knewe
> And dradde him most in ure doing.

[38] See, for example, a work formerly attributed to Vincent of Beauvais, *Speculum Morale,* 1.1.10 on the question of whether knowledge is the prerequisite to love: Pseudo-Vincent of Beauvais, *Speculum Maius* (Douai, 1624), vol. 4.

The next (seventh) chapter (7.567–636) occupies itself with the relation of man to the world, that is, it pursues the theme of man's *dignitas* from its creation to its consequences. The entire creation is subject to him and stands at his service so that he for his part may serve his creator. This mastery, naturally, is meant only for man as God conceived him, for prelapsarian man. Accordingly, the chapter is formally addressed to Adam and Eve, beginning with an apostrophe:

> *Dic, Adam, dic, Eva parens, dic unus et alter,*
> *Dic tibi si desit gracia plena dei.* 7.567–568

> [Tell me, Adam, tell me, Mother Eve, tell me both one and the other, tell me if you lack God's abounding grace. (Trans. Stockton.)]

The contents do not completely suit the form, since the last section (619–636) ranges in time far beyond the situation in Paradise and speaks of the Fall and of the incarnation of Christ. Technically, this conclusion is unquestionably a part of the theme, since Christ's labor of redemption represents the last chapter in the history of mankind's creation *ad imaginem et similitudinem dei.* After man's similarity to God was reduced by the Fall to an indissoluble natural likeness—while the supernatural likeness was lost—the creation of a new man in Christ was necessary in order to complete the original divine programme:[39]

> *Set pietate prius qui condidit omnia solus,*
> *Ille reformavit et reparavit opus.* 7.629–630

> [But He who single-handed founded all things through His goodness restored and amended His work. (Trans. Stockton.)]

Thence follows a new and greater duty of love and obedience upon which the happiness of man is based. The conclusion of the seventh chapter is a repetition and intensification of the conclusion of Chapter 6.

The eighth chapter introduces a new concept into the argument, that of man as a microcosm. Gower is hardly affected by the complicated development of the idea of the microcosm in scholastic thought.[40] Of the various possibilities according to which man can be understood as a microcosm, he uses only the most familiar. The one, of which he made abundant use in the *Mirour*,[41] derives from the doctrine of the elements. The other, widespread, he got from Gregory, according to the evidence of the *Confessio Amantis*.[42] It is based on the correlation of man's existence with that of every single member of the hierarchy of creation, and

39 See Col. 3:10; 2 Peter 1:4; and esp. Rom. 8:29 and 2 Cor. 3:18.
40 See L. S. B. MacCoull, "Neoplatonism," *ODMA* 3:1200–1.
41 See *Mirour* 26617.
42 *Confessio Amantis*, Prol.945.

occurs in the *Mirour*, in the *Vox Clamantis*, and in the *Confessio*. According to it, man shares the faculty of cognition with the angel, the five senses with the beast, growth with the plant, and being with the stone.[43] Thus he stands, in being and essence, in an indissoluble connection with the entire cosmos. If man is corrupt, he infects, with the inevitability of a natural law, the whole creation:

> *Si tamen inmundus est, que sunt singula mundi*
> *Ledit, et in peius omne refundit opus.* 7.649–650
>
> [If he is impure, however, he is injurious to everything which pertains to the world, and redirects the whole fabric for the world. (Trans. Stockton.)]
>
> *Qui minor est mundus, fert mundo maxima dampna,*
> *Ex inmundiciis si cadat ipse reus:*
> *Qui minor est mundus, si non inmunda recidat,*
> *Cuncta suo mundi crimine lesa gravat.* 7.653–656
>
> [One who is a microcosm brings the greatest misfortune upon the world, if he falls because guilty of impurities. If one who is a microcosm does not check his impurities, he weighs heavily upon everything in the world, which is impaired by his wickedness. (Trans. Stockton.)]

The same thought occurs in the Prologue of the *Confessio Amantis* (957–958):

> And whan this litel world mistorneth,
> The grete world al overtorneth.

Here the nature of the effect of human sin upon the entire creation is described more minutely than in the *Vox Clamantis*:

> For ferst unto the mannes heste
> Was every creature ordeined,
> Bot afterward it was restreigned:
> Whan that he fell, thei fellen eke,
> Whan he wax sek, thei woxen seke;
> For as the man hath passioun
> Of seknesse, in comparisoun
> So soffren othre creatures. *Confessio,* Prol.910–919

In these verses Gower understands the influence of human corruption on the condition of the world as a disease that spreads from man to creature in rather

[43] See *Vox Clamantis* 7.637–644.

the same manner as the fall of Adam contaminated the entire human race,[44] or as the lapses of a ruler confound an entire people.[45] Besides the involvement of the creatures, however, there is something like an active revolt of creation against man when he rebels against his creator. This is caused with reference to the duty of obedience by the parallelism of the equation: creature:man::man:God. The conception is so familiar that Gower only hints at it in the *Vox Clamantis*: *Celum deiecit set et odit terra superbum* [Heaven cast down the proud man and earth despises him] (7.621). He works it out more precisely in the *Confessio:*

> The Lond, the See, the firmament,
> Thei axen alle jugement
> Ayein the man and make him were:
> Therewhile himself stand out of herre,
> The remenant wol noght acorde. Prol.959–963

The idea is important in two ways. It is characteristic of the voluntaristic conception of nature, and it reaches beyond the immediate issue into the realm of politics. Naturally there can be no question of its originality.[46] However, it is good to

---

44 Bromyard, *Summa Praedicantium, s.v. homo*, may again serve as an illustration: *In natura . . . aptum est, quod moriente corde, a quo est omnium membrorum vitale principium, moriuntur et membra, sicut etiam venenata . . . sic per unius delictum, immo peccatum, et omnes homines in condemnationem, et per inobedientiam unius hominis peccatores constituti multi.* [In nature . . . it is proper that when the heart dies, from which is the vital beginning of all the members, the members too die, as if likewise poisoned . . . in this way through the fault, rather the sin, of the one, all men {are}also under sentence of death, and through the disobedience of the one man, many sinners {are} created.]

45 Bromyard, *Summa Praedicantium, s.v. regimen: Quorum* [sc. *male regentium*] *error licet in proprium periculum redundet eternum, tamen interim in damnum redundat subditorum . . . Est enim in talibus respectu ad subditos . . . sicut de stomacho respectu ad membra, et sicut de sole in medio planetarum, quorum si stomachus et cor bene disponantur, membra sunt sana. Sed ubi hec male disponuntur et ubi sol ecclipsatur, necesse est alia membra esse indisposita et alias stellas ecclipsari.* [Granted that their {*sc.* those ruling badly} error should redound to their own eternal danger, nevertheless, in the meantime it redounds to the harm of the subjects . . . For it is in such things with respect to subjects just as concerning the stomach with respect to the members and just as concerning the sun in the midst of the planets; of these if the stomach and heart are well-disposed, the members are healthy. But when these are badly indisposed, and when the sun is eclipsed, it is necessary that the other members are indisposed and the other stars eclipsed.] Gower designates the *rex iustus* the *salus* of his subjects.

46 See by way of example the powerful passages in the *Sermo de Miseria Humana* ascribed to Bernard of Clairvaux: *O homo! . . . Omnia propter te fecit Deus; et tu propter omnia relinquis eum. Propter omnia quae occurrunt tibi, dimittis Deum; et idcirco omnia dimittunt te. Propter creaturas relinquis Creatorem; et ideo contra te insurgent omnes creaturae. Quia offendendo Creatorem offendisti omnem creaturam: ideo creaturae quae factae sunt in minis-*

make clear again with such an opportunity that not only the historical but also the natural event was clearly determined ethically for the average man of the fourteenth century.

The Old Testament had presented the history of the chosen people as a continual manifestation of God. Augustine and Orosius had based the Christian view of history on the same principle. It is not poetry, but an interpretation of history when in the *Visio* Gower describes the events of 1381 in apocalyptic form. Such interpretation does not attempt to inquire into events as they have actually taken place, but to illuminate the causes that have motivated God's will to such a manifestation and to recognize the means that lead to the mitigation of divine wrath. The two factors that determine the course of history are the will of God and the moral behavior of man. The course of natural events depends on the same factors. Thus the fate of man and the world lies in man's own hands. His *dignitas* surpasses that of all other creatures. What task arises for him out of this majesty?

> *Convenit ergo satis, humili quod corde rependat*
> *Digna creatori dona creatus homo:*
> *Restat ut ipse sui factoris querat amorem,*
> *Restat ut ipse sciat quid sit et unde venit.* 7.661–664
>
> [Therefore, it is most fitting that man born of the creator return Him worthy gifts with humble heart. It remains for him to seek the love of his maker: it remains for him to know what he is and whence he came. (Trans. Stockton.)]
>
> *Noscere te studeas et amare deum, duo namque*
> *Hec sunt, que tibi, rex, scire necesse iubet.*
> *Hec est condicio sub qua tibi contulit esse*
> *Vivendique modum conditor ipse tuus.* 6.1035–1038
>
> [You should strive to know yourself and to love God, for these are the two things, O king, which He decrees indispensable for you to know. This is the condition under which your Maker has conferred existence and your way of life upon you. (Trans. Stockton.)]

We touched earlier on the problem of self-knowledge: now we must go into it in greater detail. It is the central problem of Gower's three major works and it, more

---

terium et utilitatem tuam, convertentur in vindictam et poenam tuam. [O man! . . . God made everything because of you and you because of everything abandon him. Because of all the things which come to you, you renounce God; and therefore all things renounce you. Because of the creation you abandon the Creator, and therefore all the creation rebels against you. Because in offending the Creator you have offended the entire creation; therefore the creatures that were made to your service and utility have turned into your rod and punishment.] *PL* 184:1111.

than anything else, unites the *Mirour*, *VC*, and *Confessio*. The two passages cited derive from the seventh book and from the Mirror for a Prince. Self-knowledge and love of God are accordingly the two basic demands that God makes of mankind as well as of the prince. In the first quotation they are termed *dona* of man's creaturely gratitude, in the second a vital law of human existence. Lines 7.661–664 remind one slightly of a passage from Bernard of Clairvaux, knowledge of which Gower betrays in the second book of the *Vox Clamantis*.[47] Bernard's concern, however, is only with the obligation of grateful love. How the apparently heterogeneous pair come about in Gower requires investigation.

That self-knowledge is not an end in itself for a medieval author is obvious. The two cited quotations classify it in the broader context of the relationships between man and God. Yet self-knowledge has several functions. Because it is a part of human knowledge, one must first ask about the purpose of knowledge generally. In the medieval school system the student learned to enumerate four or five objectives, of varying ethical value, for the sake of which man acquires knowledge. In a notebook from the school of Gilbert of Porrée, the anonymous *Sententiae Divinitatis*, they are stated in the following manner:

> . . . *Quidam enim sunt, qui ad hoc legunt et discunt, ut sciant, quod curiositas est. Alii, ut sciantur, quod vanitas est. Alii, ut vendant, quod simoniaca pravitas est. Alii, ut aedificant, quod caritas, alii, ut aedificentur, quod prudens humilitas est.*[48]
>
> [For there are some who read and learn to the end that they might know; that is curiosity. Others, that they might be known; that is vanity. Others,

---

[47] *Quid rependam domino pro omnibus his non habeo?* (cf. Psalm 115:12 Vulg.) *Nam quicquid sum, erit sicut stella ad solem, stilla ad flumen, pulvis ad montem; quid ergo retribuam domino pro omnibus que retribuit mihi* (=Ps. 115:12) *nisi ut ipsum diligam?* [What should I return to the Lord for all those things I do not have? For whatever I am, it will be just as a star to the sun, a drop to the river, a mote of dust to a mountain; what therefore should I recompense the Lord for all the things which he has given me but that I should love him?] (Bernard of Clairvaux, *Sermo* 22.6, *PL* 183.598B [reading *gutta* for *stilla*]). I have taken this from Jacobus de Gruytrode, *Lavacrum Conscientie Omnibus Sacerdotibus Summe Utile ac Necessarium* (Cologne: Quentell, 1501), fol. 44r. See Gower, *VC*, 2.475–478:

> *Una quid ad solem scintilla valet, vel ad equor*
> *Gutta, vel ad celum quid cinis esse potest?*
> *Vult tamen a modicis inmensus, summus ab ymis,*
> *Vult deus a nobis mentis amore coli.*
>
> [What does one spark avail the sun, or one drop the sea, or what can our ashes be worth to heaven? Nevertheless, God wishes to be worshipped by us with a loving spirit, the Infinite wishes to be worshipped by us insignificant ones, the Most High by the lowest. (Trans. Stockton.)]

[48] Ed. B. Geyer, "Die *Sententiae Divinitatis*" (Ph. D. diss., Münster, 1907), 8.

> that they might sell {i.e., knowledge}; that is simoniacal wickedness. Others, that they might edify; that is charity. Others that they might be edified; that is prudent humility.]

Knowledge as an end in itself, knowledge from ambition, and knowledge as a means of enrichment are rejected. Only two kinds of thirst for knowledge are morally justifiable: that which leads to the instruction of others as a form of brotherly love, and that which leads to self-knowledge as a way to humility.[49]

Bernard of Clairvaux grants first place to self-knowledge, first because it constitutes the prerequisite for all further knowledge, above all, however, because it is the most useful form of knowledge.[50] Self-knowledge leads to *humilitas*, to *humiliatio*, and to *dolor*, a progression which is often verified in medieval

[49] Similar enumerations occur in Bernard of Clairvaux, *Sermo XXXVI in Canticum Canticorum*, *PL* 183:968; John of Salisbury, *Policraticus*, VIII. 15; Hugh of St. Victor, *Eruditione Didascaliae*, *PL* 176:798; Vincent of Beauvais, *De Eruditione Regalium Filiorum*, 13.

[50] *Volo proinde animam primo omnium scire se ipsam, quod id postulet ratio et utilitatis et ordinis. Et ordinis quidem, quoniam quod nos sumus primum est nobis; utilitatis vero, quia talis scientia non inflat, sed humiliat, et est quaedam praeparatio ad aedificandum. Nisi enim super humilitatis stabile fundamentum, spirituale aedificium stare minime potest. Porro ad se humiliandum nihil anima invenire vivacius seu accommodatius potest, quam si se in veritate invenerit . . . Convertetur. . . ad lacrimas, convertetur ad planctus et gemitus, convertetur ad Dominum, et in humilitate clamabit: Sana animam meam, quia peccavi tibi.* Ps. 40:5. [Hence I wish first of all to know the mind itself, because the reason both of utility and of order requires it. And of order indeed because what we are is foremost to us; of utility truly because such knowledge does not puff up but humbles and is a certain preparation for building. For a spiritual building is not at all able to stand unless upon a firm foundation of humility. Furthermore, the mind can find nothing more lasting or suitable to its humbling than if in fact it finds itself . . . Let him turn to tears, let him turn to laments and groans, let him turn to the Lord, and in humility he will shout, "Heal my soul, for I have sinned against Thee."] At the end of the sermon, Bernard establishes the connection between self-knowledge and the knowledge and thus the love of God: *Ego quamdiu in me respicio, in amaritudine moratur oculus meus. Si autem suspexero et levavero oculos ad divinae miserationis auxilium; temperabit mox amaram visionem mei visio laeta Dei . . . Tali itaque experimento et tali ordine salubriter innotescit Deus, cum prius se homo noverit in necessitate positum, et clamabit ad Dominum, et exaudiet eum, et dicet: Eruam te, et honorificabis me [Ps. 49:15]. Atque hoc modo erit gradus ad notitiam Dei cognitio tui.* [As long as I look into myself, my eye lingers in anguish. If, however, I look up and I raise my eyes to the aid of divine pity, the joyous vision of God will soon temper my bitter vision . . . And when thus by such a trial and in such a manner God becomes more salubriously known, then first man will know himself placed in distress and he will shout to the Lord and He will hear him and say, "I shall deliver thee and thou shalt glorify me" (Ps. 49:15). And in this way a knowledge of yourself will be a step to the knowledge of God.] *Sermo XXXVI in Cantica Canticorum*, *PL* 183:969–970.

texts with Ecclesiastes 1:18: *Qui addit scientiam, addit et dolorem* [He that addeth knowledge, addeth also labor]. And the value of this self-knowledge is that it impels man towards divine forgiveness, for *humiliatum cor et contritum non despicies* [a humbled and contrite heart, O God, thou wilt not despise] (Ps. 50:19). It is the most important step of the human soul along the path of redemption. It is so highly regarded for that reason that Augustine can say: *Summa ergo philosophia est seipsum cognoscere* [Therefore the highest philosophy is to know yourself].[51] Next to it all other knowledge is vain and transient.[52]

The best way to attain self-knowledge is to contemplate the impermanence of mankind:

> *Est tibi nil melius igitur, quam providus illam*
> *Prospicias mortem, que tibi finis erit.* 7.711–712
>
> [Therefore, there is nothing better for you than to provide for that death which will be your end. (Trans. Stockton.)]

For that reason Gower links the themes of self-knowledge and contemplation of death and discusses death and judgment for eleven chapters (9–19). What he had only briefly suggested in the Mirror for a Prince he here paints in broad and vivid strokes. Their portraits in death and decay are held up to the envious and wrathful man, to the miser, sluggard, glutton, and lecher. The sense of these detailed descriptions is the same as that stated in the portrayal of bodily decomposition in the *Myrour of Synners*:

> Bihold now brother, this is an horrible syht but it is a ful profitable myrour. Oo ful happy is he that besyly biholdith himself in this myrour. Ffor there is no crafte, medycyne ne techyng that so soone distroyeth vices and plaunteth vertues as doth inwardly byholdying thus of a mannys laste thinges.[53]

After death comes judgment, in the description of which Gower uses every stylistic means to engender solemnity. Then, with Chapter 20, we reach the point at which Bernard's *convertetur ad lacrimas, convertetur ad Dominum* [let him turn to tears, let him turn to the Lord] can be employed:

---

[51] Cited in Bromyard, *s.v. sapientia*. Cf. Augustine, *In Joan. Ev.* 98.2–3, *PL* 35:1881.

[52] See 7.699–704:

> *Quid penetrasse iuvat studiis archana Platonem,*
> *Natureque suos composuisse libros? Etc.*
>
> [What help was it for Plato to have penetrated mysteries through his studies, and to have compiled his books of natural philosophy? (Trans. Stockton.)]

[53] Oxford, Bodleian Library, MS. Laud 174, fol. 96v.

Non poterit melius hominis caro viva domari,
Quam quod mente gerat mortua qualis erit.
Fletibus assiduis, est dum data gracia flendi,
Penituisse iuvat estque salubre satis:
Nec deus ethereus hec crimina vendicat ulli,
Que confessa dolens non residiva facit. 7.1119–1124

[Man's living flesh cannot be better subdued than by the fact that he bear in mind what it will be when dead. It is helpful and quite beneficial to have repented with continual weeping, as long as opportunity for weeping is granted. God on high does not punish any man for those crimes which he does not repeat, once he has confessed them penitently. (Trans. Stockton.)]

One would expect that Chapter 24, which returns from the universal necessity for man to rue and repent to specifically English circumstances, would have been joined directly to this introduction of a new theme. However, Gower inserts here three chapters about the decay of the times as it is documented in the failure of all classes. The inspection seems inappropriate or superfluous after the reader has already worked through three extensive books of class critique. It could simply be repetition; however, there is another conceivable explanation to which we shall presently return.[54]

Chapter 24 begins with an acknowledgement of involvement in the national misfortune that is one of Gower's best passages:

Singula que dominus statuit sibi regna per orbem,
Que magis in Cristi nomine signa gerunt,
Diligo, set propriam super omnia diligo terram,
In qua principium duxit origo meum.
Quicquid agant alie terre, non subruor inde,
Dum tamen ipse foris sisto remotes eis;
Patria set iuvenem que me suscepit alumpnum,
Partibus in cuius semper adhero manens,
Hec si quid patitur, mea viscera compaciuntur,
Nec sine me dampna ferre valebit ea:
Eius in adversis de pondere sum quasi versus;
Si perstet, persto, si cadat illa, cado.
Que magis ergo gravant presenti tempore, saltem
Ut dicunt alii, scismata plango michi. 7.1289–1302

[I love all the kingdoms which the Lord has established for Himself throughout the world and which bear standards in Christ's name. But above all I love my own land, in which my family took its origin. Whatever other lands may do, I am not shaken by it, as long as I stand apart at a

[54] See below, 161–63.

distance from them. But if the native land which bore me as a young child, and within whose realms I always remain fixed—if she suffers anything, my innermost feelings suffer with her, and she shall not be able to suffer her misfortune apart from me. I am almost overwhelmed by the weight of her adversities. If she stands firm, I stand firm; if she falls, I fall. Therefore, I bewail the schisms which, at least so others say, are so oppressive at this present time. (Trans. Stockton.)][55]

In Book II Gower spoke, referring to the prosperous national past, of the special election of the English people.[56] His expression of patriotism here is entirely free from the notion of "God's own people"; on the contrary, the restrained passion of his love appears to increase under the threat of God's anger. As in Book II, the author again contrasts the golden past and the depraved present, which has corrupted even nature in the land (1417 and following). Gower had already explained earlier that nature withholds her services from the sinner, and thus nothing is more natural than that the fields bring forth thorns and thistles (cf. Genesis 3:18) and that the precious metals of the land be exhausted. The only way out of the present situation is sinful mankind's self-awakening and return to God:

Prospera qui veteris vult temporis esse renata,
Reddat et emendet facta priora nouis. 7.1417–1418

[Let the man who wishes the prosperity of old returned give up his former ways and repair them by his new ones. (Trans. Stockton.)]

Thus the book ends with a prayer for forgiveness, which with the restoration of the correct relationship between God and man will lead to a better future for the nation:

Nos, deus alme, tui servi, quamvis modo tardi,
Te, non fortunam, credimus esse deum:
Scimus te solum super omnes esse colendum;
Sic nostri solus tu miserere, deus! 7.1439–1442

[We, Thy servants, dear God, even though we are dilatory at present, believe that Thou, not Fortune, art God. We know that Thou alone art to be cherished above all, so Thou alone take pity on us, O God! (Trans. Stockton.)]

Finally, we have yet to clarify a few questions connected with the structure of the *VC*. They concern the two versions of the last chapter of the Mirror for a Prince,

[55] Cf. above, 58 n. 14.

[56] See 2.17.

the internal relationship of the *Fortuna* and *Mundus* themes, and the concise repetition of the class critique in Book VII.

We attempted to demonstrate in an earlier chapter that Gower had already conceived the plan of the *VC* before the Peasants' Revolt (1381) and most likely before the Great Schism (1378), and, be it in whole or in part, had already executed it. In doing so we depended chiefly on divergences in the manuscript tradition. Now the last chapter of the Mirror for a Prince (Book VI, Chapter 18) in the A-Text is in form essentially different from that in the B-Text.[57] The passage in question is the last part of the letter to the young king. The B-Text presents the greater part of the chapter in the objective form of the third person singular and, until line 1184, speaks simply of the *rex*. Richard II is first addressed personally in the last section,[58] in order to show him the alternatives with which he is confronted:

> *Hec tibi, rex, scribo pro tempore nunc que futuro;*
> *Semper in ambiguo sors variatur homo.* 6.1199–1200
>
> [I write these things, O king, for now and future times,
> On earth is ever doubtful destiny.]

The earlier tradition, which fashions the last chapter of the open letter into an epilogue, differs. It opens with an invocation to God in typical prayer style, a doxology in five relative clauses comprising four distiches (6.1159–1166). There follow benedictions, likewise in four distiches, two of which direct themselves to God, two to the young king (1167–1174). Now the direct address to the king begins and in eight fervid distiches the author expounds on his hopes for the ruler (1175–1190). The conclusion is again four distiches long. It deals with the relationship of author to poem to king:

> *Ac decus imperii, Rex, ista tui metra scripsi*
> *Servus ego Regni promptus honore tibi.*
> *Hec tibi que, pie Rex, humili de corde paravi,*
> *Scripta tue laudi suscipe dona dei:*
> *Non est ista mea tantum doctrina, sed eius*
> *Qui docet, et dociles solus ab ore creat.*
> *O iuvenile decus, laus Regia, flos puerorum,*
> *Ut valor est in te, sic tibi dico vale.* 6.1191–1198
>
> [To your rule's glory I wrote these meters, O king,
> Eager servant of the realm, to your praise.

[57] Two MSS., L and L2, have the two versions back to back.

[58] *O rex, ergo tui detergas crimina regni, etc.* (6.1185) [Therefore, O king, erase your kingdom's crimes, etc.]

Accept, O pious king, these written gifts of God
I, humble in heart, have made in your praise.
This doctrine is not mine but His[59] Who teaches and
Alone makes men with His words teachable.
O youthful virtue, royal honor, flower of youths,
As you are valorous, I bid farewell.]

Gower obviously devoted painstaking care to the epilogue of the A-Text. The proportionate relationship of units of verse and thought is well balanced: 4+4:8:4. The corresponding chapter of the B-Text, on the other hand, is neither balanced nor unified. The play of words on *valor* and *vale* in the last pentameter of the A-Text indicates the twofold character of the concluding *vale*. It comprises more than a simple farewell; it is at the same time a benediction. However, the element of closure is not diminished as a result. The poet presents his verse to the king and takes his leave. It is conventional to do both at the end of a work; midway in Book VI of the *Vox Clamantis*, however, it is extraordinary. Unless the open letter and dedication are fictions, Gower expects the king to seek out a treatise respectfully presented to him in the midst of a more than substantial work. There are two possible explanations for the epilogue of the A-Text. Either Gower had an older work, a *speculum principis* composed for Richard and presented to the king upon an earlier occasion—perhaps his accession—which he transferred without essential change to the sixth book of the *Vox Clamantis*, or the *VC* originally ended with the Mirror for a Prince.

That Gower, unlike Chaucer, courted the favor of the reigning monarch his whole life long is shown by the original dedication of the *Confessio* to Richard and of the *Balades* to Henry IV, by the poem on Henry IV's accession that borrows the *invocatio* from the epilogue of the Mirror for a Prince (A-Text), and by the importunately flattering conclusion of the *Cronica Tripertita*. Nothing can be said about the *Mirour* in this respect, since it lacks beginning and end. The idea of introducing himself to the new monarch with a Latin work may therefore have suggested itself to Gower toward the end of the 70s. It is quite conceivable that, considering the king's youth, Gower would pursue his didactic bent and at the same time think to fulfill a moral mission. Because it was an occasional poem, moreover, one can hardly blame him for seizing upon material that he had already treated in the *Mirour*. The choice of Latin as linguistic medium may have been determined by the specialness of the occasion. Political writings to princely addressees tended to be written in Latin. A *speculum principis* in the vernacular—be it Anglo-Norman, be it English—could easily have given rise to a suspicion that the addressee was illiterate, or stamped the contents as light reading. One may assume that Gower, in joining the Mirror for a Prince to a substantial class critique, departed from the class critique's usual arrangement (as discussed

[59] Cf. John 7:16.

in Chapter 4) in order that the open letter would appear as the end and climax of the work. He also distinguished it formally from the other sections by going from the markedly general treatment of the other classes to a personal address, from an objective form of report to a subjective form of epistle. The goal of the work was obviously to instruct the royal youth about the condition of the state in its class divisions and to explain to him the duties which devolved upon him out of the general situation and his own position. The *Fortuna* book may have been an accommodation, even though superficial, to courtly taste and the literary mode of the day. Gower packs into it as much as possible of the *siècle* argument of the *Mirour* that was so important to him. If the title *Vox Clamantis* already belonged to this original complex, it too could have been chosen with regard to Richard. For John the Baptist appears to have been something like the special patron saint of the king.[60] There is a poem from the year 1393 that celebrates the reconciliation of the king with the citizens of London. The author, John of Maidstone, describes processions, entertainments, and living pictures in honor of the king. Among other things had been erected a zoological garden, in the midst of which stood John the Baptist. And on this occasion it was said of the Baptist that Richard II venerated him especially ardently before all other saints.[61]

I am inclined to view as a later addition everything in the *Vox Clamantis* that follows the Mirror for a Prince. It must remain an open question whether this material constitutes a special composition, after the manner of *de contemptu mundi* literature, that Gower incorporated into the work when he added the

---

[60] Cf. D. Gordon et al., eds., *The Regal Image of Richard II and the Wilton Diptych* (Coventry: Harvey Miller, 1977), esp. S. Mitchell, "Richard II: Kingship and the Cult of Saints," 115–24, 119–22.

[61] *Astitit his medius sanctus Baptista Joannes,*
Indicat hic digito, agnus et ecce Dei!
Inspicit attente rex hunc, quia quem notat iste,
Illius ut meminit mitior inde fuit.
Nam quia devotus colit hunc constanter eidem
Prae reliquis sanctis porrigit ipse preces.
Hujus ad intuitum, si quid sibi manserat irae,
Extitit exstinctum protinus usque nihil.

[In the midst of these stands St. John the Baptist,
Points with a finger, "Behold the Lamb of God!" [John 1:29, 36]
The king views him attentively, since that one whom he notes
Was meeker then, as he remembers, than the Baptist.
Therefore devoted he worships him constantly and pours
Out prayers to him in preference to the rest of the saints.
At whose sight, if any anger had been left in him,
It became quenched immediately to nothing.]

John de Maidstone, "The Reconciliation of Richard II with the City of London," ed. Thomas Wright, *Political Poems and Songs*, 1:294.

Visio, or whether the rest of the sixth and the entire seventh book were written *ad hoc* when Gower felt, after the convulsion of 1381, the need to sound a last great warning cry to the educated classes of the nation. The short survey of the estates in the seventh book, which appears superfluous after the substantial class critique of Books III-VI, speaks for the first supposition. Also, the considerable overlappings of the *Fortuna* book and the *Mundus* argument are thus most easily comprehensible. For the second supposition can be advanced the close of the seventh book, which, however, could be a piece of touching up that was intended to fit the passage to the *Vox Clamantis*. Be that as it may, what is new and important in the work as it stands before us in the B-Text version is an alteration of the poem's character that results from the change of the addressee and of the contemporary situation. From a princely *vade mecum* it became a substantial work of edificational literature that differs from similar efforts only in that it undertakes to explain a concrete historical situation, the Peasants' Rebellion, in its metaphysical bases and earthly consequences.

The change-over from the original plan to the final form was facilitated because the Mirror for a Prince belongs by its nature to the realm of ethics rather than political theory, and itself has strong edificational inclinations. The profit that accrued to the *Vox Clamantis* from the expansion of 1381 is considerable. The trite subjects—*Fortuna*, class critique, *speculum principis*—receive new life from the thrust of events. The author's genuine concern gives his verses a restrained power in the newly added parts, and the homilist reveals himself not as the prophet of a cheap morality but as a man who shows his people, with the means at his disposal, a way out of the chaos of their time—to a moral regeneration without which a political regeneration is inconceivable.

Chapter Six

Gower's Narrative Technique

Gower's narrative ability manifests itself in a direct and taut style that typically establishes a striking tempo. Yet he avoids the bareness of excessive moral concern into which the exempla style frequently degenerates and at the same time a solemn pomposity and verbose transparency that Chaucer himself does not always escape. I will begin my illustration of the special characteristics of Gower's narrative technique with an example that does not put him in competition with Chaucer. It is the story of Acteon (Ovid's Actaeon) in the *Confessio Amantis*,[1] not one of Gower's best tales, hardly, indeed, one of his better. However, for that very reason it seems appropriate as an illustration of the strength of his technique and at the same time of its limitations and dangers. It has the advantage of being suitably brief, and it also prevents the reader from applying inappropriate criteria derived from a comparison with Chaucer. Finally, the tale stems from a Latin author whose own narrative art follows such totally different paths that one does not run the risk of investigating the characteristics of the model rather than the specifically Gowerian.

[1] *Confessio Amantis* 1.333–378. [Wickert's contribution to the study of Gower's narrative art is rare in its tight focus on Gower's characteristics as a storyteller apart from any argument for a given tale's thematic or dramatic positioning within the *Confessio Amantis* viewed as a whole. The closest studies to it, neither of which keeps its focus so exclusively on technique, are Derek Pearsall, "Gower's Narrative Art," *PMLA* 81:7 (1966): 475–84 and Arno Esch, "John Gowers Erzählkunst," in *Chaucer und seine Zeit: Symposion für Walter F. Schirmer*, ed. idem (Tübingen: University of Tübingen Press, 1968), 207–39; trans. Linda Barney Burke, "John Gower's Narrative Art," in *Gower's Confessio Amantis: A Critical Anthology*, ed. Peter Nicholson (Cambridge: D.S. Brewer, 1991), 81–108. The explosion of important work on the *Confessio Amantis* since Wickert wrote can hardly be accommodated in a footnote. The reader is urged to consult the chronological bibliography in Echard, *A Companion to Gower*, 251–73 and the online bibliography of the John Gower Society. (Trans.)]

The contentual relationship of Gower's story to Ovid's can be defined in a few words.[2] In Ovid the story requires 115 verses, in Gower 45. Gower therefore reduces the narrative to a scant third, if one considers the quantitative relationship of the Latin hexameter to the iambic tetrameter of the *Confessio*, a relationship which, of course, is in part further balanced by the greater syllabic conciseness of English. Yet only the description of the action is shortened, not the action itself, which is rendered *in toto*. A substantial economy is achieved in the character apparatus, which Gower reduces to the absolutely essential. That is apparent in both Acteon and Diana, the two chief figures. Ovid surrounds Acteon with a troop of hunters (3.144–154); Gower suppresses them. Ovid has Diana step into her bath surrounded by her nymphs, whose names and functions are individually introduced (3.165–172); Gower foregoes the names and disposes of the entire ceremony in one verse (1.365). A third reduction of character apparatus concerns the pack of hounds. Ovid allows it no fewer than twenty lines (3.206–225) and makes it the subject of a highly skilled parody of heroic-epic technique. The two champions are presented with monstrous solemnity, as if they were Homeric heroes on their way to battle:

> . . . *primumque Melampus*
> *Ichnobatesque sagax latratu signa dedere,*
> *Gnosius Ichnobates, Spartana gente Melampus.* 3.206–208

> [. . . and first come Melampus and keen-scented Ichnobates, baying loud on the trail—Ichnobates a Cretan dog, Melampus a Spartan.]

Signa dare, the epithet *sagax*, above all the solemn ethnic note, are in imitation of epic style. The names and characteristics of the rest of the pack are gathered in a kind of Homeric hero catalogue—extremely precious, well-nigh masterly. Gower has no use for such artistry and reduces hounds and hunters alike to a minimum. Names are, of course, not used.

So much for the simplification of character apparatus. It causes a more powerful concentration on the chief characters as well as on the action, but it would hardly be remarkable in itself if Gower had stopped with the quantitative change. He goes considerably further. Ovid's story is bipolar. The narrative begins with Acteon and the picture of the heated hunting company lying down to rest (143–154). There then follows in narrative succession what in reality is simultaneous: the figure of the goddess preparing herself for a bath (3.155–172). Each of these "scenes" is introduced by a description of locale: *Mons erat* . . . (3.143); *Vallis erat* . . . (3.155). The parallelism is manifestly conscious and intended, and any tran-

[2] Ovid, *Metamorphoses*, ed. Rudolf Merkel, 2nd ed. (Leipzig: Teubner, 1904), 3.138–252. [The English translations of Ovid are throughout those of Frank Justus Miller in the Loeb Classical Library (Cambridge, MA: Harvard University Press, 1916). Trans.]

sition is most painstakingly avoided. Thus the two main figures stand—each in his or her own space—separate before the eyes of the reader until fate sets them in motion towards each other in 3.174 and destiny runs its course. Ovid therefore has two carriers of the action, whom he introduces successively and independently of each other in order to have them then collide. He employs this scheme again after Acteon's metamorphosis, when he first presents the stag transformation with the corresponding explanation, then the pack of hounds, in order to loose the two finally upon each other and so arrive at the tragic finale.

Gower follows a fundamentally different method. He tells the story of Acteon, a man who, uncontrolled, allowed his gaze all too free a course. Gower's moral position is clear. Ovid had generously given full scope to *fatum*;[3] in his attitude of weighing and waiting he had interpreted the story as the fatal, but in the last analysis not culpable, collision between two elements that must lead to a tragic end. This is reflected in the construction of the narrative. Gower, because he weights Acteon morally, creates an essentially different structure for the story. For him Diana has no inherent right to exist; she only serves the purpose of making known Acteon's serious lack of discipline. Consequently, it is only natural that Gower does not proceed according to the Ovidian scheme, but regards the entire action from beginning to end from the same perspective. Like Ovid he begins with Acteon; however, there is no passage like that in Ovid at 3.155. Rather, Gower incorporates the *locus amoenus*, with which Ovid introduces the Diana episode, into the perspective of Acteon. Thus Ovid's objective description becomes something like Acteon's personal experience. The marks of this adaptation can be pursued into the syntactic construction, which also firmly retains Acteon as the grammatical subject:

On his hunting as he cam ride,
In a Forest al one he was:
He syh upon the grene gras
The faire freisshe floures springe,
He herde among the leves singe
The Throstle with the nyhtingale:
Thus er he wiste into a Dale
He cam, where was a litel plein
All round aboute wel besein
With buisshes grene and Cedres hyhe;
And ther withinne he caste his yhe. 1.350–360

[3] See 3.141–142:

At bene si quaeras, fortunae crimen in illo,
Non scelus invenies, quod enim scelus error habebat?

[But if you seek the truth, you will find the cause of this in fortune's fault and not in any crime of his. For what crime had mere mischance?]

And 3.176: . . . *sic illum fata ferebant* [for so fate would have it].

The landscape has no objective reality, occurring rather in the gaze of the main figure. Gower thus achieves three different effects: the description of scenery does not interrupt the action, it does not divert the reader, and it is itself incorporated into the action. In this way the *topos* of the *locus amoenus* is varied so that it supports a living function and no longer operates as a cliché. The landscape, personally experienced by Acteon, forms the natural transition to the meeting with the goddess.

What is important in this meeting is the fact that Acteon sees Diana nude. Ovid prepared the climax carefully—one could say shrewdly—leading up to it step by step. The goddess lays aside bow and quiver, steps out of her sandals, slips the robe from her shoulders. Ovid thus employs a kind of subtraction process that a modish public undoubtedly relished. At the last moment, with masterful piquancy, he does not reveal the vision of the unveiled goddess. The attendant nymphs notice Acteon and conceal with their own bodies the mistress, who in divine nobility towers over them by a head. The combination of lustfulness and hypocritical decency in Ovid is not to be equaled. How does Gower deal with the episode? He does two things. First, he follows the eyes of Acteon and does not reveal Diana to the reader until she appears in his field of vision:

> Amidd the plein he syh a welle,
> So fair ther myhte noman telle,
> In which Diana naked stod
> To bathe and pleie hire in the flod. 1.361–364

Thus the reader is not granted a furtive sneak preview. And the second difference, which results from the first, is that the youth's gaze and the goddess's complete nudity collide unexpectedly, without having been modified or weakened. The changes in the aesthetic and moral atmospheres are so tightly interwoven here that one can hardly treat them separately. The abruptness of the meeting is on no account attributable to primitiveness in Gower's style. Needless to say, one should not efface the difference in rank between the two storytellers, yet Ovid's subtle subtraction technique was not beyond Gower's stylistic capabilities. His description of the house of Morpheus in the "Tale of Ceyx and Alcyone" proves that.[4] There, in order to show that nothing diverts the senses and disturbs the sleeper, Gower evokes a series of optical and acoustical images only in order to eliminate them again immediately and achieve, through a process of subtraction, the sensation of complete lethargy:

> Ther is no fyr, ther is no sparke,
> Ther is no dore, which mai charke,
> Wherof an yhe scholde unschette,

[4] *Confessio Amantis* 4.2927–3123.

> So that inward ther is no lette,
> And forto speke of that withoute,
> Ther stand no gret Tree nyh aboute
> Wher on ther myhte crowe or pie
> Alihte, forto clepe or crie:
> Ther is no cok to crowe day,
> Ne beste non which noise may
> The hell . . . 4.2995–3005

The method is extremely effective and, as far as this story is concerned, Gower's own improvisation. Neither Ovid nor Chaucer chanced upon it, and it is only later, in Spenser, that one finds a similar approach.[5] It is not due to inability that Gower foregoes the use of this technique in the story of Acteon.

With that we come to the question of morality, an unpleasant question, for since Chaucer there has prevailed the notion of the "moral Gower."[6] The usual explanation holds that prudery prevented the "moralistic" author from following in Ovid's footsteps, and may add some general observations about the lateness of the Renaissance in England and about how Shakespeare's contemporaries were the first Englishmen to have eyes for the beauty of the human body. But did Gower really have moral scruples along these lines? One would suppose, then, that he would have taken offense not only at the piquancy of Ovid's description but at the story itself; if he needed an *exemplum* for unbridled visual curiosity, he could just as well have chosen the harmless tale of Lot's wife. Instead, he freely chose Acteon. And if he does not join in Ovid's sensual subtlety, yet he by no means veils the phenomenon of divine nudity. On the contrary, he calls attention to it twice in the course of a few verses,[7] while Ovid, significantly, employs the epithet *nudus* only for the nymphs. Obviously Gower thought it important that the unexpected encounter have a powerful, undiminished impact—on Acteon as well as on the reader. It attains this again through the most extreme stylistic economy and through the intentional concentration of events into Acteon's perspective. Acteon remains the subject in action and syntax, whereas in Ovid—who sees in the story only the fatal coincidence of unfortunate circumstances—he is condemned to passivity in syntax and action. Not for an instant does the Augustan author inquire into Acteon's reaction to the divine apparition, but abandons him to a paralysis that leaves him only when he becomes sentimentally and elegiacally conscious of his metamorphosis into a stag. Gower, on the other hand, sharply emphasizes the question of the decision with which the Diana experience confronts the young man, because that is the essential point for

[5] The cave or grotto of Morpheus appears in Ovid, *Met.* 2.592; in Chaucer, *The Book of the Duchess* 153–65; in Spenser, *The Faerie Queene* 1.1.39.

[6] Chaucer, *Troilus and Criseyde* 5.1856–1857: "O moral Gower, this book I directe / To the. . . ." See S. Echard, "Gower's Reputation," in *Companion*, ed. eadem, 1–22, 3–6.

[7] See 1.363 and 367.

the *Confessio*. Acteon's sin lies not in the encounter itself, but in his reaction to it. He remains—and not only grammatically—the carrier of the action even when he forgets to act at all:

> But he his yhe awey ne swerveth
> Fro hire, which was naked al. 1.366–367

The goddess' anger concerns this failure, not the accidental trespass on her forest privacy. In Ovid Acteon's metamorphosis is an act of divine self-defense; in Gower it is punishment for Acteon's lack of discretion. It is comparatively unimportant how he himself submits to this punishment, and therefore Gower tells the end of the story summarily, without any emotion. One almost receives the impression that his interest in Acteon flagged and that the clamor of the hunt occupied him more than the youth's death. In any case, the conclusion is strikingly weak, architectonically, stylistically, metrically, syntactically—I almost venture to add psychologically, for psychologically absolutely nothing more happens after Acteon fails to do the morally correct thing. Here the weakness of Gower's narrative technique becomes apparent. He takes no pleasure in the depiction of a situation and lacks the imagination that develops an image for its own sake. He is the "moral" Gower in the sense that he pushes his heroes and stories with high-principled directness towards a question of moral decision. This point attained, he loses interest and becomes mediocre, curiously inept, and—not infrequently—dull. Even Gower's best stories suffer from these sudden lapses of interest that follow the climax.[8]

To speak of a development of Gower's narrative technique is dangerous insofar as we know nothing about the chronology of the individual parts of the *Confessio Amantis*. When in what follows any statement is made about the development of technique, it is with the reservation that nothing is being said about the temporal order of the tales. Any such statement should be viewed as an aesthetic judgment with no claim to chronological correctness. In this sense one can show a development of narrative technique in the Pygmalion story of Book 4.[9] It moves in the direction that the Acteon story showed to be characteristic of the author: the action is tight, the tempo quick, and the perspective unified. The story thus gains a narrative intensity that matches the intensity with which Pygmalion's passion grows. Let us look at the story itself.

The immediate source is again Ovid.[10] It is unlikely that Gower used in addition the *Ovide Moralisé*.[11] The criterion of names, successfully employed to

---

[8] Compare the end of "Mundus and Paulina," 1.761 following.

[9] *Confessio* 4.371–436.

[10] *Met.* 10.243–297.

[11] After comparing eleven stories, I am unable to establish a single conclusive correspondence between the *Confessio Amantis* and the *Ovide Moralisé*.

clarify Chaucer's relationship to French poetry, fails because the differences in the forms of the names here prove nothing. The distribution of emphasis and the moral interpretation of the story are so different that a dependence hardly appears likely. The author of the *Ovide Moralisé* interprets the tale after the fashion of a George Bernard Shaw: the nobleman elevates to his station, by means of appropriate clothing and instruction, a lower-class beauty, perchance his maidservant, whom he finds naked (=poor) and mute (=uneducated), makes her his wife, and has a son by her. Gower's point, on the other hand, is a warning against false timidity in dealing with women:

> And if he wolde have holde him stille
> And nothing spoke, he scholde have failed. 4.426–427

There is no difference this time in the length of Ovid's and Gower's narratives. Gower found the following in Ovid: a woman-hating artist creates the figure of a girl whose extraordinary beauty and vivacity fill him with desires. He conducts himself toward the object of his love as one would toward a courtesan: he flatters her and shows himself to be generous. His gifts include everything that can please a woman: jewels and precious stones, flowers, small birds, and costly gowns. At the festival of Venus the artist begs the goddess to give him the ivory maiden, or one like her, for a wife. His prayer is heard and the image awakens to real life. There follows a prayer of thanks, Venus blesses the marriage, and the result is the birth of the boy Paphos.

What Gower makes of the story is something entirely different. Because his story is supposed to illustrate the rewarded persistence of the lover, he cannot use a woman-hater. A woman-hater would be absurd in the role of a gallant who persistently woos against all likelihood of success. Thus Ovid's bachelor becomes Gower's "lusti man of youthe" (4.373). The alteration appears of little significance, but it contains two important factors. It indicates the abandonment of the double aspect hinted at by Ovid, namely that not only is the statue transformed as a favor to the man, but also that the man, under the influence of beauty, undergoes a transformation—there is a delicate interrelation of events, a latent symmetry, which tacitly forms the background of Ovid's story. Furthermore, it involves an alteration of the dynamic. Gower's "lusti man of youthe" sets to work with a fresh, joyous unconcern; in Ovid love strikes like a devastating flame[12] and causes the utmost confusion.[13]

If Gower simplifies the story and renders it inoffensive after his fashion, however, he does not merely diminish it. He improves it in directness and tautness because he eliminates the subjective point of view, thereby bringing the beginning and end a little closer together. The directness is further reinforced because Gower again unifies the perspective: Pygmalion is the grammatical subject almost throughout. Ovid has several intrusions of an objective character (10.250–252; 265–266) and an entirely new beginning with the festival of Venus (10.270). Gower avoids the intrusions by interweaving the objective description of the statue with references to its creator Pygmalion:

Riht as a lyves creature
Sche semeth, for of yvor whyt
He hath hire wroght of such delit,
That sche was rody on the cheke
And red on bothe hire lippes eke;
Wherof that he himself beguileth. 4.382–387

He expunges the festival of Venus entirely and presses to the climax in a steady crescendo. Despite all its outward similarities, this passage (4.388–414) contrasts most strongly with Ovid. In content it is entirely after the manner of the courtly Middle Ages, in form entirely after the manner of Gower. In Ovid the denouement is sultry with eroticism. Physicality is the dominant element, a physicality to which the statue is delivered up, with no will of her own, passive, and without any individual character. In Gower, on the other hand, she has from the very beginning something like a soul, a human individuality, not only a power of erotic attraction, that determines Pygmalion's relationship to her:

For with a goodly lok sche smyleth,
So that thurgh pure impression
Of his ymaginacion
With al the herte of his corage
His love upon the faire ymage
He sette, and hire of love preide. 4.388–393

---

12 *Met.* 10.252–253:

. . . miratur, et haurit
Pectore Pygmalion simulati corporis ignes.
[. . . Pygmalion looks in admiration and
Is inflamed with love for this semblance of a form.]

13 *Met.* 10.254: *Saepe manus operi temptantes admovet* [Often he lifts his hands to the work]. 10.258: *Et metuit, pressos veniat ne livor in artus* [And then he fears lest he leave marks of bruises on them {her limbs}].

She is the mistress, Pygmalion her humble servant. Instead of an almost enraptured physicality and a suppressed eroticism, we have in Gower a "pure impression of his ymaginacion"; instead of the statue's passivity, a smile, a little personality in which the process of becoming human quietly suggests itself, even though she remains mute at first ("Bot sche no word ayeinward seide" [4.394]). Even her silence, moreover, appears to be made radiant by that mysterious smile. It would be presumptuous to try and treat her as a courtesan and bribe her with presents, which Ovid allows to be done to his statue. Gower expunges all the gay fripperies. The statue's presence alone is the *sine qua non* of life for Pygmalion, and therefore Gower allows her to share work, meal, and bed with him (4.395–403). Here the lines are run-on. They become shorter and choppier as passion grows, and they employ anaphora to signal endlessly repeated efforts. At last the ends of lines and clauses coincide in a rhythmical succession of tetrameters that calls to mind the lover's breathing. The subject of the passage remains always Pygmalion, nor is he allowed to rest for even one short verse:

> And after, whan the nyht was come,
> He leide hire in his bed al naked.
> He was forwept, he was forwakid,
> He keste hire colde lippes ofte,
> And wissheth that thei weren softe,
> And ofte he rouneth in hire ere,
> And ofte his arm now hier now there
> He leide, as he hir wolde embrace,
> And evere among he axeth grace. 4.402–410

Pygmalion's restlessness and tortured agitation are manifested stylistically as a mass of verbs that hardly leave room for a substantive. Everything centers on a constantly repeated "he," always unaccented in order not to interrupt the action. Of course, the English line was more susceptible to verb expression than the Latin hexameter, but even in Chaucer it seldom achieves such intensity as it does here in Gower. The release of the tension then follows in a few clauses that operate even rhythmically as a pleasant relaxation from the breathtaking tetrameters. That Gower grants Venus only a modest role is connected with his point. Had he over-emphasized the fact that the intervention of a goddess is necessary to arouse a stony beauty to the humanness of love, the prospects for the indefatigable lover would have been slim.

The dissimilar behavior of the two authors at the moment when the statue awakens to life is again characteristic. Ovid describes the incident objectively, while Gower, incomparably more effective, transmits it through the medium of Pygmalion:

> Be nyhte and whan that he worst ferde,
> And it lay in his nakede arm,

The colde ymage he fieleth warm
Of fleissh and bon and full of lif. 4.420–423

Thus is the climax attained. Gower does not spoil it by going into detail. Ovid's account is not bad, and perhaps necessary in order to allow his statue, hitherto patently inert and unloving, to become convincingly alive:

> *. . . dataque oscula virgo*
> *Sensit, et erubuit, timidumque ad lumina lumen*
> *Attollens pariter cum caelo vidit amantem.* 10.292–294

> [The maiden felt the kisses, blushed and, lifting her timid eyes up to the light, she saw the sky and her lover at the same time.]

Such was not necessary for Gower. For him the before and after are not unrelated conditions: the metamorphosis to humanness is present in nucleus from the beginning on. What appears as a miracle in Ovid is almost a natural process of development in Gower. Not the "moral" Gower—Ovid is also thoroughly decent here—but the practiced, consciously-shaping Gower ended just at the right moment. Of course, for the sake of completeness the birth of Paphos could not be excluded; however, it is unobtrusively appended to the interpretation of the tale (4.431). It is amusing to observe that the cunning Ovid speaks of a marriage between Pygmalion and the *eidolon*, from which Paphos results. The "moral" Gower, on the other hand, unconcernedly follows the precepts of courtly love and allows the pair a night together without making a middle-class attempt to legitimate the affair.

With the "Tale of Pygmalion" Gower has surpassed by a good bit his "Acteon." There the unification of perspective and the acceleration of action served above all to focus attention on the moral problem. The tempo at which Acteon moved towards Diana was basically unimportant; on the other hand, it was important that no digressions diminish Acteon's responsibility for his conduct or divert the reader's interest from the question of decision. The same means serve to increase the psychological depth in "Pygmalion." The unity of perspective effects a special intimacy in the relationship between Pygmalion and his *eidolon*. The statue is rarely exposed directly to the gaze of the reader; rather, it is seen through the medium of Pygmalion. The accelerating speed of the tempo is the stylistic equivalent of the accelerating intensity of desire, whereby emotion is intentionally and consistently expressed as action. Gower proves his complete mastery, however, in breaking off the story at just the right moment.

As a third example I have chosen a story that Gower as well as Chaucer attempted without having altogether controlled. It is the tale of the knight

Florent,[14] who falls into the hands of his enemy and can hope for pardon only if he learns within a year's time the correct answer to a question—it contains, therefore, a fairy-tale motif combined with other elements, for the question itself belongs not to the fairy-tale type, but rather to the province of the French parliament of love. It is: what do women most desire in the world? The knight seeks the answer in vain, until, in a solitary place, he meets—just before the expiration of the appointed time—an ancient hag who professes to know the correct answer. She will teach it to him if he will promise to make her his wife after the happy outcome. He gives his promise, the answer proves to be the right one, and the knight's dilemma begins. After various complications, the loathsome hag becomes an enchanted princess in the bridal bed.

Gower's story, like Chaucer's, is bound to a specific milieu (in Chaucer so much that the story almost seems an intrusion, in Gower not so conspicuously) from which it becomes by progressive action more and more independent. Most disturbing in Chaucer is the heteronomy of moods. He locates his story in Arthur's court and in a magic world: the knight belongs to Arthur's circle, the lady to the fairy kingdom. That these two worlds were intrinsically related and could be artistically blended with one another is obvious even if one forgets about Spenser. Chaucer proceeds, therefore, from a world removed from history, transfigured by magic, in which the tale must run its course. Perhaps it is still tolerable when he expects the reader to include in this illusion an episode from the sophisticated frivolity of the French parliament of love. However, when his fairy opens her mouth and begins to speak with the incessant fluency of the Wife of Bath, the illusion is seriously endangered. Her efflorescence, her sarcasm, and her feeling of superiority are in themselves refreshing, but they explode the unity of atmosphere. Irony and the mood of fairy tale preclude each other. One sees Chaucer's delight in experimentation; one sees his pellucid rationalism, which never suffers for long the twilight of the fairy-tale mood. One sees his humor, and one sees the huge profit, the psychological mastery, which leads to the metamorphosis of the tale in the teller's conception. Only when one has reasons, as in the present instance, for divorcing the narrative from its frame and considering it for itself can it not be denied that the experiment has the character of a brilliant operation that the patient unfortunately did not survive.

Gower also divorces his story from the milieu of its beginning, but he proceeds more slowly and cautiously and with another goal in mind. Unlike Chaucer's, his story takes place at the emperor's court in a semi-historical, clearly defined sociological milieu. Florent is a model knight without individual characteristics:

He was a man that mochel myhte,

[14] Gower, "The Tale of Florent," *Confessio Amantis* 1.1407–1861; Chaucer, *The Wife of Bath's Tale*.

Of armes he was desirous,
Chivalerous and amorous,
And for the fame of worldes speche,
Strange aventures forto seche,
He rod the Marches al aboute. 1.1412–1417

In addition, he gets into his precarious position through the caprice of *Fortuna*, not through personal guilt:

Fortune, which may every thred
Tobreke and knette of mannes sped,
Schop, as this knyht rod in a pas,
That he be strengthe take was. 1.1419–1422

His exemplary standing and his illustrious ancestry are respected by his enemies, and, instead of putting him to death, they grant him a period of time in which to find the answer to the question of what women most desire. If unsuccessful, he will die. He returns to the emperor's court and a conference of philosophers is convened; however, the question remains unsolved.

So far, Gower's narrative is proper, colorless, and tedious. The chief figure does not step out of the social milieu. His emotional reactions do not appear to have occupied the author for a moment. As long as Florent moves in a firmly outlined, familiar setting, as long as he conducts himself as a member of a specific social class according to the rules of this society—in an extreme situation, indeed, but yet in one for which social customs are alleged—he has something automatic about him and the motive powers of individual actions or passions remain obscure. Gower's art in general is insufficient to individualize his figures convincingly within a social milieu; they easily become types. Or perhaps it is more correct to say that Gower never strove for realism in Chaucer's sense because differentiation within a sociological reality did not attract him. His realism, if one wishes to apply the notion to him in a general way, is psychological—one could almost say moral. His characters remain types until they are thrust into a situation that demands a moral decision. Driven psychically into a corner, they lose their typicality and become human beings. Of course, Gower's psychological realism nowhere exhibits a tendency towards the working out of the accidental. Because all his stories contain exemplary characters, there clings to them, even in the situation of moral decision, a certain universal validity. All of his characters have something about them of the chief figure of a morality play: they represent the *genus humanum*, be they called Acteon, Pygmalion, or Florent. What distinguishes them from types in this situation, however, is the fact that they represent, in the uniqueness of their painful personal experience, a universally meaningful human problem. There appears to be a law of that literature not yet fully developed in its means of expression—as long as it is not of a dramatic nature—that psychological realism test itself first on the description of painful experience, a law from which probably only great masters are exempted. Thus Gower's attempts at realistic description are indebted in part to the pressure of the situation. In other respects, however, they are inherent in him, especially in the means of expression that he employed.

The turning point from *typus* to *individuum* in the "Tale of Florent" is located after 1.1521. It is the moment when Florent quits the emperor's court to meet his fate. The stylistic means that effects this transformation is the double use of the accented word "alone," an extremely simple means with a remarkable power of expression:

> And thus he wente forth his weie
> Alone as knyht aventurous,
> And in his thoght was curious
> To wite what was best to do:
> And as he rod alone so . . . 1.1522–1526

Here the man is quite undramatically and yet with the surest hand divorced from his social setting and put on his own, at first only externally. However, the external isolation is only the preliminary condition or the mirror image of the inner solitude in which fate and the author place the man in order to shape him individually. It is not only so in this story. One encounters isolation in Gower again and again as the mental/spiritual context in which all important events take place. To the solitude is joined, moreover, a retarding element: deliberation. So far Florent has behaved correctly, competently, without hesitation. He has signed a covenant, made a report, given his testamentary instructions. There has been no trace of reflection. Now, because scarcely anything remains to be done, the solitary knight suddenly emerges:

> And in his thoght was curious
> To wite what was best to do. 1.1524–1525

There is no restlessness in it, nor angst, nor rebellion, but, rather, a bemused astonishment. Florent rides on his way, considers his situation more passively than actively, and thus comes to his meeting with the ugly old woman, the loathly lady.

For the time being we will not speak of her. In Chaucer she immediately seizes the reins of the action, just as she seizes the reins of the horse, in order to accompany, or rather to lead, Florent to the king's court. Not for another moment is one free from her and her torrent of words. She is determined to dominate, and she dominates. Chaucer's Florent proceeds unsuspectingly into a situation over which he gradually loses control, and thus becomes more and more colorless. Gower leaves the conduct of the action to his Florent, just as he leaves him freedom of decision. Because the tale is supposed to illustrate the theme of obedience, we must examine the situation and this freedom of decision before we can talk about active obedience. Gower foregoes the mass of tension-producing elements that in Chaucer effectively bring about the climax at the king's court.

Florent encounters the loathly lady, discovers from her that she possesses the correct answer, learns the price of this answer, and is faced with a decision. Although the encounter took place in direct address, here the narrative reverts to objective description. The dialogue, naturally a dramatic element, is here oddly still, while the neutral description is full of realistic vivacity. The method is again frugal, the sentence structure simple, and nowhere is there a trace of emotion. The inner unrest is converted into external motion:

> Tho fell this knyht in mochel thoght,
> Now goth he forth, now comth ayein,
> He wot noght what is best to sein,
> And thoghte, as he rod to and fro,
> That chese he mot on of the tuo,
> Or forto take hire to his wif
> Or ells forto lese his lif. 1.1568–1574

Again the doubling ("Now goth he forth, now comth agein"; "as he rod to and fro"; "Or forto take . . . Or forto lese") causes an increase in intensity. Moreover there is, in addition to Florent's restlessness and perplexity, yet another element in the to and fro of his physical motion. One receives the impression of a bird in a cage, of confinement between two equally unacceptable alternatives, which are stated in the last two lines. The parallelism between "Now goth he forth, now comth ayein" and "Or forto take hire to his wif / Or elles forto lese his lif" is a true reflection of the inner and outer motion. The weight of his psychic burden is expressed in the plainest way imaginable, in a simple statement of quantity without any psychological differentiation ("Tho fell this knyht in mochel thoght") that is later followed by an equally simple "he wot not" and "and thoghte." Perhaps what is left unsaid is equally important in this emphasized simplicity. The knight does not sigh, as Gower's heroes are prone to do otherwise. There prevails that anxious silence that is more impressive than eloquent description. The loathly lady does not observe him, nor does he pay her any heed at this moment. That means that Gower, in order to isolate his hero completely and guarantee him the freedom of painful decision, suspends in this situation the relationship of the two figures which just now was manifested in the dialogue and which is reestablished with the moment when Florent arrives at a decision and breaks his silence.

Florent reaches his decision—with an inner reservation, to be sure, but one which has no great importance for the course of the action—and receives the answer that should deliver him. With it he sets out for his destination, while the loathly lady remains behind.

The threat of death in itself induced in Florent nothing other than impersonal reactions. It belonged to situations for which there was a class-bound, formulaic approach. It isolated him only externally and led him into solitude. The threat to his freedom through the voluntary-involuntary wedding, however, matches no conventional pattern and requires a personal inner strife. It presses heavily upon the man, not the knight. Florent is different from now on: "He goth him forth with hevy chiere" (1619). He does know the correct answer, but it does not make him free. It means only a short reprieve, after which he must return to his real problem:

> Florent of his answere is quit:
> And tho began his sorwe newe,
> For he mot gon, or ben untrewe,
> To hire which his trowthe hadde. 1.1664–1667

Unlike Chaucer, Gower confronts his knight for a second time with the decision with which he must already have wrestled in the first encounter with the loathly lady, and thus deepens that decision's moral intensity. He gives Florent the opportunity to evade the consequences of his oath by not returning to her. Only now does Florent accept his fate in its full significance. When he gave his oath there existed the possibility either that an answer other than the one thus purchased would save him, or that this answer itself would prove to be a deception. Moreover, his choice was made under the threat of death. Now Gower gives Florent complete freedom of moral decision and he must choose yet again. Also, the choice's alternatives have been changed in the meantime. At first they consisted of death or an unwanted marriage, and perhaps this choice was the easier because it dealt with two very real matters. Now Florent is confronted with the question of an odious marriage or dishonor, a dishonor that would possibly remain secret since the loathly lady does not appear publicly in Gower. One sees that what Gower lost in dramatic power when he did not have the loathly lady appear at court is pure profit psychologically. He is thus in a position to present and develop the problem of obedience in all its complexity.

Florent makes the right decision:

> Bot he, which alle schame dradde,
> Goth forth in stede of his penance,
> And takth the fortune of his chance,
> As he that was with trowthe affaited. 1.1668–1671

He achieves obedience—an obedience that consists for the time being in the joyless acceptance of the penance that fate demands from him—and prepares to return to the ugly hag. Gower is sparing of direct expression of emotion and says nothing of Florent's feelings along the way. Yet, as he reaches his destination,

> Florent his wofull heved uplefte
> And syh this vecke wher she sat. 1.1674–1675

There are only two lines, but they remind one involuntarily of Auerbach's interpretation of Genesis 22:4 (from the story of the sacrifice of Isaac):[15] "On the third day he [Abraham] lifted up his eyes and saw the place from afar." Florent's arrival to the old woman and Abraham's arrival at the place of sacrifice—both under the pressure of an obligation of obedience that strains their strength to the utmost—are of course only rough parallels. Yet, Florent's raising of his head is to be understood in the same fashion as Abraham's lifting of his eyes to Mount Moriah: the weight of silent obedience, the burden of impending sacrifice until then kept Florent's eyes depressed. Of course, the young man raises his eyes not in order to recognize his destination, but to look upon the object of his grief.

At their first meeting Florent had been confronted with the phenomenon of repulsive ugliness as a totality:

> In a forest under a tre
> He syh wher sat a creature,
> A lothly wommannysch figure,
> That forto speke of fleisch and bon
> So foul yit syh he nevere non. 1.1528–1532

Here Gower renders an impression and foregoes a description of the ugly hag. Not so at Florent's return. The approach is again according to Gower's technique of subjective experience. Now, however, there ensues an inventory of all the repulsive particulars that produces an objective character:

> Florent his wofull heved uplefte
> And syh this vecke wher sche sat,
> Which was the lothlieste what
> That evere man caste on his yhe:
> Hire nase bass, hire browes hyhe,
> Hire yhen smale and depe set,
> Hire chekes ben with teres wet,
> And rivelen as an emty skyn
> Hangende doun unto the chin,
> Hire lippes schrunken ben for age,
> Ther was no grace in the visage,
> Hir front was nargh, hir lockes hore,
> Sche loketh forth as doth a More,
> Hire necke is schort, hir schuldres courbe,
> That myhte a mannes lust destourbe,
> Hire body gret and nothing smal,
> And schortly to descrive hire al,

---

15 See Erich Auerbach, *Mimesis* (Berne: Francke, 1946), 14. [Trans. Willard Trask, *Mimesis: The Representation of Reality in Western Literature* (Princeton: Princeton University Press, 1953; repr. New York: Doubleday Anchor, 1957), 7.]

Sche hath no lith without a lak;
Bot lich unto the wollesak
Sche proferth hire unto this knyht. 1.1674–1693

The old hag is not only the ugliest woman that Florent ever met, but the ugliest creature that ever came under a man's gaze. Thus within a passage the narrative quietly changes from subjective ("Florent syh") to objective ("That evere man caste on his yhe"). Yet one can just as easily consider the catalogue of details that follows the result of Florent's observation as the objective proof of the generalizing relative clause (1676–1677). It seems to me there is artistic intent in this uncertainty of reference. Florent proceeds slowly, adding up the overwhelming sum of ugliness with which he must share his life in the future. The idea of ugliness, until now vague in its generality, becomes clear to him in its drastic details.

The catalogue of ugliness itself is noteworthy because of a realism such as Gower never achieved in the description of beauty. Had he wished to follow the conventional catalogue of beauty provided by poetics, with reverse symptoms so to speak, he certainly would not have found it difficult to use grotesque or repugnant objects of comparison instead of the objects of value that poetics furnished for the praise of beauty. One could let lips be withered tree bark instead of coral, convert eyes into guttering candles instead of twinkling stars. The negative catalogue of beauty certainly does not first appear in England with Shakespeare,[16] but it belongs to a non-narrative genre. There exist two satirical love poems of this type from the early fifteenth century, the one by Hoccleve ("Of my lady, wel me reioise I may"),[17] the other attributed to Lydgate ("My fayr lady so fresshe of hew").[18] In addition, two anonymous satirical verse letters by a pair of lovers survive in a manuscript that belongs paleographically to the second half of the fifteenth century.[19] Because they are included in a small omnibus manuscript, the pieces could conceivably have been written considerably earlier, but not, of course, before Chaucer had become the recognized model of style.[20] In all these poems the negative catalogue of beauty is employed with parodic intent. In his opening lines Hoccleve, like Shakespeare later, adheres closely to the customary scheme:

Of my lady, wel me reioise I may:

---

[16] Compare Shakespeare, Sonnet 130.

[17] *Hoccleve's Works: The Minor* Poems, vol. 2, ed. Israel Gollancz, EETS O.S. 73 (London: Oxford University Press, 1925), 37–38.

[18] Ed. J. O. Halliwell, *A Selection from the Minor Poems of Dan John Lydgate*, Percy Society (London: Richards, 1840), 2:199.

[19] Ed. R. H. Robbins, "Two Middle English Satiric Love Epistles," *MLR* 37 (1942): 415–21.

[20] See line 8 of the second poem: "The Ynglysch of Chaucere was nat in youre mynd": Robbins, "Satiric Love Epistles," 417.

Hir golden forheed is ful narw and smal;
Hir browes been lyk to dym reed coral;
And as the jeet hir yen glistren ay.

Later on he improvises more freely (11–12):

Hir nose a pentice is, that it ne shal
Reyne in hir mowth thogh shee vp-rightes lay.

The anonymous author offers the following variations on the theme:

The Goodlynesse of your persone is esye to endyte
For he leuyth nat that can youre persone appayre
So comly best shapyne of feture most fayre
Most fresch of contenaunce euyn as an oule

Ys best and most fauoryd of ony odyr foule
Youre manly visage shortly to declare
Your forehed mouth and nose so flatte
In short conclusyon best lykened to an hare
Of alle lyvyng thynges saue only a catte. I. 3–11

In the second poem he makes a two-fold point in the following detailed simile:

Youre caumsyd nose with nose-thryllys brode
Vnto the chyrch a noble instrument
To quenche tapers brennyng afore the roode
Ys best apropred at myne avysement. II. 22–25

Even when an author writes with the intent to parody, however, he cannot compress loathsomeness with complete success into a catalogue of similes, since the grotesque simile mitigates in that it objectifies. Because these poems do objectify, they all mention plain, realistic features—Hoccleve in the fourth stanza and the anonymous pieces in I stanza 4 and II stanza 6.

Now Gower had to shun parody at all events if he wished convincingly to shape Florent's inner turmoil by such a sight. Therefore, with the exception of line 1686, he foregoes simile. He gives the overall impression (1.1676–1677) that he resolves the sight into its components with naturalistic precision and dryness (1.1678–1689), that is, he presents its physical details as if in close-up and only sums it up at the end in the one striking image of the wool sack (1.1690–1693). The "wollesak" works so much more effectively than Hoccleve's "foot-bal"[21] because it is active and asserts a claim upon Florent:

[21] Line 13: "Hir comly body shape as a foot-bal."

Bot lich unto the wollesak
Sche proferth hire unto this knyht.

Hoccleve's simile, on the other hand, is static and but one among many. Perhaps, however, it was not only his fear that simile would bring an unwanted comic element into the tension of the situation that determined Gower's realistic description. Perhaps the convincing impression of ugliness can only be attained through naturalistic precision, whereas there appears to be inherent in beauty a latent connection with an absolute value that either illuminates the lovely subject transcendentally or challenges it to competitive comparison with other lovely subjects.

However, we must return to the story. The old woman takes the knight at his word, the horse by the reins, and sets the action once again in motion. Florent thinks that his heart must break (1.1700). In order to clarify the knight's mental condition, Gower employs in this passage one of his infrequent lengthy similes, and in it a change takes place. From now on Florent accepts his fate: the uncertainty and the dreadful burden of decision are past:

Ia Loke, how a sek man for his hele
b Takth baldemoine with canele
c And with the mirre takth the sucre.
Ryht upon such a maner lucre
Stant Florent, as in this diete:
IIc He drinkth the bitre with the swete,
b He medleth sorwe with likynge,
a And liveth, as who seith, deyinge. 1.1703–1710

The image is based on antitheses. The first three lines present them in material form, the next two relate the object of comparison to the subject of comparison (they are something like a formal axis around which the metaphor revolves), and the following three lines, which repeat the antitheses in a slightly more abstract form, constitute the conclusion. Formally the construction is very attractively done, not too schematic, but pleasing, with an unexaggerated but nevertheless clearly perceptible balance and with a reciprocal relationship to content, syntax, and meter. The two groups of antithetical verses are situated around the axis, ll. 1706–1707, in such a way that they form an expanded chiasmus. If one designates the two groups I and II, then the arrangement Ia, b, c matches the arrangement IIc, b, a. Proceeding from the axis, that means that Ic ("mirre . . . sucre") is answered by IIc ("bitre . . . swete") and Ib ("baldemoine . . . canele") less stringently by IIb ("sorwe . . . lyking"). The parallelism of the contents is reflected in syntactical similarity, which, though it does not lead to a complete similarity of sentence structures, nevertheless clearly removes the two groups of verses from the different constructions of the surrounding lines and binds them to each other. The metrical parallelism is effected when the paired antitheses appear each time in the same position in the line. The relationships between Ia and IIa are much less evident, are, in fact, merely hinted at in the similarity of the images: "sek man . . . hele" (Ia) and "liveth . . . deyinge" (IIa). It is as if the more rigorous scheme of correspondence relaxes the farther one moves away from the axis, a sign of a wholesome freedom that is able to renounce mechanical symmetry in favor of lively ease.

One could conclude that the accentuation of the antitheses must reflect Florent's inner strife, as do the antitheses in lines 1.1568 following. That is not at all the case. In fact, a change is at hand. For the antitheses here are no longer merely juxtaposed to each other, as in "Now goth he forth, now comth ayein" (1564), but are joined together: "he drinkth the bitre with the swete." Clearly Florent is still a long way from an organic synthesis, but in his conduct he does overcome the apparent irreconcilables. And the choice of images proclaims a positive conclusion. Florent is the sick man who must take bitters for his recovery, but at least one is able to speak of recovery. Thus the new phase of the tale begins under positive auspices.

Florent keeps his promise conscientiously and the wedding takes place. Gower devotes some space to detail, while Chaucer, to good effect, cuts the ceremony short. In return, Gower makes amends with the description of the bridal night, which is one of his really good pieces. He introduces it with an overstatement *topos* in plainest form:

> So wo begon was nevere knyht
> As he was thanne of mariage. 1.1762–1763

To it he attaches the following couplet, which contrasts in mood and in vivacity of expression:

> And sche began to pleie and rage,
> As who seith, I am wel ynowh. 1.1764–1765

Then the climax slowly begins. She wishes to be kissed, while, on the other hand,

> His body myhte wel be there,
> Bot as of thoght and of memoire
> His herte was in purgatoire. 1.1774–1776

"Purgatoire" recalls the earlier-used "penance" and has a twofold aspect. The cleansing fire is indeed agonizing as a place of residence, but it also has the character of a transitional stage. Gower probably wishes to call forth both associations simultaneously, painful torment with reference to Florent's present situation, suggestive promise for the further course of the story.

The next step is for him to go to bed with the hag. Chaucer compressed the situation into a single couplet (*Wife of Bath's Tale* 1085–1086):

He walweth and he turneth to and fro.
His olde wyf lay smylynge evermo.

The contrast between the tortured restlessness of the knight—which is above all distinctly marked in the monosyllables at the ends of lines and in the modest alliteration of the tenues—and the smiling superiority of the old woman—whose person is emphasized by the caesura, whose well-being is stressed by the smooth flow of the last half of the second verse—is first-rate. But Chaucer's terseness permits no elaboration of the scene, no possibility of a climax. The rest is direct address, but didactic address, not dramatic dialogue. Gower develops the situation for its own sake, not as an occasion for moralizing observations. He looks, and allows the reader to look:

And whan thei were abedde naked,
Withoute slep he was awaked;
He torneth on that other side,
For that he wolde hise yhen hyde
Fro lokynge on that foule wyht.
The chambre was al full of lyht,
The courtins were of cendal thinne. 1.1781–1787

Florent, who tries in vain to hide his eyes for shame; the room, which is so bright that the diaphanous bed curtains cannot create a softening semi-darkness; the oppressive and humiliating consciousness of unconcealed nakedness; the inescapable conclusion that the loathly lady draws from the situation ("For now, sche seith, we ben bothe on," 1.1743); and Florent's deathly despair ("And he lay stille as eny ston," 1.1794)—all that is masterfully done. All emotion is shunned; the curve of the psychological experience appears clearly and distinctly. "Wo begon," "purgatoire," "stille as eny ston," mark the three stages that lead Florent to a kind of inner death. Earlier he had accepted the marriage as an unavoidable bond; now he must accept it as a *fait accompli*:

He herde and understod the bond,
How he was set to his penance. 1.1798–1799

Because he finds himself in a state of lethargy after the death of his physical pride, he acts "as it were a man in trance"—but he acts. He turns to the old woman—and finds her transformed.

Gower does not say in so many words that the knight's inner change occasions or causes the loathly lady's outer transformation, although this is basically the theme of his story. Rather, he maintains that Florent's submissive reply to a vexatious question is the deciding factor. That was part of the story as Gower and Chaucer found it and neither has actually altered it much. The story betrays its courtly origin by the kind of question and answer on which Florent's life depends in the first part. The question is: what do women most desire? It requires an answer in the spirit of courtly love culture: mastery in love ("Sovereynetee," says Chaucer, *Wife of Bath's Tale*, 1038; "Be soverein of mannes love," says Gower, 1.1609). This answer, however, must be not only recognized and acknowledged, but also experienced. Therefore, the second part ties the transformation of the ugly old woman into a dawn-lovely princess to the willingness of the knight to submit himself unconditionally to the loathly lady. This willingness is tested with a second question that is put to the knight on the evening of the forced wedding. He must choose whether he would rather have his wife young and beautiful or ugly and faithful (as in Chaucer); or whether he would rather see his beloved young and beautiful by day but old and ugly by night, or, vice versa, beautiful and young by night but ugly and old by day (as in Gower).

Florent passes the test because he leaves the decision to the lady, and thus acknowledges her "sovereynetee." Now it is curious that this point is elucidated so altogether differently in Chaucer's and Gower's versions. Gower prepared so well psychologically that the decision seems almost to be anticipated and the correct answer to the test question loses some significance. Thus in Gower Florent already demonstrated obedience in a much more bitter sense when he went back to accept the loathly lady, in all her ugliness, as bedfellow. According to the logic of the story, the transformation occurs at this moment. Florent's readiness to submit himself to her decision—whether she will be ugly only by day or only by night—has by far the lesser effect and in Gower affects only the permanence of the transformation. Thus the force of the spiritual transformation impairs the originally sensational effect of the point. Likewise, the denouement then degenerates utterly. It is technically necessary to complete the plot, but it contains no further moral problem and thus Gower reels it off with little sympathy.

Chaucer does not anticipate the transformation. Yet he endangers the point with another element, namely with the lecture that the old hag gives the knight after she has put the test question to him. The alternatives in Chaucer are young, lovely, and faithless, or old, ugly, and true. The loathly lady points to the answer—old, ugly, and true—with every rhetorical and dialectical means, and with an unequalled loquacity. In the event that the content of the lecture is not intended ironically, then one would expect that Florent would derive profit from it and now, without further ado, be in a position to give the correct answer. Yet suddenly the reader discovers to his considerable astonishment that the correct answer consists in the renunciation of decision. A slight flaw in the logic is the result. It is to a certain extent compensated for by the moment of surprise that the unexpected denouement causes. This combines with the subsequent unexpected, final transformation of the loathly lady for a cumulative effect such as Chaucer loved.

When one weighs this phase of Gower's and Chaucer's stories, one must for a moment consider the different wording of the test question. It has been supposed that the choice with which Chaucer confronts his knight is of greater moral significance than the choice between beauty by day or by night with which Gower confronts Florent. That is no doubt correct. But in so determining one fails to see that the choice *qua* choice is unimportant since it remains unchosen; instead of decision, the story demands submission to the will of the lady. With this submission the goal of the story is attained. One cannot avoid the impression that Chaucer's narrative frame impaired the value of the story at this point, for the demand for submission accords all too well with the character of the teller, the Wife of Bath, and is thus flavored with a barely concealed irony. It almost seems as if the self-characterization of the Wife of Bath is Chaucer's chief concern. In this he succeeded incomparably, but the story suffers as a result. Florent shares the inglorious fate of the aforesaid lady's five husbands when he laconically and submissively accepts his newfound conjugal bliss.

Chaucer's narrative is the story of the loathly lady, or, indirectly, of the Wife of Bath. He works with the coarser means of conflict of moods, an occasional brilliance of expression, and irony. Gower makes his task less simple, and actually tells the story of Florent. He is not as concerned with the moment of surprise and the happy ending as he is with what matters above all to him: proper conduct in a situation of moral decision. If we may employ the idea of development yet once more in the context of Gower's narrative art, this story is new in that the moral decision does not ensue suddenly—as in "Acteon," where everything seems pointed to the one end—but passes through more phases. In this way the tale receives a gradual intensification and a psychological deepening that necessitate a new descriptive technique. In the other two tales Gower tightened the action and quickened the tempo; in "Florent" he takes as his artistic task the shaping of the retarding moment. Gower sacrifices surprise to the greater credibility of his knight's inner development and often achieves astonishing results with economical means, although Chaucer deals with his material in a superior manner. Gower pursues the moral and psychological problem with great care and is superior in this respect even to the sixteenth-century novel. He scarcely heeds what lies to the right and left of the way, and may sometimes for that reason appear pedantic and tedious. One cannot expect in him a fullness of life, but he undertook earnestly and persistently, as did hardly any of his contemporaries, the attempt to understand and describe man from the moral motives of his behavior. His narrative art is the living expression of this endeavor.

Bibliography

Primary Sources

Gower, John. *Poema quod dicitur Vox Clamantis necnon Chronica Tripertita*, ed. H. O. Coxe. London: Nicol for the Roxburghe Club, 1850.

———. *The Complete Works of John Gower*, ed. G. C. Macaulay. 4 vols. EETS O.S. 81–84. Oxford: Oxford University Press. 1899–1902; repr. Grosse Pointe, MI: Scholarly Press, 1968.

———. *The Major Latin Works of John Gower*, trans. E. W. Stockton. Seattle: University of Washington Press, 1962.

———. *Mirour de l'omme (The Mirror of Mankind)*, trans. W. B. Wilson and N. W. Van Baak. East Lansing, MI: Colleagues Press, 1992.

———. *The Minor Latin Works with In Praise of Peace*, ed. and trans. R. F. Yeager with M. Livingston. Kalamazoo: Medieval Institute Publications, 2005.

———. *Poems on Contemporary Events: The Visio Anglie (1381) and Cronica Tripertita (1400)*, trans. D. R. Carlson and A. G. Rigg. Toronto: Pontifical Institute of Mediaeval Studies, 2011.

———. *Vox Clamantis* Book VI. Trans Robert J. Meindel. The Gower Project Translations at https://gowertranslations.pbworks.com/w/page/53715438/Vox%20Clamantis%20Translations

Alanus de Insulis. *Liber Sententiarum ac Dictorum Memorabilium. PL* 210:229–252.

———. *Summa de Arte Praedicatoria. PL* 210:109–198.

Alexander of Hales. *Summa Theologica.* 4 vols. Ad Aquas Claras (Quaracchi): Typographia Collegii S. Bonaventurae, 1924–1948.

Anon. "Die *Sententiae Divinitatis*," ed. B. Geyer. Ph.D. diss., Universität Münster, 1907.

Anon. Early Fifteenth-Century Sermon. Oxford, Bodleian Library, MS. 649.

Anon. *Myrour of Sinners.* Oxford, Bodleian Library, MS. Laud 174.

Anon. "Seldom Seen is Soon Forgot." In *The Minor Poems of the Vernon Manuscript*, ed. F. J. Furnivall and C. Horstmann, 1:715–18. 2 vols. EETS O.S. 117. London: Kegan Paul, Trench, Trübner, 1901.

Anon. *Speculum Christiani,* ed. G. Holmstedt. EETS O.S. 182. London: Oxford University Press, 1933.

Augustine. *De Civitate Dei*, ed. B. Dombert. 2 vols. Leipzig: Teubner, 1905–1909.

———. *The City of God*, trans. M. Dods. New York: Random House, 1950.

Bacon, Roger. *Secretum secretorum.* In *Opera hactenus inedita Rogeri Baconi*, ed. R. Steele. 5 vols. Oxford: Clarendon Press, 1920.

———. *Three Prose Versions of the Secretum secretorum*, ed. R. Steele. EETS E.S. 74. London: Kegan Paul, Trench, Trübner, 1898.

Bernard of Clairvaux. *Sermo de miseria humana. PL* 184:1109–1114.

———. *Sermo XXXVI in Canticum Canticorum. PL* 183:967–971.

Ps.-Bernard of Clairvaux. *Meditationes piissimae de cognitione humanae conditionis. PL*184:485–508.

Bernardus Silvestris. *Commentum Bernardi Silvestris super sex libros Eneidos Virgilii*, ed. R. Riedel. Greifswald: J. Abel, 1924.

———. ———, trans. C. G. Schreiber and T. E. Maresca. Lincoln: University of Nebraska Press, 1979.

Boethius. *De Consolatione Philosophiae*, ed. A. Fortescue. London: Burns, Oates & Washburne, 1925.

———. ———, ed. L. Bieler. CCSL 94. 2nd ed. Turnhout: Brepols, 1984.

———. ———, ed. and trans. E. K. Rand et al. Loeb Classical Library. Cambridge, MA: Harvard University Press, 1918.

Bonaventura. *Commentarius in Evangelium S. Lucae.* In *Opera Omnia.* 10 vols. Ad Aquas Claras (Quaracchi): Typographia Collegii S. Bonaventurae, 1882–1902.

Ps.-Bonaventura. *Liber Salutaris Beati Bonaventurae Cardinalis Ordinis Minorum Pharetra vocatus.* Paris: B. Rembolt, 1518.

Bracton, Henry de. *De Legibus et Consuetudinibus Angliae*, ed. G. E. Woodbine. 4 vols. New Haven: Yale University Press, 1915–1942.

———. *On the Laws and Custons of England*, trans. S. E. Thorne. 4 vols. Cambridge, MA: Belknap Press for Harvard University Press, 1968.

Bromyard, John. *Summa Praedicantium.* Venice: D. Nicolinus, 1586.

Cassiodorus. *Variae*, ed. T. Mommsen. MGH Auctores Antiquissimi 12. Berlin: Weidmann, 1894.

Chaucer, Geoffrey. *The Works of Geoffrey Chaucer*, ed. F.N. Robinson. 2nd ed. Boston: Houghton Mifflin, 1957.

(Ps.-)Cyprian. *De duodecim abusivis saeculi. PL* 4:869–882.

Donne, John. *Devotions Upon Emergent Occasions*, ed. J. Sparrow. Cambridge: Cambridge University Press, 1923.

Epistolae Karolini Aevi, ed. E. Dümmler. MGH. 4 vols. Berlin: Weidmann, 1895.

Francis of Hales. *Summa Theologica.* 5 vols. Ad Claras Aquas (Quaracchi): Typographia Collegii S. Bonaventurae, 1924–1948.

Gregory the Great. *Homiliae in Evangelia. PL* 76:1075–1312.

———. ———, ed. R. Etaix. CCSL 141. Turnhout: Brepols, 1999.
———. *Homiliae in Ezechiel. PL* 76:785–1072.
———. ———, ed. M. Adriaen. CCSL 142. Turnhout: Brepols, 1971.
———. *Moralia in Job. PL* 75:509–1162.
———. ———, ed. M. Adriaen. 2 vols. CCSL 143–143A. Turnhout: Brepols, 1963–1979.
Guibert of Nogent. *Liber quo ordine sermo fieri debet. PL* 156:21–32.
———. ———, trans. J.M. Miller. *Today's Speech* 17 (1969): 45–56.
Higden, Ranulph. *De Forma Praedicandi*. Oxford, Bodleian Library, MS. 316, Canon.Misc. 522.
———. *Ars componendi sermones*, ed. and trans. M. Jennings and S.A. Wilson. Paris: Peeters, 2003.
Historia Anglicana, ed. H. T. Riley. 2 vols. Rolls Series. London: Longman, Green, 1963.
History of Reynard the Fox, ed. H. Morley. London: Routledge, 1889.
Hoccleve, Thomas. *Hoccleve's Works: The Minor Poems*, ed. I. Gollancz, vol. 2. EETS O.S. 73. London: Oxford University Press, 1925.
Honorius of Autun. *Expositio in Canticum Canticorum. PL* 172:347–496.
Hugh of St Victor. *De Arca Noe morali. PL* 176:617–680.
———. *De Arca Noe mystica. PL*176:681–704.
———. *De Sacramentis Christianae fidei. PL* 176:173–618.
———. *Eruditionis Didascaliae. PL* 176:739–838.
———. *Speculum Ecclesiae*. Seville: J. Kronberger, 1512.
Humbert De Romanis. *Liber de Eruditione Praedicatorum*, ed. J. J. Berthier. 2 vols. Rome: n.p., 1889.
Isidore of Seville. *Etymologiae*, ed. W. M. Lindsay. 2 vols. Oxford: Clarendon Press, 1911.
———. *Sententiae. PL* 83:537–738.
———. ———, ed. P. Cazier. CCSL 111. Turnhout: Brepols, 1998.
Jacobus de Gruytrode. *Lavacrum Conscientie omnibus sacerdotibus summe utile ac necessarium*. Cologne: Quentell, 1501.
John of Salisbury. *Policraticus*, ed. C. J. Webb. 2 vols. London: Oxford University Press, 1909.
———. ——— *I–IV*, ed. K. S. B. Keats-Rohan. CCCM 118. Turnhout: Brepols, 1993.
———. ———, trans. C. J. Nederman. Cambridge: Cambridge University Press, 1990.
Langland, William. *The Vision of William concerning Piers the Plowman*, ed. W. W. Skeat. 2 vols. Oxford: Oxford University Press, 1886.
———. *Piers Plowman*, ed. E. T. Donaldson. New Haven: Yale University Press, 1949.
Lorens d'Orléans. *Somme le Roi*, trans. anon., *The Book of Vices and Virtues*, ed. W. N. Francis. EETS O.S. 217. London: Oxford University Press, 1942.

Lydgate, John. *A Selection from the Minor Poems of Dan John Lydgate*, ed. J.O. Halliwell. 2 vols. Percy Society. London: Richards, 1840.

Maidstone, Richard. *Concordia (The Reconciliation of Richard II with London)*, ed. D. R. Carlson, verse trans. A. G. Rigg. Kalamazoo: Medieval Institute Publications, 2003. Available from TEAMS.

Martin of León. *Sermo II Sancti Joanne Baptista. PL* 209:13–20.

The Minor Poems of the Vernon Manuscript, ed. F. J. Furnivall and C. Horstmann. 2 vols. EETS O.S. 98, 117. London: Kegan Paul, Trench, Trübner, 1901.

Nicholas de Lyra. *Postilla Litteralis super Biblia*. Rome, 1471–1472.

Ovid. *P. Ovidius Naso*, ed. R. Merkel. 2nd ed. 3 vols. Leipzig: Teubner, 1904–1907.

———. *Metamorphoses*, ed. and trans. F. J. Miller. Loeb Classical Library. Cambridge, MA: Harvard University Press, 1916.

———. *Tristia*, ed. and trans. A. L. Wheeler. Loeb Classical Library. Cambridge. MA: Harvard University Press, 1924.

Peter Riga. *Aurora*. Oxford, Bodleian Library, MS. 822.

———. ———, ed. P. E. Beichner. 2 vols. Notre Dame: University of Notre Dame Press, 1965.

Political Poems and Songs, ed. T. Wright. 2 vols. Rolls Series. London: Longman, Green, 1859–1861.

Raymond of Pennaforte. *Summa Theologiae Moralis*. Oxford, Bodleian Library, MS. 316 Canon. Misc. 522.

Robert de Basevorn. *Forma Praedicandi*, trans. L. Krul. In Murphy, *Three Medieval Rhetorical Arts*, 109–215.

Roger of Waltenham. *Compendium morale de virtuosis dictis et factis exemplaribus antiquorum*. Oxford, Bodleian Library, MS. Fairfax 4.

Speculum Gy de Warewyke: An English Poem, ed. G. L. Morrill. EETS E.S. 75. London: Kegan Paul, Trench, Trübner, 1898.

Vincent of Beauvais. *De Eruditione regalium filiorum*, ed. A. Steiner. Cambridge, MA: Medieval Academy of America, 1938.

———. *Speculum Historiale*, ed. D. Bernardi. Venice: D. Nicolinus, 1591.

———. *Speculum Quadruplex (Speculum Maius)*. 4 vols. 1: *Speculum Doctrinale*; 2: *Speculum Naturale*; 3: *Speculum Historiale*; 4 (ps.-Vincent): *Speculum Morale*. Douai, 1624; repr, Graz: Akademische Druck- und Verlagsanstalt, 1965.

Waldeby, John. *Sermones*. Oxford, Bodleian Library, MS. 687.

William of Auvergne. *Ars Praedicandi*, ed. A. de Poorter. Bruges: n.p., 1927.

Wyclif, John. *Tractatus de civili dominio*, ed. R. Lane Poole. London: Trübner, 1885.

———. *Sermones*, ed. J. Loserth. 4 vols. London: Trübner, 1890.

Secondary Works

Aers, David. "Representations of the Third Estate: Social Conflict and its Milieu around 1381." *Southern Review* (Australia) 16 (1983): 335–49.

———. "*Vox Populi* and the Literature of 1381." In *The Cambridge History of Medieval English Literature,* ed. D. Wallace, 432–53. Cambridge: Cambridge University Press, 1999.

Auerbach, E. *Mimesis.* Bern: Francke, 1946. Trans. W. R. Trask. Princeton: Princeton University Press, 1953; repr. New York: Doubleday Anchor, 1957.

Balogh, J. "*Rex a recte regendo.*" *Speculum* 3 (1928): 580–82.

Beichner, P. E. "Gower's Use of *Aurora* in *Vox Clamantis.*" *Speculum* 30 (1955): 582–95.

Bertolet, C. E. "Fraud, Division, and Lies: John Gower and London." In *On John Gower,* ed. Yeager, 43–70.

Carlson, D. R. "Gower's Early Latin Poetry: Text-Genetic Hypotheses of an *Epistola ad regem* (c.1377–1380), from the Evidence of John Bale." *Mediaeval Studies* 65 (2003): 293–317.

———. "Gower's Beast Allegories in the 1391 *Visio Angliae.*" *Philological Quarterly* 87 (2008): 257–75.

———. "The Parliamentary Source of Gower's *Cronica Tripertita* and Incommensurable Styles." In *Trilingual Poet,* ed. Dutton et al., 98–111.

Carlyle, R. W., and A. J. Carlyle. *A History of Medieval Political Theory in the West.* 6 vols. Edinburgh: Blackwood, 1903–1936.

Charland, T. M. *Artes Praedicandi*: *Contribution à l'histoire de la rhétorique au moyen âge.* Paris: Vrin, 1936.

Coffman, G. R. "John Gower in his Most Significant Role." In *Elizabethan Studies and Other Essays in Honor of George F. Reynolds,* 52–61. Boulder: University of Colorado Press, 1945.

———. "John Gower, Mentor for Royalty: Richard II." *PMLA* 69 (1954): 953–64.

Curtius, E.R. *Europäische Literatur und lateinisches Mittelalter.* Bern: Francke, 1948.

———. *European Literature and the Latin Middle Ages.* Trans. W. R. Trask. New York: Pantheon, 1953.

Dutton, E., et al., eds. *John Gower, Trilingual Poet: Language, Translation, and Tradition.* Cambridge: Boydell & Brewer, 2010.

Echard, S. "Gower's Books of Latin: Language, Politics and Poetry." *Studies in the Age of Chaucer* 25 (2003): 123–56.

———. "Gower's Reputation." In *Companion,* ed. eadem, 1–22.

———, ed. *A Companion to Gower.* Cambridge: D. S. Brewer, 2004.

Esch, A. "John Gowers Erzählkunst." In *Chaucer und seine Zeit: Symposion für Walter F. Schirmer,* ed. idem, 207–39. Tübingen: Universität Tübingen, 1968.

———. "John Gower's Narrative Art," trans. L. B. Burke. In *Gower's* Confessio Amantis: *A Critical Anthology*, ed. P. Nicholson, 81–108. Cambridge: D. S. Brewer, 1991.

Fisher, J. H. *John Gower, Moral Philosopher and Friend of Chaucer.* New York: New York University Press, 1964.

Fox, G. G. *The Medieval Sciences in the Works of John Gower.* New York: Haskell, 1931, repr. 1966.

Galloway, A. "Gower in his Most Learned Role and the Peasants' Revolt of 1481." *Mediaevalia* 16 (1993 [1990]): 329–47.

———. "Reassessing Gower's Dream-Visions." In *Trilingual Poet*, ed. Dutton et al., 288–303.

Gilson, E. *Les idées et les lettres.* Paris: Vrin, 1932.

Haferkorn, R. *'When Rome is Removed into England': eine politische Prophezeihung des 14. Jahrhunderts.* Beiträge zur englischen Philologie 19. Leipzig: Tauchnitz, 1932.

Hamilton, G. L. "Some Sources of the Seventh Book of Gower's *Confessio Amantis.*" *Modern Philology* 9 (1911/12): 323–45.

Irvin, M. "Genius and Sensual Reading in the *Vox Clamantis.*" In *Trilingual Poet*, ed. Dutton et al., 196–205.

Jarrett, B. *Social Theories of the Middle Ages, 1200–1500.* London: Benn, 1926.

Justice, S. *Writing and Rebellion: England in 1381.* Berkeley: University of California Press, 1994.

Kendall, E. "Saving History: Gower's Apocalyptic and the New Arion." In *Trilingual Poet*, ed. Dutton et al., 46–58.

Kienzle, B. M. *The Sermon.* TSMAO 81–83. Turnhout: Brepols, 2000.

Kleineke, W. *Englische Fürstenspiegel vom* Policraticus *Johanns von Salisbury bis zum* Basilikon Doron *König Jakobs I.* Studien zur englischen Philologie 90. Halle: Niemeyer, 1937.

Kobayashi, Y. "The Voice of an Exile: From Ovidian Lament to Prophecy in Book I of John Gower's *Vox Clamantis.*" In *Through a Classical Eye: Transcultural and Transhistorical Visions in Middle English, Italian and Latin Literature in Honour of Winthrop Wetherbee*, ed. A. Galloway and R. F. Yeager, 363–80. Toronto: University of Toronto Press, 2009.

Kuczynski, M.P. "Gower's Virgil." In *On John Gower*, ed. Yeager, 161–87.

Langlois, C. V. *La vie en France au moyen âge.* 3 vols. Paris: Hachette, 1925–1928.

Leclercq, J. "Le magistère du prédicateur au XIIIe siècle." *Archives d'histoire doctrinale et littéraire du Moyen Age* 15 (1946): 105–47.

Legouis, E., and L. Cazamian. *A History of English Literature*, trans. A. D. Irvine. Rev. ed. London: Macmillan, 1940.

Lewis, C. S. *The Allegory of Love.* Oxford: Oxford University Press, 1936.

———. *The Discarded Image.* Cambridge: Cambridge University Press, 1964.

MacCoull, L. S. B. "Neoplatonism." *ODMA* 3:1200–1.

Mann, J. "Beast Fable and Epic." *ODMA* 1:237–39.

Middleton, A. "The Idea of Public Poetry in the Reign of Richard II." *Speculum* 53 (1978): 94–114.

Miller, P. "John Gower, Satiric Poet." In *Gower's* Confessio Amantis: *Responses and Reassessments*, ed. A. J. Minnis, 79–104. Cambridge: D. S. Brewer, 1983.

Mitchell, S. "Richard II: Kingship and the Cult of Saints." In *The Regal Image of Richard II and the Wilton Diptych*, ed. D. Gordon et al., 115–24. Coventry: Harvey Miller, 1997.

Mommsen, T. *Römisches Staatsrecht.* 3rd ed. 3 vols. Leipzig: Hirzel, 1887–1888.

Morley, H. *English Writers.* 10 vols. London: Cassell, 1864–1888.

Murphy, J. J. *Three Medieval Rhetorical Arts.* Berkeley: University of California Press, 1971; repr. Tempe: ACMRS, 2001.

Nicholson, P. *Love and Ethics in Gower's Confessio Amantis.* Ann Arbor: University of Michigan Press, 2005.

Nolan, M. "The Poetics of Catastrophe: Ovidian Allusion in Gower's 'Vox Clamantis'." In *Medieval Latin and Middle English Literature: Essays in Honour of Jill Mann*, ed. C. Cannon and eadem, 113–33. Cambridge: D. S. Brewer, 2011.

Olsson, K. "John Gower's *Vox Clamantis* and the Medieval Idea of Place." *Studies in Philology* 84 (1987): 134–58.

Owst, G. R. *Preaching in Medieval England.* Cambridge: Cambridge University Press, 1926.

———. *Literature and Pulpit in Medieval England.* Cambridge: Cambridge University Press, 1933.

Pearsall, D. "Gower's Narrative Art." *PMLA* 81 (1966): 475–84.

———. "The Manuscripts and Illustrations of Gower's Works." In *Companion*, ed. Echard, 73–97.

Peck, R. A. *Kingship and Common Profit in Gower's Confessio Amantis.* Carbondale: Southern Illinois University Press, 1978.

———. "The Politics and Psychology of Governance in Gower: Ideas of Kingship and Real Kings." In *Companion*, ed. Echard, 215–38.

Rigg, A. G. *History of Anglo-Latin Literature 1066–1422.* Cambridge: Cambridge University Press, 1992.

———, and E. S. Moore. "The Latin Works: Politics, Lament, and Praise." In *Companion*, ed. Echard, 153–64.

Robbins, R. H. "Two Middle English Satiric Love Epistles." *MLR* 37 (1942): 415–21.

Salisbury, E. "Violence and the Sacrificial Poet: Gower, the *Vox*, and the Critics." In *On John Gower*, ed. Yeager, 124–43.

Schirmer, W. *Kurze Geschichte der englischen Literatur.* Halle: Niemeyer, 1945.

Spitzer, L. "Note on the Poetic and the Empirical 'I' in Medieval Authors." *Traditio* 4 (1946): 414–22.

Taylor, A. B. *An Introduction to Medieval Romance.* London: Heath Cranton, 1930; repr. New York: Barnes & Noble, 1969.

Taylor, R. *The Political Prophecy in England.* New York: Columbia University Press, 1911.

ten Brink, B. *Geschichte der englischen Literatur*, ed. A. Brandl. 2 vols. Strassburg: Trübner, 1893.

Trevelyan, G. M. *England in the Age of Wycliffe.* 4th ed. London: Longmans, Green, 1946.

Tucker, S. M. *Verse Satire in England before the Renaissance.* New York: Columbia University Press, 1908.

Urban, M., ed. *John Gower: Manuscripts, Readers, Contexts.* Turnhout: Brepols, 2009.

———. "Gower's *Vox Clamantis* and the Authority of History." In *Fragments: Past and Present in Chaucer and Gower*, 57–84. Bern: Peter Lang, 2010.

Ward, A. W., and A. R. Waller, eds. *The Cambridge History of English Literature.* 14 vols. New York: Putnam, 1907–1921.

Wenzel, S. *Macaronic Sermons: Bilingualism and Preaching in Late-Medieval England.* Ann Arbor: University of Michigan Press, 1994.

Wogan-Browne, J., ed. *Medieval Britain: The French of England, c. 1100–1500.* York: York Medieval Press, 1009.

Yeager, R. F. *John Gower's Poetic: The Search for a New Arion.* Woodbridge: Boydell & Brewer, 1990.

———. "John Gower's French." In *Companion*, ed. Echard, 137–51.

———, ed. *On John Gower: Essays at the Millennium.* Kalamazoo: Medieval Institute Publications, 2007.

Zarins, K. "From Head to Foot: Syllabic Play and Metamorphosis in Book I of Gower's *Vox Clamantis.*" In *On John Gower*, ed. Yeager, 144–60.

Updated online:
http://gowerbib.lib.utsa.edu
http://home.gw.edu/~jhsy/gower.html#biblio